Nikon® D7100™

FOR DUMMIES®
A Wiley Brand

by Julie Adair King

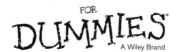

FOR DUMMIES
A Wiley Brand

Nikon® D7100™ For Dummies®

Published by: John Wiley & Sons, Inc., 111 River Street, Hoboken, NJ 07030-5774, www.wiley.com

Copyright © 2013 by John Wiley & Sons, Inc., Hoboken, New Jersey

Published simultaneously in Canada

No part of this publication may be reproduced, stored in a retrieval system or transmitted in any form or by any means, electronic, mechanical, photocopying, recording, scanning or otherwise, except as permitted under Sections 107 or 108 of the 1976 United States Copyright Act, without the prior written permission of the Publisher. Requests to the Publisher for permission should be addressed to the Permissions Department, John Wiley & Sons, Inc., 111 River Street, Hoboken, NJ 07030, (201) 748-6011, fax (201) 748-6008, or online at http://www.wiley.com/go/permissions.

Trademarks: Wiley, For Dummies, the Dummies Man logo, Dummies.com, Making Everything Easier, and related trade dress are trademarks or registered trademarks of John Wiley & Sons, Inc. and may not be used without written permission. Nikon and D7100 are trademarks of Nikon Corporation. All other trademarks are the property of their respective owners. John Wiley & Sons, Inc. is not associated with any product or vendor mentioned in this book.

For general information on our other products and services, please contact our Customer Care Department within the U.S. at 877-762-2974, outside the U.S. at 317-572-3993, or fax 317-572-4002. For technical support, please visit www.wiley.com/techsupport.

Wiley publishes in a variety of print and electronic formats and by print-on-demand. Some material included with standard print versions of this book may not be included in e-books or in print-on-demand. If this book refers to media such as a CD or DVD that is not included in the version you purchased, you may download this material at http://booksupport.wiley.com. For more information about Wiley products, visit www.wiley.com.

Library of Congress Control Number: 2013937650

ISBN 978-1-118-53046-7 (pbk); ISBN 978-1-118-53040-5 (ebk); ISBN 978-1-118-53049-8 (ebk); ISBN 978-1-118-53055-9 (ebk)

Manufactured in the United States of America

10 9 8 7 6 5 4 3 2 1

Contents at a Glance

Table of Contents

Introduction

*N*ikon. The name has been associated with top-flight photography equipment for generations. And the introduction of the D7100 has only enriched Nikon's well-deserved reputation, offering all the control a die-hard photography enthusiast could want while at the same time providing easy-to-use, point-and-shoot features for the beginner.

In fact, the D7100 offers so *many* features that sorting them all out can be more than a little confusing, especially if you're new to digital photography, SLR photography, or both. For starters, you may not even be sure what SLR means or how it affects your picture-taking, let alone have a clue as to all the other techie terms you encounter in your camera manual — *resolution, aperture, white balance,* and so on. And if you're like many people, you may be so overwhelmed by all the controls on your camera that you haven't yet ventured beyond fully automatic picture-taking mode. Which is a shame because it's sort of like buying a Porsche and never actually taking it on the road.

Therein lies the point of *Nikon D7100 For Dummies.* Through this book, you can discover not just what each bell and whistle on your camera does, but also when, where, why, and how to put it to best use. Unlike many photography books, this one doesn't require any previous knowledge of photography or digital imaging to make sense of things, either. In classic *For Dummies* style, everything is explained in easy-to-understand language, with lots of illustrations to help clear up any confusion.

In short, what you have in your hands is the paperback version of an in-depth photography workshop tailored specifically to your Nikon picture-taking powerhouse.

A Quick Look at What's Ahead

This book is organized into four parts, each devoted to a different aspect of using your camera. Although chapters flow in a sequence that's designed to take you from absolute beginner to experienced user, I've also tried to make each chapter as self-standing as possible so that you can explore the topics that interest you in any order you please.

Here's a brief preview of what you can find in each part of the book:

- **Part I: Fast Track to Super Snaps:** Part I contains four chapters to help you get up and running. Chapter 1 offers a tour of the external controls on your camera, shows you how to navigate camera menus, and walks you through initial camera setup. Chapter 2 explains basic picture-taking options, such as shutter-release mode and Image Quality settings, and Chapter 3 shows you how to use the camera's fully automatic exposure modes. Chapter 4 explains the ins and outs of using Live View, the feature that lets you compose pictures on the monitor, and also covers movie recording.

✔ **Part II: Working with Picture Files:** This part offers two chapters dedicated to after-the-shot topics. Chapter 5 explains how to review your pictures on the camera monitor, delete unwanted images, and protect your favorites from accidental erasure. Chapter 6 offers a look at some photo software options — including Nikon ViewNX 2, which ships free with your camera — and guides you through the process of downloading pictures to your computer and preparing them for printing and online sharing.

✔ **Part III: Taking Creative Control:** Chapters in this part help you unleash the full power of your camera by moving into the advanced shooting modes (P, S, A, and M). Chapter 7 covers the critical topic of exposure, and Chapter 8 explains how to manipulate focus and color. Chapter 9 summarizes all the techniques explained in earlier chapters, providing a quick-reference guide to the camera settings and shooting strategies that produce the best results for portraits, action shots, landscape scenes, and close-ups.

✔ **Part IV: The Part of Tens:** In famous *For Dummies* tradition, the book concludes with two "top ten" lists containing additional bits of information and advice. Chapter 10 covers the photo-editing and effects tools found on the camera's Retouch menu and also shows you how to use the Effects exposure mode to add special effects to movies and photos as you record them. Chapter 11 wraps up the book by detailing some camera customization features that, although not found on most "Top Ten Reasons I Bought My Nikon D7100" lists, are nonetheless interesting, useful on occasion, or a bit of both.

Icons and Other Stuff to Note

If this isn't your first *For Dummies* book, you may be familiar with the large, round icons that decorate its margins. If not, here's your very own icon-decoder ring:

A Tip icon flags information that will save you time, effort, money, or some other valuable resource, including your sanity. Tips also point out techniques that help you get the best results from specific camera features.

When you see this icon, look alive. It indicates a potential danger zone that can result in much wailing and teeth-gnashing if ignored. In other words, this is stuff that you really don't want to learn the hard way.

Lots of information in this book is of a technical nature — digital photography is a technical animal, after all. But if I present a detail that is useful mainly for impressing your technology-geek friends, I mark it with this icon.

I apply this icon either to introduce information that is especially worth storing in your brain's long-term memory or to remind you of a fact that may have been displaced from that memory by some other pressing fact.

Additionally, I need to point out these extra details that will help you use this book:

- **Other margin art:** Replicas of some of your camera's buttons and onscreen symbols also appear in the margins next to some paragraphs. I include these to provide a quick reminder of the appearance of the button or feature being discussed.

- **Software menu commands:** In sections that cover software, a series of words connected by an arrow indicates commands that you choose from the program menus. For example, if a step tells you to "Choose File⇨Convert Files," click the File menu to unfurl it and then click the Convert Files command on the menu.

- **Online updates:** Occasionally, Wiley's technology books are updated. If this book has technical updates, they'll be posted at www.dummies. com/go/nikond7100updates.

eCheat Sheet

As a little added bonus, you can find an electronic version of the famous *For Dummies* eCheat Sheet at www.dummies.com/cheatsheet/nikond7100. The eCheat Sheet contains a quick-reference guide to all the buttons, dials, switches, and exposure modes on your camera. Print it out, and tuck it in your camera bag for times when you don't want to carry this book with you.

Practice, Be Patient, and Have Fun!

To wrap up this preamble, I want to stress that if you initially think that digital photography is too confusing or too technical for you, you're in very good company. *Everyone* finds this stuff a little mind-boggling at first. So take it slowly, experimenting with just one or two new camera settings or techniques at first. Then, each time you go on a photo outing, make it a point to add one or two more shooting skills to your repertoire.

I know that it's hard to believe when you're just starting out, but it really won't be long before everything starts to come together. With some time, patience, and practice, you'll soon wield your camera like a pro, dialing in the necessary settings to capture your creative vision almost instinctively.

So without further ado, I invite you to grab your camera, a cup of whatever it is you prefer to sip while you read, and start exploring the rest of this book. Your D7100 is the perfect partner for your photographic journey, and I thank you for allowing me, through this book, to serve as your tour guide.

Part I
Fast Track to Super Snaps

getting started
with your
Nikon
D7100

In this part . . .

- ✔ Get familiar with the basics of using your camera, from attaching lenses to using the Information display and Control panel.

- ✔ Find out how to select the shutter-release mode, exposure mode, picture resolution, file type (JPEG or Raw), and image area.

- ✔ Discover tips for getting good results in the automatic exposure modes.

- ✔ Start taking creative control by stepping up to Scene modes.

- ✔ Switch to Live View mode to compose pictures by using the monitor.

- ✔ Record, play, and trim digital movies.

1

Getting the Lay of the Land

*I*f you're like me, shooting for the first time with a camera as sophisticated as the Nikon D7100 produces a blend of excitement and anxiety. On one hand, you can't wait to start using your new equipment, but on the other, you're a little intimidated by all its buttons, dials, and menu options.

Well, fear not: This chapter provides the information you need to start getting comfortable with your D7100. Along with an introduction to the camera's external controls, I offer details about working with lenses and memory cards, viewing and adjusting camera settings, and choosing basic camera setup options.

Looking at Lenses

One of the biggest differences between a digital point-and-shoot camera and a dSLR *(digital single-lens reflex)* camera is the lens. With a dSLR, you can change lenses to suit different photographic needs, going from an extreme close-up lens to a super-long telephoto, for example. In addition, a dSLR lens has a focusing ring that gives you the option of focusing manually instead of relying on the camera's autofocus mechanism.

I don't have room in this book to go into detail about the science of lenses, nor do I think that an in-depth knowledge of the subject is terribly important to your photographic success. But the next few sections offer advice that may help when you're shopping for lenses, figuring out whether the lenses you inherited from Uncle Ted or found on eBay will work with your D7100, and taking the steps involved in actually mounting and using a lens.

Choosing a lens

To decide which lens is the best partner for your camera, start by considering these factors:

- ✔ **Lens compatibility:** You can mount a wide range of lenses on your D7100, but some lenses aren't fully compatible with all camera features. For example, with some lenses, you can't take advantage of autofocusing and must focus manually.

  Your camera manual lists all the lens types that can be mounted on the camera and explains what features are supported with each type. For maximum compatibility, look for these types: Type D or G AF Nikkor, AF-S Nikkor, or AF-I Nikkor. (The latter is an older, expensive professional lens that is no longer sold but might be available on the resale market.)

  All the aforementioned lens types (as well as some others) offer CPU (central processing unit) technology, which allows the lens to talk to the camera. This feature is critical to getting maximum performance from the autofocusing system, exposure metering system, and so on. That's not to say that you can't use a non-CPU lens; you just lose access to some camera features.

  Information in this book assumes that you're using a CPU lens that supports all the camera's functions. If your lens doesn't meet that criteria, check the camera manual for specifics on what features are unavailable or need to be implemented differently.

- ✔ **Focal length and the crop factor:** The focal length of a lens, stated in millimeters, determines the angle of view that the camera can capture and the spatial relationship of objects in the frame. Focal length also affects *depth of field,* or the distance over which focus appears acceptably sharp.

  You can loosely categorize lenses by focal length as follows:

  - *Wide-angle:* Lenses with short focal lengths — generally, anything under 35mm — are known as *wide-angle lenses.* A wide-angle lens has the visual effect of pushing the subject away from you and making it appear smaller. As a result, you can fit more of the scene into the frame without moving back. Additionally, a wide-angle lens has a large depth of field, which means that both the subject and background objects appear sharp. These characteristics make wide-angle lenses ideal for landscape photography.

- *Telephoto:* Lenses with focal lengths longer than about 70mm are *telephoto* lenses. These lenses create the illusion of bringing the subject closer to you, increase the subject's size in the frame, and produce a short depth of field so that the subject is sharply focused but distant objects are blurry. Telephoto lenses are great for capturing wildlife and other subjects that don't permit up-close shooting.

- *Normal:* A focal length in the neighborhood of 35mm to 70mm is considered "normal" — that is, somewhere between a wide-angle and telephoto. This focal length produces the angle of view and depth of field that are appropriate for the kinds of snapshots that most people take.

Figure 1-1 offers an illustration of the difference that focal length makes, showing the same scene captured at 42mm (left image) and 112mm (right image). Of course, the illustration shows just two of countless possibilities, and the question of which focal length best captures a scene depends on your creative goals.

42mm   112mm

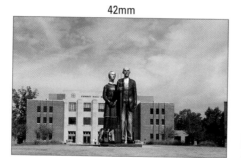 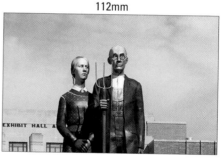

Figure 1-1: I used a focal length of 42mm to capture the first image and then zoomed to a focal length of 112mm to capture the second one.

Note, however, that the focal lengths stated here and elsewhere in the book are so-called *35mm equivalent* focal lengths. Here's the deal: For reasons that aren't really important, when you put a standard lens on most digital cameras, including your D7100, the available frame area is reduced, as if you took a picture on a camera that uses 35mm film negatives and then cropped it.

This so-called *crop factor* varies depending on the camera, which is why the photo industry adopted the 35mm-equivalent measuring stick as a standard. With the D7100, the crop factor is 1.5. So the 18–105mm kit lens, for example, captures the approximate area you would get from a 27–158mm lens on a 35mm film camera. (Multiply the crop factor by the lens focal length to get the actual angle of view.) In Figure 1-2, the red line indicates the image area that results from the 1.5 crop factor compared with the shot you would get from the same focal length lens mounted on a 35mm film camera.

When shopping for a lens, it's important to remember this crop factor to make sure that you get the focal length designed for the type of pictures you want to take.

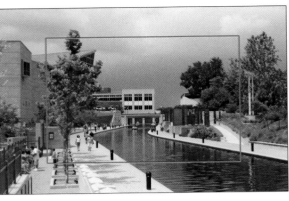

Figure 1-2: The 1.5 crop factor produces the angle of view indicated by the red outline.

Not sure which focal length to choose? Here's a really cool online tool to help you understand the subject more: Point your web browser to http://imaging.nikon.com, click the link for Nikkor lenses, and then click the link for the Nikkor Lenses Simulator. Using this interactive tool, you can see exactly how different lenses capture the same scene.

⮑ **Prime versus zoom lenses:** A *prime* lens is a single focal-length lens. With a zoom lens, you get a range of focal lengths in one unit. For example, the kit lens I feature in this book has a focal-length range of 18–105mm.

Why select a lens that offers a single focal length when a zoom lens offers a range of focal lengths? In a word, quality. Because of some lens science I won't bore you with, you typically see some reduction in picture quality at certain points in the range of a zoom lens. On the flip side, a zoom lens is certainly more convenient than carting around a bag of prime lenses with different focal lengths. And you can get exceptional image quality from many zoom lenses, even with some *super zooms,* which offer a huge range of focal lengths.

⮑ **Aperture range:** The *aperture* is an adjustable diaphragm in a lens. By adjusting the aperture size, you control the amount of light that enters through the lens and strikes the image sensor, thereby controlling exposure. The aperture setting also affects depth of field: A wide-open aperture produces a short depth of field, so the subject is sharply focused, but distant objects appear blurry; a narrow aperture produces a long depth of field so that both the subject and distant objects appear sharp.

Chapters 7 and 8 cover these issues in detail. For the purposes of lens shopping, you need to know just a few things.

- *Every lens has a specific range of aperture settings.* Obviously, the larger that range, the more control you have over exposure and depth of field.

- *The larger the maximum aperture, the "faster" the lens.* Aperture settings are stated in *f-stops,* with a lower number meaning a larger aperture. For example, a setting of f/2 results in a more open aperture than f/4. And if you have one lens with a maximum aperture of f/2 and another with a maximum aperture of f/4, the f/2 lens is said to be *faster* because you can open the aperture wider, thereby allowing more light into the camera and permitting the image to be captured in less time. This not only benefits you in low-light situations but also when photographing action, which requires a fast shutter speed (short exposure time). So, all other things being equal, a faster lens is better.

- *With some zoom lenses, the maximum and minimum aperture change as you zoom the lens.* For example, when you zoom to a telephoto focal length, the maximum aperture generally gets smaller — that is, you can't open the aperture as much as you can at a wide-angle setting. You can buy lenses that maintain the same maximum and minimum aperture throughout the whole zoom lens, but you pay more for this feature.

After studying these issues and narrowing down your choices, finding the right lens in the category you want is just a matter of doing some homework. Study lens reviews in photography magazines and online photography sites to find the best performing lens in your price range.

Attaching and removing lenses

Whatever lens you choose, follow these steps to attach it to the camera body:

1. **Turn off the camera.**

2. **Remove the cap that covers the lens mount on the front of the camera.**

3. **Remove the cap that covers the back of the lens.**

4. **Hold the lens in front of the camera so that the mounting index on the lens aligns with the one on the camera.**

   The *mounting index* is a marker found on both the lens and the camera body to indicate how to align the two when mounting the lens. On the D7100, the mounting index is the white dot labeled in Figure 1-3.

   On the 18–105mm lens that's available in a bundle with the D7100 body, the lens mounting index is also a white dot, as shown in the figure. If you buy a different lens, your mounting index may look different, so check the lens instruction manual.

5. **Keeping the index markers aligned, position the lens on the camera's lens mount.**

6. **Turn the lens in a counter-clockwise direction until the lens clicks into place.**

   To put it another way, turn the lens toward the side of the camera that sports the shutter button, as indicated by the arrow in Figure 1-3.

7. **On a CPU lens that has an aperture ring, set and lock the ring so the aperture is set at the highest f-stop number.**

   Check your lens manual to find out whether your lens sports an aperture ring and how to adjust it. (The lens featured in this book doesn't have an aperture ring.)

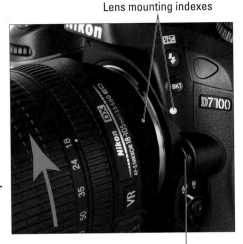

Lens mounting indexes

Lens-release button

Figure 1-3: When attaching the lens, align the index dots as shown here.

To detach a lens, take these steps:

1. **Turn off the camera and locate the lens-release button, labeled in Figure 1-3.**

2. **Press the lens-release button while turning the lens clockwise (away from the shutter button) until the mounting index on the lens is aligned with the index on the camera body.**

   When the mounting indexes line up, the lens detaches from the mount.

3. **Place the rear protective cap onto the back of the lens.**

   If you aren't putting another lens on the camera, cover the lens mount with the protective cap that came with your camera, too.

Always change lenses in a clean environment to reduce the risk of getting dust, dirt, and other contaminants inside the camera or lens. For added safety, point the camera slightly down when performing this maneuver to help prevent any flotsam in the air from being drawn into the camera by gravity.

Changing the focusing method (auto or manual)

Assuming that your lens supports autofocusing when mounted on the D7100, familiarize yourself with these two controls, which set the focusing method to manual or autofocusing:

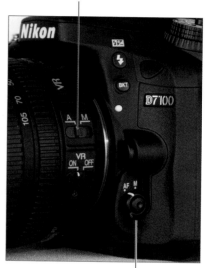

Lens focus-mode switch

Focus mode selector

Figure 1-4: Set the focus mode both on the camera body and the lens.

✔ **Lens focus-mode switch:** Assuming that your lens offers autofocusing as well as manual focusing, it has a switch that you use to choose between the two options. On the 18–105mm kit lens shown in Figure 1-4, the switch has an M setting for Manual focus and an A setting for Autofocus. Other lenses may offer different switches, so check your lens instruction guide for specifics.

✔ **Focus-mode selector:** Also shown in Figure 1-4, this switch sets the camera itself to manual focusing (M) or autofocusing (AF).

Chapter 8 details how to take best advantage of the camera's autofocusing system. Manual focusing is fairly simple: Just rotate the focus ring on the lens to bring your subject into focus. The placement and appearance of the focus ring depend on the lens; Figure 1-5 shows you the one on the 18–105mm kit lens.

Zooming in and out

If you bought a zoom lens, it has a movable zoom ring. The location of the zoom ring on the 18–105mm kit lens is shown in Figure 1-5. To zoom in or out, just rotate that ring.

The numbers at the edge of the zoom ring, by the way, represent focal lengths. The number that's aligned with the white bar at the edge of the zoom ring represents the current focal length. In Figure 1-5, for example, the focal length is 35mm.

Focus length indicator

Zoom ring Focusing ring

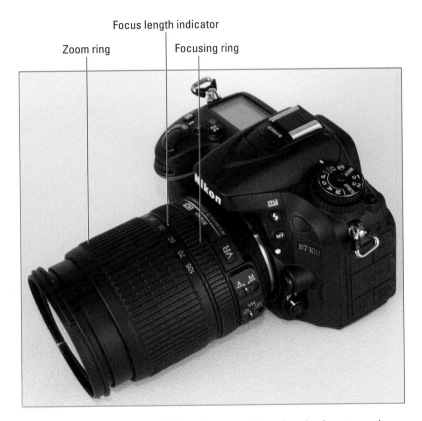

Figure 1-5: On the 18–105mm kit lens, the manual-focusing ring is set near the back of the lens.

Getting shake-free shots with Vibration Reduction (VR) lenses

Some Nikon lenses offer *Vibration Reduction.* This feature, indicated by the initials VR in the lens name, attempts to compensate for small amounts of camera shake that are common when photographers handhold their cameras and use a slow shutter speed, a lens with a long focal length, or both. That camera movement during the exposure can produce blurry images. Although Vibration Reduction can't work miracles, it enables most people to capture sharper handheld shots in many situations than they otherwise could. On the 18–105mm lens featured in this book, you enable and disable Vibration Reduction via the VR switch, labeled in Figure 1-6.

Here's what you need to know about this feature:

- ✔ **For handheld shooting, turn on Vibration Reduction.** Vibration Reduction engages when you press the shutter button halfway and after you press the button all the way to take the picture. The image in the viewfinder may appear a little blurry right after you take the picture. That's normal and doesn't indicate a problem with your camera or focus.

- ✔ **With the 18–105mm kit lens, turn off Vibration Reduction when you mount the camera on a tripod.** When you use a tripod, Vibration Reduction can have detrimental effects because the system may try to adjust for movement that isn't occurring. This recommendation assumes that the tripod is "locked down" so that the camera is immovable.

Vibration Reduction switch

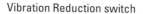

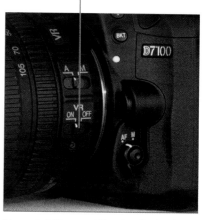

Figure 1-6: Turn on Vibration Reduction for sharper handheld shots, but turn off the feature when you use a tripod.

You don't need to disable Vibration Reduction when you want to create motion effects by panning the camera, however. (*Panning* means to move the camera horizontally or vertically as you take the shot, a technique that blurs the background while keeping the subject sharply focused, creating a heightened sense of motion.) The Vibration Reduction system is smart enough to ignore panning movement and compensate only for movement in other directions.

- ✔ **For other lenses, check the lens manual to find out whether your lens offers a similar feature.** On non-Nikon lenses, Vibration Reduction may go by another name: *image stabilization, optical stabilization, anti-shake, vibration compensation,* and so on. In some cases, the manufacturers may recommend that you leave the system turned on or select a special setting when you use a tripod or pan the camera.

Additionally, some lenses enable you to engage different types of stabilization (the settings may be called Active/Normal or something similar); again, refer to the lens manual for specifics.

Enabling automatic distortion correction

Pictures taken with wide-angle lenses often exhibit *barrel distortion,* which causes straight lines to bow outward. And telephoto lenses sometimes cause verticals to bow inward, creating *pincushion distortion.* The Auto Distortion Control feature on the Shooting menu attempts to correct both problems.

The option is turned off by default. Before enabling it, understand that some of the area you see in your viewfinder may not be visible in the final photo because the anti-distortion

manipulation requires some cropping of the scene. Also note that the feature is unavailable for movies and works only with certain types of lenses. (See the camera manual for specifics.)

Because results depend on your lens, take test shots to decide whether the feature is right for your equipment. Keep in mind that you have the option of applying a similar correction after the shot, using the Distortion Control option on the Retouch menu.

Adjusting the Viewfinder Focus

Near the upper-right side of the viewfinder is a dial that enables you to adjust the viewfinder focus to accommodate your eyesight. Figure 1-7 offers a close-up look at the dial, which is officially known as the *diopter adjustment control.*

If you don't take this step, scenes that appear out of focus through the viewfinder may actually be focused through the lens, and vice versa. Here's how to make the necessary adjustment:

Viewfinder adjustment dial

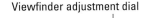

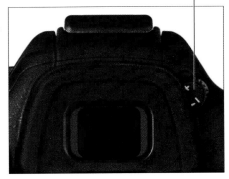

Figure 1-7: Rotate this dial to adjust the viewfinder focus to your eyesight.

1. **Remove the lens cap from the front of the lens.**

2. **Look through the viewfinder and press the shutter button halfway to display picture data at the bottom of the viewfinder.**

   In dim lighting, the built-in flash may pop up; ignore it for now and close the unit after you finish adjusting the viewfinder.

3. Rotate the diopter adjustment dial until the viewfinder data appears sharpest to your eye.

As you rotate the dial, the bracket-like marks in the center of the viewfinder, which are related to autofocusing, also become more or less sharp.

The Nikon manual warns you not to poke yourself in the eye as you perform this maneuver. This warning seems so obvious that I laugh every time I read it — which makes me feel doubly stupid the next time I poke myself in the eye as I perform this maneuver.

Ordering from Camera Menus

You access many camera features via menus, which, conveniently enough, appear when you press the Menu button. Features are grouped into six main menus, described briefly in Table 1-1.

Table 1-1	D7100 Menus	
Symbol	**Open This Menu**	**Access These Functions**
▶	Playback	Viewing, deleting, and protecting pictures
⬜	Shooting	Basic photography settings
✎	Custom Setting	Advanced photography options and some basic camera options
⚐	Setup	Additional basic camera options
✐	Retouch	Built-in photo retouching options
📑📄	My Menu/Recent Settings	Your custom menu or 20 most recently used menu options

After you press the Menu button, you see a screen similar to the one shown in Figure 1-8. The left side of the screen sports the icons shown in Table 1-1, each representing one of the available menus. The highlighted icon is the active menu; options on that menu automatically appear to the right. In the figure, the Shooting menu is active, for example.

Menu icons   Multi Selector

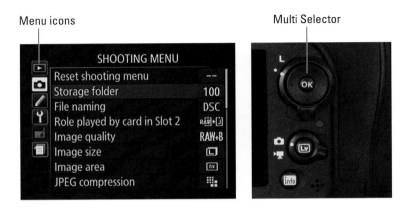

Figure 1-8: Use the Multi Selector to navigate menus.

The Multi Selector, labeled in the figure, is the key to the navigating menus. Press the edges of the Multi Selector to navigate up, down, left, and right through the menus.

In this book, the instruction "Press the Multi Selector left" means to press the left edge of the control. "Press the Multi Selector right" means to press the right edge, and so on.

Here's a bit more detail about menus:

- **Select a menu.** Press the Multi Selector left to jump to the column containing the menu icons. Then press up or down to highlight the menu you want to display. Finally, press right to jump over to the options on the menu.

- **Select and adjust a function on the current menu.** Use the Multi Selector to scroll up or down the list of options to highlight the feature you want to adjust and then press the OK button at the center of the Multi Selector. Settings available for the selected item then appear. For example, if you select Image Quality from the Shooting menu, as shown on the left in Figure 1-9, and press OK, the available Image Quality options appear, as shown on the right. Repeat the old up-and-down scroll routine until the choice you prefer is highlighted. Then press OK to return to the previous screen.

  In some cases, you may see a right-pointing triangle instead of OK next to an option. That's your cue to press the Multi Selector right to display a submenu or other list of options.

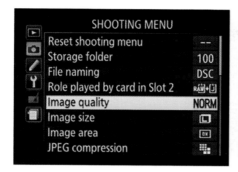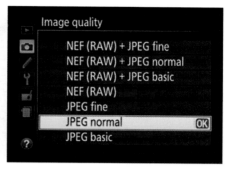

Figure 1-9: Select the option you prefer and press OK to return to the active menu.

✓ **Create a custom menu or view your 20 most recently adjusted menu items.** The sixth menu is actually two menus bundled into one: Recent Settings and My Menu, both shown in Figure 1-10. The menu icon changes depending on which of these two functions is active; Table 1-1 shows both menus. Each menu contains a Choose Tab option; select this option and press OK to access the screen that lets you shift between the two menus.

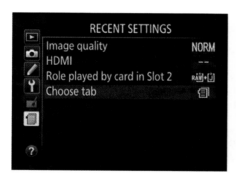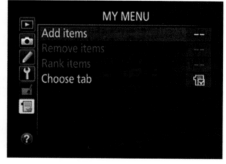

Figure 1-10: The Recent Settings menu offers quick access to the last 20 menu options you selected; the My Menu screen lets you design a custom menu.

Here's what the two menus offer:

- *Recent Settings:* This screen lists the 20 menu items you ordered most recently. If you want to adjust those settings, you don't have to wade through all the other menus looking for them — just head for the Recent Settings menu.

  To remove an item from the Recent Settings menu, highlight it and press the Delete button. Press again to confirm your decision.

- *My Menu:* Through this screen, you can create a custom menu that contains your favorite menu options. Chapter 11 details the steps.

Decoding the Displays

Your D7100 gives you three ways to monitor picture settings:

- ✓ **Control panel:** Figure 1-11 offers a look at this display, found on top of the camera. You can illuminate the panel temporarily by rotating the On/Off switch past the On position to the light bulb marker and then releasing the switch.

Battery status   Illuminate control panel

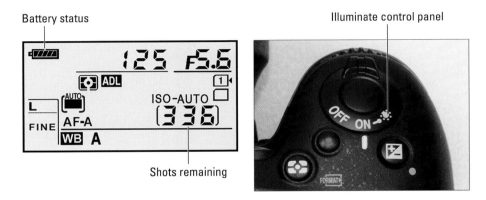

Shots remaining

Figure 1-11: Rotate the On/Off switch to the light bulb position to illuminate the Control panel.

- ✓ **Information display:** If your eyesight is like mine, making out the tiny type on the Control panel can be difficult. Fortunately, you can press the Info button on the back of the camera to display the Information screen on the monitor. As shown in Figure 1-12, this screen displays the current shooting settings at a size that's easier on the eyes.

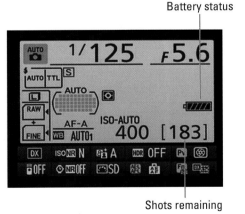

Battery status

Shots remaining

Figure 1-12: Press the Info button to view picture-taking settings on the monitor.

The Information screen has a hidden power, too: After the screen is displayed, you can press the *i* button to activate the control strip at the bottom of the screen, as shown on the left in Figure 1-13. You then can quickly adjust any of the settings on the two rows of the strip. Use the Multi Selector to highlight a setting — a little *tooltip* (text label) appears to identify it — and then press OK. The camera then zips you directly to the menu containing the available settings, as shown on the right in the figure. Make your choice and press OK again to exit the menu. You can then adjust another setting or press the *i* button one more time to deactivate the control strip. Press the shutter button halfway to return to shooting mode.

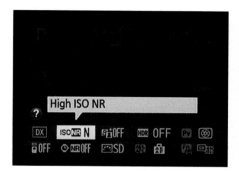
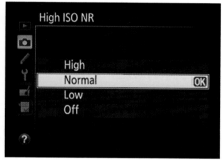

Figure 1-13: Press the *i* button while the Information screen is displayed to gain quick access to the settings on the control strip at the bottom of the screen.

✔ **Viewfinder:** You can view some settings in the viewfinder as well, as shown in Figure 1-14.

Don't worry if you don't have any clue what all the symbols and numbers shown in Figures 1-11 through 1-14 mean — most of them relate to options explored in later chapters. But do note the following points of data now:

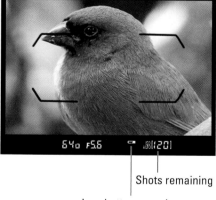

Shots remaining

Low battery warning

Figure 1-14: You also can view some camera settings at the bottom of the viewfinder.

✔ **Battery status indicator:** A full battery icon like the one in Figures 1-11 and 1-12 shows that the battery is fully charged. Bars disappear from the icon as the battery runs down. When the battery gets very low, the viewfinder displays a warning symbol, as shown in Figure 1-14. If the battery is beyond the point where you can take any more photos, the symbol flashes in the displays.

✔ **Shots remaining:** Labeled in Figures 1-11, 1-12, and 1-14, this value indicates how many additional pictures you can store on the current memory card (or cards if you put one in each of the camera's two card slots).

When the shots-remaining number is greater than 999, the initial K appears next to the value to indicate that the first value represents the picture count in thousands. (*K* being a universally accepted symbol indicating 1,000 units.) The number is rounded down to the nearest hundred. So if the number of shots remaining is, say, 1,230 more pictures, the value reads as 1.2K.

Working with Memory Cards

Instead of recording images on film, digital cameras store pictures on memory cards. Your D7100 uses a specific type of memory card — an *SD card* (for *Secure Digital*).

To enable you to shoot oodles of pictures without having to swap out cards, the D7100 has two card slots. Open the cover on the right side of the camera, as shown in Figure 1-15, to reveal them. The top slot is Slot 1; the bottom slot is Slot 2.

The next section explains some details you need to know when you use two cards at a time, but first, here are some general guidelines about using SD cards:

✔ **Understanding card specifications:** Most SD cards carry the designation SDHC (for *High Capacity*) or SDXC (for *eXtended Capacity*), depending on how many gigabytes (GB) of data they hold. SDHC cards hold from 4GB to 32GB of data; the SDXC moniker indicates a capacity greater than 32GB.

Memory card access light

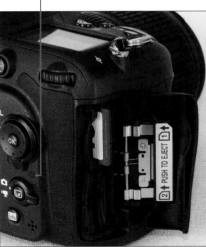

Figure 1-15: Insert cards with the labels facing the back of the camera.

Cards are also assigned a speed rating from 2 to 10, with a higher number indicating a faster data-transfer rate. The Powers That Be recently added a new category of speed rating — Ultra High Speed

(UHS). UHS cards also carry a number designation; at present, there is only one class of UHS card, UHS 1. These cards currently are the fastest the planet has to offer.

Of course, a faster card means a more expensive card. But to maximize your camera's performance, I recommend that you make the investment in Class 10 or UHS 1 cards. Especially for video recording, a faster card translates to smoother recording and playback. A faster card also can improve performance when you're shooting a burst of images using the camera's continuous capture feature.

✔ **Inserting a card:** Turn off the camera and then place the card in the slot with the label facing the back of the camera, as shown in Figure 1-15. Push in the card until it clicks into place; the card access light (labeled in the figure) blinks for a second to let you know the card is inserted properly.

✔ **Removing a card:** After making sure that the card access light is off, indicating that the camera has finished recording your most recent photo, turn off the camera. Open the memory card door, depress the memory card slightly until you hear a little click, and then let go. The card pops halfway out of the slot, enabling you to grab it by the tail and remove it.

When both memory card slots are empty, the symbol [-E-] appears in the shots remaining area of the viewfinder, Control panel, and Information screen. If you have a card in the camera and you get these messages, try taking the card out and reinserting it.

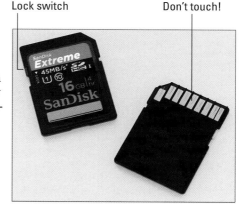

Figure 1-16: Avoid touching the gold contacts on the card.

✔ **Handling cards:** Don't touch the gold contacts on the back of the card. (See the right card in Figure 1-16.) When cards aren't in use, store them in the protective cases they came in or in a memory card wallet. Keep cards away from extreme heat and cold as well.

✔ **Locking cards:** The tiny switch on the side of the card, labeled "Lock switch" in Figure 1-16, enables you to lock your card, which prevents any data from being erased or recorded to the card. Press the switch toward the bottom of the card to lock the card contents; press it toward the top of the card to unlock the data.

Using two cards at the same time

When you install two memory cards, you can specify how you want the camera to use the card installed in Slot 2. You have three choices:

- **Overflow:** This setting is the default; the camera fills the card in Slot 1 (the top slot) and then switches to the second card.

- **Backup:** The camera records each picture to both cards. This option gives you some extra security — should one card fail, you have a backup on the other card.

- **Raw Slot 1 - JPEG Slot 2:** This setting relates to the Image Quality option, which Chapter 2 explains. If you select one of the Raw (NEF) + JPEG settings, Raw files go on the card in Slot 1 and the JPEG files go on the card in Slot 2.

Make your wishes known via the Role Played by Card in Slot 2 option on the Shooting menu, shown in Figure 1-17.

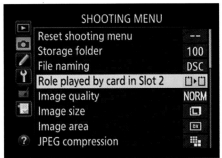

Figure 1-17: This option tells the camera how to use the card in Slot 2.

A few other critical points about using two cards:

- **Monitoring card use in the Information display:** You can tell which secondary slot function is in force by looking at the Image Quality readout of the Information screen, highlighted on the left in Figure 1-18. The card symbols tell you what's going where. In the figure, the symbols show that the camera is set up to send Raw files to Slot 1 and the JPEG versions to Slot 2. (*Fine* represents one of three available settings for JPEG files.) If you see the same data for each card — for example, the word *Raw* appears in both cards — the Backup option is selected. And if the file type label appears in only one card, with the other card appearing empty, the Overflow option is selected.

- **Monitoring card use in the Control panel:** Symbols representing each card also appear in the Control panel, as shown on the right in Figure 1-18. If you set the slot function to Overflow, the number of the card currently in use appears (1 or 2). At the other settings, you see both a 1 and a 2, as in the figure, showing that both cards are in use.

- **Determining how many more shots you can take:** When you set the second card to the Backup or Raw/JPEG option, the shots remaining value is based on whichever card contains the least amount of free

space. When either card is out of space, you can't take any more pictures. For the Overflow option, the shots remaining value tells you how
many pictures you can fit on the card in Slot 1 until you fill that card.
Then it changes to indicate the space on the second card.

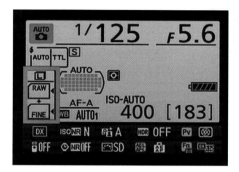 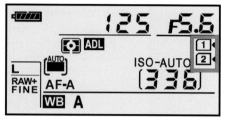

Figure 1-18: These symbols represent your memory cards.

✏ **Selecting a card to store movie files:** Movie recording throws a wrench
in the card configuration system. No matter what setting you chose for
the Role Played by Card in Slot 2 menu option, movie files always go on
the card in Slot 1 by default. But if Card 2 has more space, you may want
to send your movie files to it so that you can record a longer movie.
(Choosing Overflow doesn't work because the camera can't put part of
the file on one card and the rest on the other.)

To change the movie-storage setup, select Movie Settings on the
Shooting menu and press OK. Then set the Destination option to Card 2.
See Chapter 4 for complete details about movie recording.

✏ **Copying pictures from one card to another:** You can take this step by
choosing the Copy Image(s) option on the Playback menu. For details,
see Chapter 6.

Formatting cards

The first time you use a new memory card or insert a card that's been used
in other devices, *format* it to ensure that the card is properly prepared to
record your pictures. Formatting after you download pictures to your computer is also a good idea. However, don't use your computer's file-manage-
ment tools to format the card; the camera is better equipped to do the job.

Formatting erases everything on your memory card. So before formatting,
copy any pictures or other data to your computer.

You can format a card in two ways:

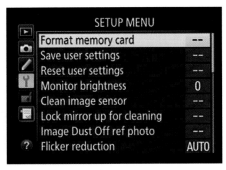

SETUP MENU

Format memory card	--
Save user settings	--
Reset user settings	--
Monitor brightness	0
Clean image sensor	--
Lock mirror up for cleaning	--
Image Dust Off ref photo	--
Flicker reduction	AUTO

- ✔ **Choose the Format Memory Card command from the Setup menu, as shown in Figure 1-19.** When you select the command, you're asked to select which card you want to format. After taking that step, you see a screen where you confirm your decision to format the card. Highlight Yes and press OK to go forward.

Figure 1-19: Formatting removes all data from the memory card.

- ✔ **Simultaneously press and hold the Metering Mode and Delete buttons.** See the red Format labels next to the buttons? They're reminders that you use these buttons to quickly format a memory card. Hold the buttons down for about two seconds, until you see the letters *For* blink in the Control panel.

After you press the buttons, the Control panel also displays the icon for the card that will be formatted if you go forward. If you have two cards installed in the camera, you can switch to the other card by rotating the Main command dial (back of the camera, upper-right corner). You also see the shots remaining value, which indicates how many pictures you can fit on the memory card at the current Image Quality and Image Size settings.

While the display is blinking, press and release both buttons again. When formatting is complete, the *For* message disappears, and the Control panel display returns to normal.

If you insert a memory card and see the letters *For* blink in the Control panel or viewfinder, you must format the card before you can do anything else.

Exploring External Camera Controls

In later chapters, I detail all your camera's buttons, dials, and switches. For now, just cruise through the next several sections, which provide a basic road map to the external controls.

One note: Many buttons perform multiple functions and so have multiple "official" names. I think that's a little confusing, so I always refer to each button by the first moniker you see in the lists here. To avoid any confusion over which button I'm referencing, a picture of the button appears in the margin.

Topside controls

Your tour begins with the birds-eye view shown in Figure 1-20:

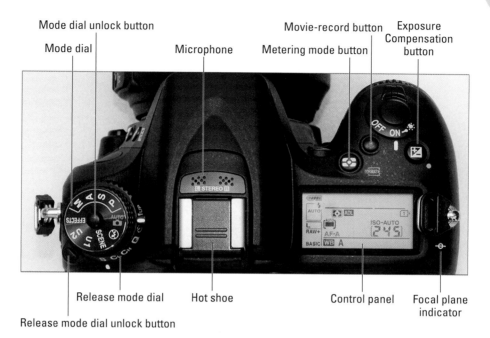

Mode dial unlock button

Mode dial

Microphone

Movie-record button

Metering mode button

Exposure Compensation button

Release mode dial unlock button

Release mode dial

Hot shoe

Control panel

Focal plane indicator

Figure 1-20: Press and hold the Mode dial unlock button before rotating the dial.

- **Control panel:** You can view many picture-taking settings on this LCD panel. See the earlier section "Decoding the Displays" for more info.

- **On/Off switch and shutter button:** Okay, I'm pretty sure you already figured out this combo button. Just remember that you can illuminate the Control panel by rotating the On/Off switch past the On position to the little light bulb icon. Moving the switch to that position also activates the exposure meters. After you release the switch, the panel backlight and meters remain active for about six seconds or until you take a picture. You can also turn off the panel light by rotating the switch to the light bulb position again.

- **Exposure Compensation button:** When working in the three semi-automatic exposure modes (P, S, and A), you can apply an exposure-adjustment feature called Exposure Compensation by pressing this button while rotating the Main command dial (the one on the back of the camera; see upcoming Figure 1-21). Chapter 7 details this feature.

- **Metering Mode button:** Press this button while rotating the Main command dial to select an exposure *metering mode,* which determines what part of the frame the camera considers when calculating exposure. Look to Chapter 7 for information on this feature, too.

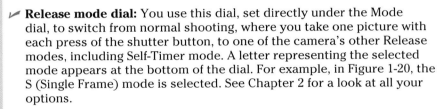

✔ **Movie-record button:** After setting the camera to movie mode, you press this button to start and stop recording. (You engage movie mode by setting the Live View switch shown in Figure 1-21 to the movie camera icon and then pressing the LV button.)

✔ **Mode dial:** With this dial, you set the camera to a fully automatic, semi-automatic, or manual exposure mode. You also can set up and select two of your own modes, U1 and U2 (*U* for *user*). Chapter 3 details the fully automatic modes (Auto, Auto Flash Off, and the Scene modes); Chapter 7 explains semi-automatic and manual modes (P, S, A, and M); and Chapter 10 discusses Effects mode. Chapter 11 shows you how to create your two custom modes.

Before you can rotate the dial, you must press and hold the mode dial unlock button in the center of the dial, labeled in Figure 1-20.

✔ **Release mode dial:** You use this dial, set directly under the Mode dial, to switch from normal shooting, where you take one picture with each press of the shutter button, to one of the camera's other Release modes, including Self-Timer mode. A letter representing the selected mode appears at the bottom of the dial. For example, in Figure 1-20, the S (Single Frame) mode is selected. See Chapter 2 for a look at all your options.

To rotate the dial, you must press and hold the Release mode dial unlock button labeled in Figure 1-20.

✔ **Microphone:** The holes labeled Microphone in Figure 1-20 lead to the camera's built-in microphone.

✔ **Flash hot shoe:** A *hot shoe* is a connection for attaching an external flash head. The contacts on the shoe are covered by a little black insert when the camera ships from the factory, as shown in Figure 1-20. Keep the cover in place to protect the contacts until you want to attach a flash.

✔ **Focal plane indicator:** Should you need to know the exact distance between your subject and the camera, the focal plane indicator labeled in Figure 1-20 is key. This mark indicates the plane at which light coming through the lens is focused onto the image sensor. Basing your measurement on this mark produces a more accurate camera-to-subject distance than using the end of the lens or some other external point on the camera body as your reference point.

Back-of-the-body controls

The back side of the camera, shown in Figure 1-21, sports the following smorgasbord of controls:

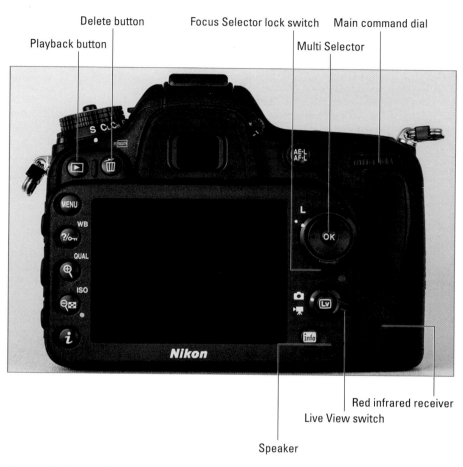

Figure 1-21: Here's a look at the backside controls.

✔ **Main command dial:** After you activate certain camera features, you rotate this dial, labeled in Figure 1-21, to select a setting. For example, to choose a White Balance setting, you press the WB button as you rotate the Main command dial.

 ✔ **AE-L/AF-L button:** When taking pictures in some automatic modes, you can lock focus and exposure settings by holding down this button. Chapter 7 explains.

If you don't use the button's normal function often, you can assign another job to it. Instructions in this book assume that you stick with the default button function, but if you want to explore your options, see Chapter 11.

✔ **Multi Selector/OK button:** This dual-natured control, labeled in Figure 1-21, plays a role in many camera functions. You press the outer edges of the Multi Selector left, right, up, or down to navigate camera menus and access certain other options. At the center of the control is the OK button, which you press to finalize a menu selection or other camera adjustment.

✔ **Focus Selector Lock switch:** Just beneath the Multi Selector, this switch relates to the camera's autofocusing system. When the switch is set to the position shown in Figure 1-21, you can use the Multi Selector to tell the camera to base focus on a specific focusing point. Setting the switch to the L position locks in the selected point. See Chapter 8 for details.

✔ **Live View switch:** *Live View,* detailed in Chapter 4, is the feature that enables you to use the monitor to compose your shots for still photography. You also must use the monitor for composition when you record movies; the viewfinder is disabled for movie recording.

Rotate the Live View switch, labeled in Figure 1-21, to the camera symbol to use Live View for still photography; move the switch to the movie-camera symbol for movie recording. Either way, press the LV button at the center of the switch to actually turn on Live View.

✔ **Info button:** Press this button to display the Information screen on the camera monitor. Press again to turn the display off. See the earlier section "Decoding the Displays" for details on the Information display.

✔ **Playback button:** Press this button to switch the camera into picture review mode. Chapter 5 details picture playback.

✔ **Delete button:** Sporting a trash can icon, the universal symbol for delete, this button enables you to erase pictures. Chapter 5 has specifics.

✔ **Menu button:** Press this button to access menus of camera options. See the earlier section "Ordering from Camera Menus," in this chapter, for help using menus.

WB

✔ **WB/Help/Protect button:** This button serves several purposes:

• *White Balance control:* For picture-taking purposes, the button's main function is to access white balance options, a topic you can explore in Chapter 8. Press the button while rotating the Main command dial to adjust the setting.

• *Help:* When menus are displayed, you can press the button to display helpful information about certain menu options. See "Asking Your Camera for Help," later in this chapter, for details.

• *Protect:* In playback mode, pressing the button locks the picture file — hence the little key symbol that appears on the button face — so that it isn't erased if you use the picture-delete functions. (The picture *is* erased if you format the memory card, however.) See Chapter 5 for details.

QUAL

✔ **Qual (Quality)/Zoom In button:** In playback mode, pressing this button magnifies the image and also reduces the number of thumbnails displayed at a time. Note the plus sign in the middle of the magnifying glass — plus for zoom in.

In picture-taking mode, pressing the button gives you fast access to the Image Quality and Image Size options, both of which you can explore in Chapter 2.

ISO

✔ **ISO/Zoom Out/Thumbnail button:** In picture-taking mode, pressing this button while rotating the Main command dial adjusts the ISO setting, which controls the camera's sensitivity to light. Chapter 7 has details.

In playback mode, pressing the button enables you to display multiple image thumbnails on the screen and to reduce the magnification of the current photo.

✔ *i* **button:** When the Information display is visible, pressing this button activates the control strip of options at the bottom of the screen. You can then use the Multi Selector to highlight an option and press OK to display a menu screen the offers the available settings for that option. Press the *i* button again to return to the normal Information display.

✔ **Speaker:** When you play movies that contain sound, the sound comes wafting through these little holes.

✔ **Rear infrared receiver:** This sensor, labeled in Figure 1-21, picks up the signal from the optional ML-L3 wireless remote control. There's a second sensor on the front of the camera; see the next section for a look-see.

Front-left controls

On the front-left side of the camera body, shown in Figure 1-22, you find the following:

✔ **Flash/Flash Compensation:** Pressing this button pops up the camera's built-in flash (except in automatic shooting modes, in which the camera decides whether the flash is needed). By holding the button down and rotating the Main command dial, you can adjust the Flash mode (normal, red-eye reduction, and so on). In advanced exposure modes (P, S, A, and M), you also can adjust the flash power by pressing the button and rotating the Sub-command dial. (That's the dial on the front of the camera, labeled in Figure 1-23.)

✔ **BKT (Bracket) button:** Press this button to access settings related to automatic *bracketing,* a feature that simplifies the job of recording the same subject at various exposure, flash, and white balance settings. Chapter 7 details flash and exposure bracketing; Chapter 8 discusses white balancing.

✓ **Lens-release button:** Press this button to disengage the lens from the camera body so that you can remove the lens. See the first part of this chapter for help with mounting and removing lenses.

✓ **Focus-mode selector:** This switch sets the camera to manual or autofocusing. See the earlier section "Changing the focusing method (auto or manual)" for the short story; see Chapter 8 for complete focusing details.

✓ **AF-mode button:** Pressing this button accesses two options that control autofocusing. While holding the button, you rotate the Main command dial to adjust the Autofocus mode and rotate the Sub-command dial to adjust the AF-area mode. Again, Chapter 8 explains how these settings affect the camera's autofocusing behavior.

✓ **Front infrared receiver:** Here's the second of two receivers that can pull in the signal from the optional ML-L3 wireless remote control unit. Figure 1-21 shows you where to aim the remote transmitter if you're standing behind the camera.

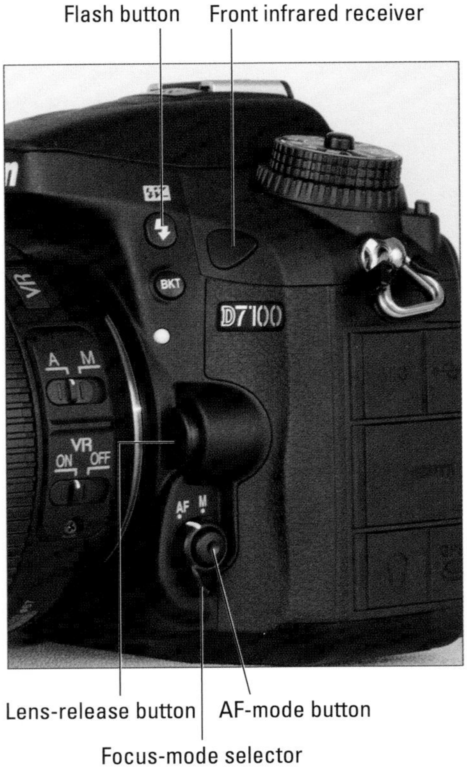

Flash button   Front infrared receiver

Lens-release button | AF-mode button

Focus-mode selector

Figure 1-22: The front-left side of the camera sports these features.

Front-right controls

Figure 1-23 offers a look at the front-right side of the camera, which houses the following controls:

✓ **Sub-command dial:** This dial is the counterpart to the Main command dial on the back of the camera. As with the Main dial, you rotate this one to select certain settings, usually in conjunction with pressing a camera button.

✔ **AF-assist lamp:** In dim lighting, a beam of light shoots out from this lamp to help the camera's autofocus system find its target. In general, leaving the AF-assist option enabled is a good idea, but if you're shooting at an event where the light may be distracting, you can disable it through the Built-In AF-Assist Illuminator option, found on the Autofocus section of the Custom Setting menu.

The lamp also lights before the shutter is released in Self-Timer mode and before the flash fires in Red-Eye Reduction Flash mode. Chapter 2 offers more information about both of these features.

✔ **Depth-of-Field Preview button:** By pressing this button, you can see how different aperture settings affect depth of field, or the distance over which focus appears sharp. Chapter 8 shows you how it works, and Chapter 11 explains how to assign a different function to the button if you don't care to preview depth of field.

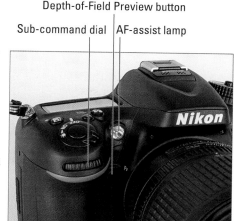

Depth-of-Field Preview button

Sub-command dial ⎮ AF-assist lamp

Fn (Function) button

Figure 1-23: You can set the Function (Fn) and Depth-of-Field Preview buttons to perform a variety of operations.

If you stick with the default setting and flash is enabled, pressing the button also causes the flash to emit a pulse of light to help you see how your subject will be illuminated. You can disable that feature via the Modeling Flash option, found in the Bracketing/Flash section of the Custom Setting menu.

✔ **Function (Fn) button:** By default, pressing this button while rotating either command dial switches the Image Area setting from the DX area mode, which captures your picture using the entire image sensor, to the 1.3 crop mode, which uses a smaller area at the center of the sensor. For details on this setting, see the first part of Chapter 2.

As with the Depth-of-Field Preview button, you can change the operation that's accomplished by pressing the button. Again, see Chapter 11 for the scoop.

Hidden connections

Under the doors on the left side of the camera, you find the following connections, labeled in Figure 1-24.

✔ **Microphone jack:** If you're not happy with the quality provided by the internal microphone, you can plug in an external microphone here. The jack accepts a 3.5mm microphone plug.

✔ **USB port:** One way to download images to your computer is to connect the camera and computer via the USB cable provided in the camera box. The small end of the cable goes into this port. Chapter 6 explains the downloading process.

You also use this port to connect the optional WU-1a wireless adapter, which permits wireless transfer of photos from the camera to a smart phone and certain tablet computers. Chapter 6 offers more information about this accessory.

✔ **HDMI port:** You can connect the camera to a high-def (HDMI) television via this port, but you need to buy a Type C mini-pin HDMI cable to do so. Chapter 5 has details about connecting your camera to a TV.

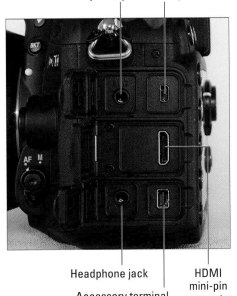

Microphone jack USB port

Headphone jack

Accessory terminal

HDMI mini-pin connector

Figure 1-24: Connection ports for various cables and accessories are found under the covers on the left side of the camera.

✔ **Headphone jack:** To enable you to monitor movie audio, you can attach headphones via this port. Your headphones need a 3.5mm plug.

✔ **Accessory terminal:** Here's where you attach the optional Nikon GP-1 GPS (Global Positioning System) unit, the WR-1 and WR-R10 wireless remote controllers, and the MC-DC2 wired remote control. I don't cover these optional devices, so refer to the manuals that ship with them to find out more.

If you turn the camera over, you find a tripod socket, which enables you to mount the camera on a tripod that uses a ¼" screw, plus the battery chamber. The other little rubber cover is related to the optional MB-D15 battery pack; you remove the cover when attaching the battery pack. Along the side of the battery cover, a little flap covers the connection through which you can attach the optional AC power adapter; the camera manual provides specifics on running the camera on AC power.

Asking Your Camera for Help

Your camera offers a built-in help line — a great tool for times when you forget the purpose of a particular menu option.

If you see a question mark in the lower-left corner of a menu, as shown on the left in Figure 1-25, press and hold the WB button to display information about that option, as shown on the right. (The little question mark symbol on the button reminds you of this function.) If you need to scroll the screen to view all the help text, keep the button pressed and scroll by using the Multi Selector. Release the button to close the help screen.

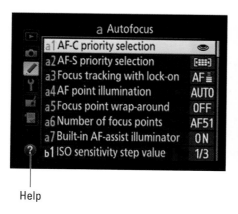
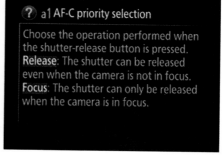

Help

Figure 1-25: Press and hold the WB button to display onscreen help.

Reviewing Basic Setup Options

You can customize your camera in scads of ways, and I address all of them throughout later chapters. However, you should review a few settings before you take your first pictures; the rest of this chapter covers these basic setup options.

Cruising the Setup menu

Among the initial customization options to consider are the following settings, all found on the Setup menu. It's a three-page affair, with the first two pages shown in Figure 1-26. Press the Multi Selector up and down to scroll through the pages of options.

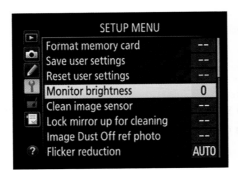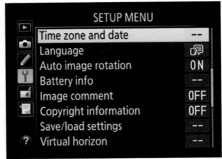

Figure 1-26: The Setup menu contains options that control basic camera operations.

✔ **Monitor Brightness:** This option enables you to make the camera monitor brighter or darker. If you take this step, though, what you see on the display may not be an accurate rendition of your image. Crank up the monitor brightness, for example, and an underexposed photo may look just fine. So I recommend sticking with the default setting (0).

✔ **Clean Image Sensor:** Your D7100 has an internal cleaning system designed to keep a filter that's fitted onto the image sensor free of dust and dirt. By choosing the Clean Image Sensor command, you can perform a cleaning at any time. Just choose the command, press OK, select Clean Now, and press OK again. Set the camera on a flat surface when performing the cleaning for best results.

You also can tell the camera to perform automatic cleaning every time you turn the camera on or off, only at startup, only at shutdown, or never; to do so, select Clean at Startup/Shutdown instead of Clean Now. Then press the Multi Selector right, highlight the cleaning option you prefer, and press OK.

✔ **Lock Mirror Up for Cleaning:** This feature is necessary when manually cleaning the camera image sensor (or technically, the aforementioned filter) — an operation that I don't recommend that you tackle yourself because you can easily damage the camera if you don't know what you're doing. If you *are* comfortable with the sensor-cleaning process, be sure that the camera battery is charged before you start; the menu option disappears when the battery is low.

✔ **Image Dust Off Ref Photo:** This feature enables you to record an image that serves as a point of reference for the automatic dust-removal filter available in Nikon Capture NX 2. I don't cover this accessory software, which must be purchased separately, in this book.

✔ **Time Zone and Date:** When you turn on your camera for the first time, it displays this option and asks you to set the current date and time. Keeping the date/time accurate is important because that information is recorded as part of the image file. In your photo browser, you can then see when you shot an image and, equally handy, search for images by the date they were taken.

On a related note: If you see the message "Clock" blinking in the Information display and you already set the date and time, the internal battery that keeps the clock running is depleted. Simply charging the main camera battery and then putting that battery back in the camera sets the clock ticking again, but you need to reset the camera time and date.

✔ **Language:** This option determines the language of text on the camera monitor.

✔ **Battery Info:** Select this option to view detailed information about your battery, as shown in Figure 1-27. The Charge data shows you the current power remaining as a percentage value, and the No. of Shots value tells you how many times you've pressed and released the shutter button since the last time you charged the battery. The final readout, Battery Age, lets you know how much more life you can expect out of the battery before it can no longer be recharged. When the display moves toward the right end of the little meter, it's time to buy a new battery.

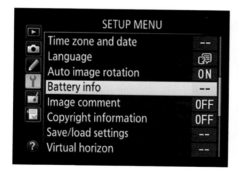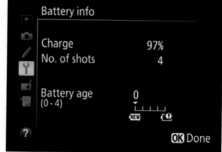

Figure 1-27: You can check the health of your battery via the Battery Info menu item.

The screen in Figure 1-27 shows the display as it appears when you use the regular camera battery. If you attach the optional battery pack, see its manual and the camera manual to find out how to interpret the data that's reported.

✔ **Save/Load Settings:** Through this feature, available only when you shoot in the P, S, A, or M exposure modes, you create a file that records the current major menu settings and store the file on your memory card. (The camera manual contains a list of settings that are stored.) If you later want to use all those settings again, you just load the file from the memory card. The camera stores your settings on the card in Slot 1, assigning the filename NCSETUPA. Don't change the filename, or you won't be able to reload the settings later.

✔ **Virtual Horizon:** Here's a cool aid for shooting pictures that requires your camera to be level with the horizon. When you select this option, as shown on the left in Figure 1-28, and then press OK, you see a screen with a built-in level, as shown on the right. When the camera is level to the horizon, the line through the middle of the display turns green, as shown in the figure. (If the entire display is gray, the camera is tilted too far forward or backward for the system to do its thing.) Unfortunately, the display shows only on the monitor and not in the viewfinder, so it's mostly of use setting up your camera on a tripod.

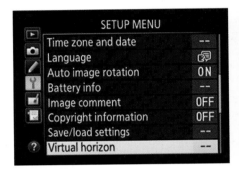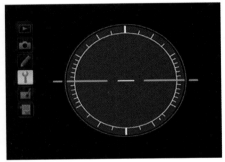

Figure 1-28: The Virtual Horizon display helps you make sure the camera is level.

During Live View shooting, you can enable a display option that super-imposes the Virtual Horizon tool over the live image on the monitor. Just press the Info button to cycle through the various display modes until the virtual horizon graphic appears. Chapter 4 details Live View shooting.

Although you can't see the virtual horizon indicator in the viewfinder, you can set the Fn (Function) button or Depth-of-Field Preview button to display a roll-bar-type level indicator in the viewfinder. However, the buttons then no longer perform their default functions, which are to access the Image Area setting and preview depth of field. So leave the buttons alone for now — otherwise, my instructions through the rest of the book related to the two buttons won't work. If you want to try the roll-bar feature, Chapter 11 shows you how to assign the function to either button.

✔ **Non-CPU Lens Data:** A CPU lens is equipped with technology that enables it to transmit certain data about the lens to the camera. When you use a non-CPU lens, you lose access to certain D7100 features. (Your manual spells them out.) You can gain back a little of the lost functionality by registering your lens through this Setup menu option. You assign the lens a number — you can register up to nine lenses — and enter the maximum aperture and focal length of that lens.

✔ **GPS:** If you purchase the optional Nikon GPS unit, this item, found on page 3 of the Setup menu, holds settings related to its operation. This book doesn't cover this accessory, but the camera manual provides help to get you started.

✔ **Wireless Mobile Adapter:** This option relates to the Wu-1a mobile adapter, which enables you to send pictures over a wireless network to some smart phones and tablets. When the feature is turned on, the camera looks for a wireless signal that the unit can use for the transfer. Turn the option off in locations where wireless devices are prohibited. It's also a good idea to disable the feature when you're not using the Wu-1a device, because the signal locator uses battery power.

✔ **Network:** This function provides options related to the optional UT-1 communication unit, which enables you to transfer files to a computer via an Ethernet network connection, or, when used together with the WT-5 wireless transmitter, via a wireless network. These devices also enable you to control the camera from your computer, but only if you invest in the optional Nikon Camera Control Pro 2 software (about $180). I don't cover these devices or the software in this book, but the camera and device manuals spell out what you need to know to take advantage of these features. The option is disabled on the menu if the devices aren't plugged into the camera.

✔ **Eye-Fi Upload:** Your camera can work with some Eye-Fi memory cards, which are equipped with technology that enables you to send your pictures over a wireless network to your computer. If you put one of the cards in the camera, this option appears on the Setup menu and contains settings for making the transfer and for disabling the wireless signal in situations where wireless devices are not allowed. When no Eye-Fi card is installed, the option doesn't appear.

For the whole story on Eye-Fi, including help with setting up your wireless transfers, visit the company's website at `www.eye.fi`.

✔ **Firmware Version:** Select this option and press OK to view what version of the camera firmware, or internal software, your camera is running. You see two firmware items, C and L, which refer to firmware for different aspects of the camera operation. At the time this book was written, C was in Version 1.0, and the L was 1.008.

Keeping your camera firmware up to date is important, so visit the support section of the Nikon website regularly to find out whether your camera sports the latest version. You can find detailed instructions on how to download and install any firmware updates on the site.

Browsing the Custom Setting menu

Displaying the Custom Setting menu, whose icon is a little pencil, takes you to the left screen shown in Figure 1-29. Here you can access submenus that carry the labels A through G. Each submenu holds clusters of options related to a specific aspect of the camera's operation. Highlight a submenu and press OK to get to those options, as shown on the right.

Custom Setting menu icon

Menu subcategories

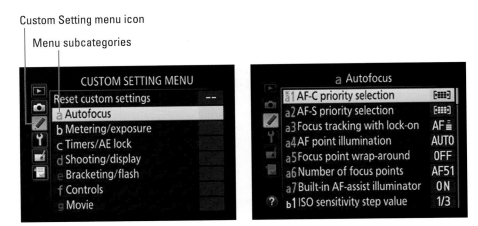

Figure 1-29: Select a submenu and press OK to access the available options.

A few important points about the Custom Setting menu:

- ⯈ After you jump to the first submenu, you can simply scroll up and down the list to view options from other submenus. You don't have to keep going back to the first screen in Figure 1-29, selecting the submenu, pressing OK, and so on.

- ⯈ Items that are dimmed in the menu are off-limits in the current exposure mode (Auto, Scene, P, M, and so on). Many options are available only in the P, S, A, and M modes.

- ⯈ An asterisk above a letter, as in the highlighted option on the right in Figure 1-29, indicates that you selected a setting other than the default.

- ⯈ In the Nikon manual, instructions sometimes reference these settings by a menu letter and number. For example, "Custom Setting a1" refers to the first option on the Autofocus submenu. I try to be more specific in this book, however, so I use the actual setting names. (Really, everyone has enough numbers to remember, don't you think?)

With those clarifications out of the way, the following sections describe customization options related to basic camera operations.

Adjusting automatic shutdown timing

To save battery power, your camera automatically shuts off the exposure meter, viewfinder display, and monitor after a period of activity. You can specify how long you want the camera to wait before taking either step through the following options, both found on the Timers/AE Lock portion of the Custom Setting menu:

✔ **Standby Timer:** This setting, highlighted in Figure 1-30, controls the exposure meter and viewfinder display shutoff. The default is 6 seconds. You can raise the value as high as 30 minutes or, by choosing the No Limit option, disable the shutdown entirely.

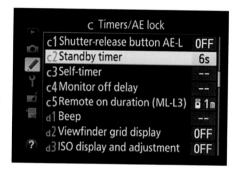

Figure 1-30: Use the Standby Timer option to adjust the auto shutdown timing of the meter and viewfinder display.

✔ **Monitor Off Delay:** Through this option, you can specify the auto-off timing for picture playback, menu displays, the Information display, and the Live View display. Additionally, you can adjust the length of time the camera displays a picture immediately after you press the shutter button, known as the Image Review period. Because the monitor is one of the biggest drains on battery power, keep the shutoff delay times as short as you find practical.

Customizing shooting and display options

Head for the Shooting/Display section of the Custom Setting menu to tweak various aspects of how the camera communicates with you, as well as to control a couple of basic shooting functions. Later chapters discuss options related to picture-taking; the following affect the basic camera interface:

✔ **Beep:** Through this option, spotlighted in Figure 1-31, you can tell the camera to emit a beep to indicate that focus is achieved when you use certain autofocus settings. The beep also sounds when you use the Self-Timer Release mode or certain Remote-Control Release modes, if you try to take a picture when the memory card is locked, and when time-lapse photography ends.

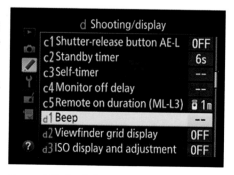

Figure 1-31: By default, the camera's beeper is disabled, enabling quieter shooting.

By default, the beep is disabled. If you want to hear the beep, choose the Beep option and then set the volume and pitch of the beep. On the Information and Control panel displays, a little musical note icon appears when the beep is enabled.

✏ **Viewfinder Grid Display:** You can display gridlines in the viewfinder by setting this option to On. The gridlines are a great help when you need to ensure the alignment of objects in your photo.

✏ **Screen Tips:** If you don't want to see the little help labels that appear when you adjust settings via the control strip in the Information display, turn this option to Off. For a look at a screen tip, see the left side of Figure 1-13, earlier in this chapter.

✏ **File Number Sequence:** This option controls how the camera names your picture files. If you set this option to Off, the camera restarts file numbering at 0001 every time you format your memory card or insert a new memory card. Numbering is also restarted if you create custom folders (an advanced option covered in Chapter 11), or if the current folder is full and the camera automatically creates a new folder.

This setup can cause problems over time, creating a scenario where you wind up with multiple images that have the same filename — not on the current memory card, but when you download images to your computer. So, I strongly encourage you to stick with the default setting, On. At this setting, file numbering continues from the previous number used or from the largest file number in the current folder. Note that when you get to picture number 9999, file numbering is still reset to 0001, however. The camera automatically creates a new folder to hold your next 9,999 images.

The Reset option tells the camera to look at the largest file number on the current card (or in the selected folder) and then assign the next highest number to your next picture. If the card or selected folder is empty, numbering starts at 0001. Then the camera behaves as if you selected the On setting.

Should you snap enough pictures to reach folder 999, and that folder contains either 9,999 pictures or a photo that has the file number 9999, the camera will refuse to take another photo until you choose that Reset option and either format the memory card or insert a brand-new one.

✏ **Information Display:** Normally, the camera tries to make the data on the display easier to read by automatically shifting from black text on a light background to light text on a black background, depending on the ambient light. If you prefer one display style over the other, visit this menu item and change the setting from Auto to Manual. You can then select either Dark on Light (for dark lettering on a light background) or Light on Dark (for light lettering on a dark background).

In this book, I show the Information screen using the Dark on Light display because it reproduces better in print.

✔ **LCD Illumination:** This setting affects a backlight that can be turned on to illuminate the Control panel. When the option is set to Off, as it is by default, you can illuminate the panel briefly by rotating the On/Off switch past the On setting, to the little light bulb marking. The backlight turns off automatically a few seconds after you release the switch.

If you instead set the LCD Illumination option to On, the backlight comes on automatically anytime the exposure meters are activated (which happens when you press the shutter button halfway). Obviously, this option consumes more battery power than simply using the On/Off switch to light up the panel when you really need it.

✔ **MB-D15 Battery Type and Battery Order:** You don't need to worry about these options unless you buy the optional MB-D15 battery adapter. If you use the battery pack, specify the type of battery you're using via the MB-D15 Battery Type menu option. Then use the Battery Order option to tell the camera whether you want it to draw power first from the battery pack or the regular camera battery when you have both installed. (See your camera manual for more details about using the battery pack.)

Shooting without a memory card (not!)

The Slot Empty Release Lock setting, found on the Controls section of the Custom Setting menu and shown in Figure 1-32, determines whether the shutter release is disabled when no memory card is in the camera. At the default setting, OK, you can take a temporary picture, which appears in the monitor with the word *Demo* but isn't recorded anywhere. (The feature is provided mainly for use in camera stores, enabling salespeople to demonstrate the camera without having to keep a memory card installed.) I suggest that you change the setting to Release Locked. It's too easy to miss that *Demo* message and think you've recorded a picture when you really haven't.

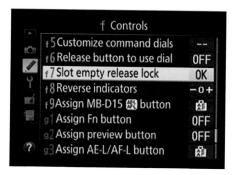

Figure 1-32: At this setting, you can take a temporary, demo-only photo when no memory card is installed.

Choosing a storage folder

By default, the camera creates an initial storage folder to hold your files; each folder can hold 999 images. When you exceed that limit, the camera creates a new folder for your next 999 shots. However, you can create a new folder at any time via the Storage Folder option on the Shooting menu; Chapter 11 tells you how. If you create your own folders, specify via the menu option which folder you want to use for your next pictures.

Restoring default settings

Should you want to return your camera to its original, out-of-the-box state, the camera manual contains a complete list of all the default settings.

You can also partially restore default settings by taking these steps:

- ✔ **Reset all Shooting Menu options:** Open the Shooting menu, choose Reset Shooting Menu, and press OK.

- ✔ **Reset all Custom Setting Menu options:** Choose the Reset Custom Settings option at the top of the Custom Setting menu.

- ✔ **Restore critical picture-taking settings *without* affecting options on the Custom Setting menu:** Use the two-button reset method: Press and hold the Exposure Compensation button and the ISO button simultaneously for longer than two seconds. (The little green dots near the buttons are a reminder of this function.) See the camera manual for a list of exactly what settings are restored.

2

Choosing Basic Picture Settings

*E*very camera manufacturer strives to provide a good *out-of-box* experience — that is, to ensure that your initial encounter with the camera is a happy one. To that end, the camera's default settings are selected to make it easy for you to take a good picture the first time you press the shutter button.

Although the default settings produce a nice picture in many cases, they're not designed to produce the optimal results in every situation. You may be able to use the defaults to take a decent portrait, for example, but you probably need to tweak a few settings to capture action. Adjusting a few options can help turn that decent portrait into a stunning one, too.

So that you can start fine-tuning camera settings to your subject, this chapter explains the most basic picture-taking options: exposure mode, shutter-release mode, picture resolution, file type, and image area. They're not the most exciting options (don't think I didn't notice you stifling a yawn), but they make a big difference in how easily you can capture the photo you have in mind.

Choosing an Exposure Mode

The first setting to consider is the exposure mode, which you select via the Mode dial, shown in Figure 2-1. To rotate the dial, you must press and hold its center button, labeled in the figure as the "Mode dial unlock button."

Your choice determines how much control you have over two critical exposure settings — aperture and shutter speed — as well as many other options, including those related to color and flash photography.

Mode dial unlock button   Auto Flash Off

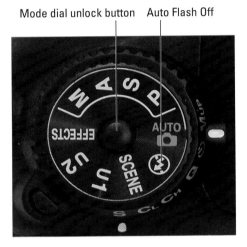

Figure 2-1: The Mode setting determines how much input you have over exposure, color, and other picture options.

Your exposure mode choices break down as follows:

- **Fully automatic exposure modes:** For people who haven't yet explored photography concepts such as aperture and shutter speed, the D7100 offers the following point-and-shoot modes:

  - *Auto:* The camera analyzes the scene and tries to select the most appropriate settings to capture the image. In dim lighting, the built-in flash may fire.

  - *Auto Flash Off:* This mode, represented by the icon labeled in Figure 2-1, works just like Auto but disables flash.

  - *Scene modes:* Set the Mode dial to Scene and then rotate the Main command dial to choose from automatic modes geared to capturing specific types of shots: portraits, landscapes, child photos, and such.

- *Effects modes:* Set the Mode dial to this setting and rotate the Main command dial to select from seven special effects, such as Night Vision mode (which creates a grainy, black-and-white photo) and Color Sketch mode (which creates a picture that resembles a drawing produced with colored pencils).

Because these modes are designed to make picture-taking simple, they prevent you from accessing many of the camera's features. You can't use the White Balance control, for example, to tweak picture colors. Options that are off-limits appear dimmed in the camera menus.

For help using Auto, Auto Flash Off, and Scene modes, travel to Chapter 3; for information about Effects mode, check out Chapter 10.

✔ **Semi-automatic modes:** To take more creative control but still get some exposure assistance from the camera, choose one of these modes:

- *P (programmed autoexposure):* The camera selects the aperture and shutter speed necessary to ensure a good exposure. But you can choose from different combinations of the two to vary the creative results. For example, shutter speed affects whether moving objects appear blurry or sharp. So you might use a fast shutter speed to freeze action, or you might go the other direction, choosing a shutter speed slow enough to blur the action, creating a heightened sense of motion. Because this mode gives you the option to choose different aperture/shutter speed combos, it's sometimes referred to as *flexible programmed autoexposure.*

- *S (shutter-priority autoexposure):* You select the shutter speed, and the camera selects the aperture. This mode is ideal for capturing sports or other moving subjects because it gives you direct control over shutter speed.

- *A (aperture-priority autoexposure):* In this mode, you choose the aperture, and the camera sets the shutter speed. Because aperture affects *depth of field,* or the distance over which objects in a scene appear sharply focused, this setting is great for portraits because you can select an aperture that results in a soft, blurry background, putting the emphasis on your subject. For landscape shots, on the other hand, you might choose an aperture that produces a large depth of field so that both near and distant objects appear sharp and therefore have equal visual weight in the scene.

All three modes give you access to all the camera's features. So even if you're not ready to explore aperture and shutter speed, go ahead and set the mode dial to P if you need to access a setting that's off-limits in the fully automated modes. The camera then operates pretty much as it does in Auto mode but without limiting your ability to control picture settings if you need to do so.

When you're ready to make the leap to P, S, or A mode, look to Chapter 7 for assistance. In addition, check out Chapter 8 to find out ways beyond aperture to manipulate depth of field.

✔ **Manual (M):** In this mode, you select both the aperture and shutter speed. But the camera still offers an assist by displaying an exposure meter to help you dial in the right settings. You have control over all other picture settings, too. For more on this mode, see Chapter 7.

✔ **U1 and U2:** These two settings represent the pair of custom exposure modes that you can create. (The *U* stands for *user.*) They give you a quick way to immediately switch to all the picture settings you prefer for a specific type of shot. For example, you might store the options you like to use for indoor portraits as U1 and store settings for sports shots as U2.

For step-by-step instructions, check out Chapter 11.

Choosing the Shutter-Release Mode

Chapter 7 explains the *shutter,* which is the thing inside the camera that controls when light is allowed to enter through the lens, strike the image sensor, and expose the image. The shutter opens when you press the shutter button, and it closes after the image is exposed. Photo lingo uses the term *shutter release* to refer to the action of the shutter opening.

By default, the D7100 is set to capture one image each time you press the shutter button. But you have a variety of other options. You can delay the shutter release for a few seconds after the button is pressed, for example, or record a continuous burst of images as long as you hold down the shutter button.

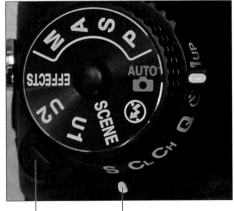

Release mode   Selected Release mode
unlock button

The primary point of control for shutter release is the Release mode dial, shown in Figure 2-2. To change the setting, press and hold the Release mode dial unlock button (labeled in Figure 2-2) while rotating the dial. The letter displayed next to the white marker represents the

Figure 2-2: You can choose from a variety of Release modes.

selected setting. For example, in Figure 2-2, the S is aligned with the marker, showing that the Single Frame mode is selected. The Information display shows you the current mode as well, as shown in Figure 2-3.

Upcoming sections explain the various Release modes and introduce you to a few menu options that also affect the shutter release.

One note in advance: If you've worked with another Nikon dSLR with a Release mode dial, you may expect to find a dial

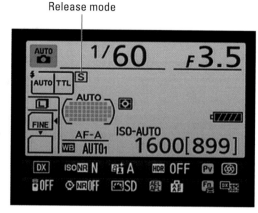

Figure 2-3: This symbol represents the current Release mode.

setting designed for use with the wireless ML-L3 remote control unit. But Nikon moved that option off the dial on the D7100. Instead, you enable wireless remote shooting via the Remote Control Mode (ML-L3) option on the Shooting menu. See "Enabling remote control shooting," later in the chapter, for details.

Single Frame and Quiet modes

S At the default Release mode setting, Single Frame, you get one picture each time you press the shutter button. In other words, this is normal-photography mode.

Q Quiet Shutter Release mode works just like Single Frame mode but makes less noise as it goes about its business. Designed for situations when you want the camera to be as silent as possible, this mode disables the beep that the autofocus system may sound when it achieves focus. (The beep sounds only if you enable it through the Beep setting on the Custom Setting menu; it's turned off by default.)

Additionally, Quiet Shutter Release mode affects the operation of the internal mirror that causes the scene coming through the lens to be visible in the viewfinder. Normally, the mirror flips up when you press the shutter button and then flips back down after the shutter opens and closes. This mirror movement makes some noise. In Quiet Shutter Release mode, you can prevent the mirror from flipping down by keeping the shutter button pressed after the shot. This feature enables you to delay the final mirror movement — and its accompanying sound — to a moment when the noise won't be objectionable.

Hey, my shutter button isn't working!

You press the shutter button . . . and press it, and press it — and nothing happens. Don't panic: Your problem is likely related to one of these two Custom Setting menu options:

✔ **AF-S Priority Selection:** By default, this option tells the camera not to release the shutter if focus can't be achieved when you use autofocusing and set the Autofocus mode to AF-S. The same thing happens if you use the AF-A mode and the camera automatically selects the AF-S mode for

you. (Chapter 8 details the Autofocus mode.) Change the setting to Release if you want the picture to be captured regardless of whether focus is achieved.

✔ **Slot Empty Release Lock:** This option controls whether the shutter button is released if you don't have a memory card in the camera. If you took my advice at the end of Chapter 1 and set the option to Release Locked, the shutter button ignores you until you insert a card.

Continuous (burst mode) shooting

Setting the Release mode dial to Continuous Low or Continuous High enables *burst mode* shooting. That is, the camera records a continuous burst of images for as long as you hold down the shutter button, making it easier to capture fast-paced action.

Here's how the two modes differ:

CL ✔ **Continuous Low:** In this mode, you can tell the camera to capture from 1 to 6 frames per second. You set the maximum frames-per-second (fps) count via the CL Mode Shooting Speed option, found on the Shooting/Display section of the Custom Setting menu and featured in Figure 2-4. The default is 3 fps.

Why would you want to capture fewer than the maximum number of shots? Well, frankly, unless you're shooting something that's moving at a really fast pace, not

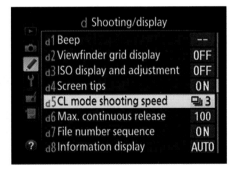

Figure 2-4: You can specify the maximum frames-per-second rate for Continuous Low Release mode.

too much is going to change between frames when you shoot at 6 frames per second. So when you set the burst rate that high, you typically wind up with lots of shots that show the exact same thing, wasting space on your memory card. I keep this value set to the default 3 fps and then, if I want a higher burst rate, I use the Continuous High setting, explained next.

The Release mode symbol in the Information display shows you the current frames-per-second setting. (Refer to Figure 2-3.)

CH

✔ **Continuous High:** This mode works just like Continuous Low except that it records up to 6 frames per second. You can't adjust the maximum capture rate as you can for Continuous Low. However, you *may* be able to boost the rate to 7 frames per second by adjusting some other camera settings. (Keep reading for details.)

For both modes, you can limit the maximum number of shots the camera takes with each press of the shutter button. Again, the idea behind this feature is simply to prevent firing off lots of wasted frames. Make the adjustment via the Max Continuous Release option, found just below the CL Mode Shooting Speed option, as shown in Figure 2-5.

A few other critical details about these two release modes:

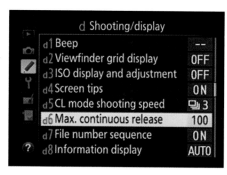

Figure 2-5: This option limits the number of shots recorded with each press of the shutter button in the Continuous Low and Continuous High modes.

✔ **You can't use flash.** Continuous mode doesn't work with flash because the time that the flash needs to recycle between shots slows down the capture rate too much. So even if the Release mode dial is set to CL or CH, you get one shot for each press of the shutter button if the flash is raised.

✔ **Images are stored temporarily in the memory buffer**. The camera has a little bit of internal memory — a *buffer* — where it stores picture data until it has time to record them to the memory card. The number of pictures the buffer can hold depends on certain camera settings, such as resolution and file type (JPEG or Raw). The viewfinder displays an estimate of how many pictures will fit in the buffer; see the sidebar "What does [r 24] in the viewfinder mean?" later in this chapter, for details.

After shooting a burst of images, wait for the memory card access light on the back of the camera to go out before turning off the camera. That's your signal that the camera has successfully moved all data from the buffer to the memory card. Turning off the camera before that happens may corrupt the image file.

✓ **The maximum frames-per-second (fps) rate depends on the Image Quality and Image Area settings.** I detail both settings later in this chapter. For now, just be aware of their impact on the actual capture rate the camera delivers:

- *If the Image Area option is set to DX (the default) and the Image Quality option is set to 14-bit NEF (Raw):* The maximum fps drops from 6 to 5 for both the Continuous Low and Continuous High Release modes. (Even if you select 6 fps as the CL Mode Shooting Speed option, the camera maxes out at 5 fps.) Why the slowdown? Because the 14-bit NEF (Raw) setting increases the image file size, and it takes more time for the camera to write the data to the memory card.

- *If the Image Area setting is 1.3x and the Image Quality setting is JPEG (the default) or 12-bit NEF (Raw):* The maximum fps for Continuous High goes up to 7 fps. The camera can achieve this faster pace because the 1.3x Image Area setting captures a smaller image than normal, resulting in a smaller file size and faster data transfer. You just have to avoid setting the Image Quality setting to the 14-bit NEF (Raw) option, or you offset the reduction in file size.

✓ **Your mileage may vary.** The actual number of frames you can capture depends on a number of other factors, too, including your shutter speed. At a slow shutter speed, the camera may not be able to reach the maximum frame rate. Enabling Vibration Reduction also can reduce the frame rate, as can a weak battery. Additionally, although you can capture as many as 100 frames in a single burst, the frame rate can drop if the buffer gets full.

Self-timer shooting

You're no doubt familiar with Self-Timer mode, which delays the shutter release for a few seconds after you press the shutter button, giving you time to dash into the picture. Here's how it works on the D7100: After you press the shutter button, the autofocus-assist illuminator on the front of the camera starts to blink. If you enabled the camera's voice via the Beep option on the Custom Setting menu, you also hear a series of beeps. A few seconds later, the camera captures the image.

What does [r 24] in the viewfinder mean?

When you look in your viewfinder to frame a shot, the initial value shown at the right end of the display indicates the number of additional pictures that can fit on your memory card. For example, in the left image below, the value shows that the card can hold 856 more images.

As soon as you press the shutter button halfway, which kicks the autofocus and exposure

mechanisms into action, that value instead shows how many pictures can fit in the camera's *memory buffer,* which is the internal storage tank used to hold picture data until it can be moved to the memory card. In the right image here, for example, the r 24 value tells you that 24 pictures can fit in the buffer.

500F5.6   ISO AUTO [856]   500F5.6   ISO AUTO [r 24]

By default, the camera waits 10 seconds after you press the shutter button and then records a single image. But you can tweak the delay time and capture as many as nine shots at a time. Set your preferences through the Self-Timer option on the Custom Setting menu, as shown in Figure 2-6. Here's what you need to know about the three settings:

- ✔ **Self-Timer Delay:** Choose a delay time of 2, 5, 10, or 20 seconds.

- ✔ **Number of Shots:** Specify how many frames you want to capture with each press of the shutter button; the maximum is nine frames.

- ✔ **Interval between Shots:** If you choose to record multiple shots, this setting determines how long the camera waits between each one. You can set the delay to a half second (the default setting), 1 second, 2 seconds, or 3 seconds.

Two more points to note about self-timer shooting:

- ✔ **Using flash disables the multiple frames recording option.** The camera records just a single image, regardless of the Number of Shots setting.

- ✔ **Cover the viewfinder if possible.** Otherwise, light may seep into the camera through the viewfinder and affect exposure. Your camera comes with a viewfinder cover made just for this purpose.

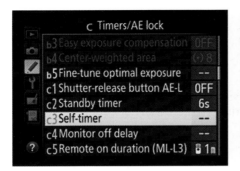
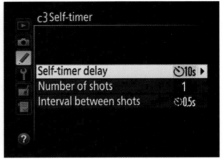

Figure 2-6: You can adjust the self-timer capture delay via the Custom Setting menu.

Mirror lockup (MUP)

One component of the optical system of your camera is a mirror that moves every time you press the shutter button. The small vibration caused by the action of the mirror can result in slight blurring of the image when you use a very slow shutter speed, shoot with a long telephoto lens, or take extreme close-up shots.

 To cope with that issue, the D7100 offers mirror-lockup shooting, which delays opening the shutter until after the mirror movement is complete. Enable the feature by setting the Release mode to Mirror Up (labeled MUP on the Release Mode dial).

 Mirror-lockup shooting requires that you press the shutter button twice to take the picture. Follow these steps:

1. **After framing and focusing, press the shutter button all the way down to lock up the mirror.**

   At this point, you can no longer see anything through the viewfinder. Don't panic — that's normal. The mirror's function is to enable you to see in the viewfinder the scene that the lens will capture, and mirror lockup prevents it from serving that purpose.

2. **To record the shot, let up on the shutter button and then press it all the way down again.**

   If you don't take the shot within about 30 seconds, the camera will record a picture for you automatically.

Remember that you still need to worry about moving the camera itself during the shot — even with the mirror locked up, the slightest jostle of the camera can cause blurring. In other words, situations that call for mirror lockup also call for a tripod. With the kit lens, turn off Vibration Reduction as well; with other lenses, check the manufacturer's recommendations about this issue.

Adding a remote-control shutter-release further ensures a shake-free shot — even the action of pressing the shutter button can move the camera enough to cause some slight blurring. Or you can just wait the 30 seconds needed for the camera to take the picture automatically, if your subject permits.

Off-the-dial shutter release features

In addition to the Release modes you can select from the Release mode dial, you have access to three other features that tweak the way the shutter is released, all explained next.

Exposure Delay mode

As an alternative to mirror lockup, you can use the Exposure Delay feature when you want to ensure that the movement of the mirror doesn't cause enough vibration to blur the shot. Through this option, you can tell the camera to wait 1, 2, or 3 seconds after the mirror is raised to capture the image.

Look for the setting in the Shooting/ Display section of the Custom Setting menu, as shown in Figure 2-7. Just don't forget you enabled the feature, or you'll drive yourself batty trying to figure out why the camera isn't responding to your shutter-button finger. (I say this from experience.) To help remind you, the Information display sports the letters DLY under the shutter speed value.

Also, the Exposure Delay feature isn't compatible with Continuous High or Continuous Low shooting — if you enable it in those modes, you get one image for each press of the shutter button rather than a burst of frames.

d Shooting/display	
d7 File number sequence	ON
d8 Information display	AUTO
d9 LCD illumination	OFF
d10 Exposure delay mode	OFF
d11 Flash warning	ON
d12 MB-D15 battery type	LR6
d13 Battery order	MB-D15
e1 Flash sync speed	1/250

Figure 2-7: Enabling Exposure Delay is another way to make sure that mirror vibrations don't cause blurring.

Enabling remote-control shooting

To use the optional Nikon ML-L3 wireless remote control unit to trigger the shutter button, you must enable the feature via the Remote Control Mode (ML-L3) option on the Shooting menu, as shown on the left in Figure 2-8, or via the Information display control strip, as shown on the right. (Press the *i* button to activate the control strip.) Either way, press OK to display a screen where you can select from the following capture options:

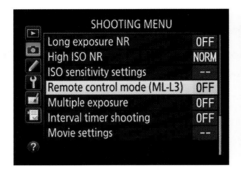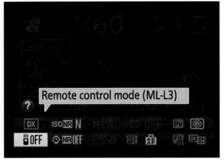

Figure 2-8: Set preferences for wireless remote control shutter release via the Shooting menu or control strip.

> ✔ **Delayed Remote:** The shutter is released 2 seconds after you press the button on the remote control unit.

> ✔ **Quick-Response Remote:** The shutter opens immediately after you press the button.

> ✔ **Remote Mirror-Up:** As its name implies, this setting enables you to use the remote for mirror-up shooting, a technique explained in the preceding section.

> ✔ **Off (default):** The camera doesn't respond to the remote control unit.

Automatic time-lapse photography

Self-Timer mode enables you to take up to nine pictures with one press of the shutter button, timing the frames at intervals of a half second to 3 seconds. If you want to record more frames or enjoy more flexibility over the interval between images, bail out of Self-Timer mode and instead enable Interval Timer Shooting.

With Interval Timer Shooting, you can record a whole memory card full of images and space the shots minutes or even hours apart. This feature enables you to capture a subject as it changes over time — a technique commonly known as *time-lapse photography*. Here's how to do it:

1. **Set the Release mode to any setting but Self-Timer or Mirror Up.**

   Those modes aren't compatible with interval-timing shooting. You also can't use the optional ML-L3 wireless remote control for this task.

2. **Choose Interval Timer Shooting from the Shooting menu, as shown on the left in Figure 2-9, and press OK.**

   The screen on the right in Figure 2-9 appears.

3. **To begin setting up your capture session, highlight Now or Start Time.**

   - *If you want to start the captures right away,* highlight Now.

   - *To set a later start time for the captures,* highlight Start Time.

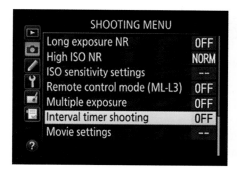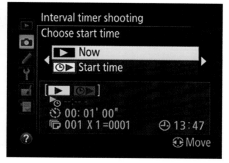

Figure 2-9: The Interval Timer Shooting feature enables you to do time-lapse photography.

4. **Press the Multi Selector right to display the capture-setup screen.**

   If you selected Start Time in Step 3, the screen looks like the one in Figure 2-10. If you selected Now, the Start Time option is dimmed, and the Interval option is highlighted instead.

5. **Set up your recording session.**

   You get three options: Start Time, Interval (time between shots), and Number of Times x Number of Shots (determines total number of shots recorded). The current settings for each option appear in the bottom half of the screen, as labeled in Figure 2-10.

At the top of the screen, value boxes appear. The highlighted box is active and relates to the setting that's highlighted at the bottom of the screen. For example, in the figure, the hour box for the Start Time setting is active. Press the Multi Selector right or left to cycle through the value boxes; to change the value in a box, press up or down.

A few notes about your options:

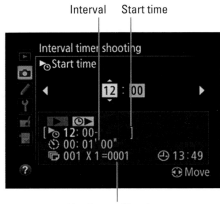

Interval   Start time

No. times x No. shots

Figure 2-10: Press the Multi Selector right or left to cycle through the setup options; press up or down to change the highlighted value.

- The Interval and Start Time options are based on a 24-hour clock. (The current time appears in the bottom-right corner of the screen and is based upon the date/time information you entered when setting up the camera.)

- For the Interval option, the left column box is for the hour setting; the middle, minutes; and the right, seconds. Make sure that the value you enter is longer than the shutter speed you plan to use.

- For the Start Time option, you can set hour and minute values only.

- The Number of Times value multiplied by the Number of Shots per interval determines how many pictures will be recorded.

6. Press the Multi Selector right until you see the screen shown in Figure 2-11.

7. Highlight On and press OK.

If you selected Now as your interval-capture starting option, the first shot is recorded about 3 seconds later. If you set a delayed start time, the camera displays a "Timer Active" message for a few seconds, and then the monitor turns off.

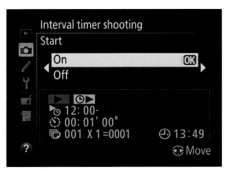

Figure 2-11: When you see this screen, highlight On and press OK to begin timed interval shooting.

A few final factoids:

- ✔ **Monitoring the shot progress:** The letters INTVL blink in the Control panel while an interval sequence is in progress. Before each shot is captured, the display changes to show the number of intervals remaining and the number of shots remaining in the current interval. The first value appears in the space usually occupied by the shutter speed; the second takes the place of the f-stop setting. You also can view the values at any time by pressing the shutter button halfway.

- ✔ **Interrupting interval shooting:** Between shots, bring up the Interval Timing menu item, press OK, highlight Pause, and press OK. You can also interrupt the interval sequence by turning off the camera — which gives you the chance to install an empty memory card if the current ones are full. When you turn on the camera again, reselect the Interval Timer Shooting menu option, press the Multi Selector right, choose Restart, and press OK to continue shooting. To cancel the sequence entirely, choose Off instead of Restart.

- ✔ **Autofocusing:** If you're using autofocusing, the camera initiates focusing before each shot.

- ✔ **Between shots:** You can view pictures in Playback mode or adjust menu settings between shots. The monitor goes dark about 4 seconds before the next shot is taken.

Choosing the Right Image Size and Image Quality Settings

Almost every review of the D7100 contains glowing reports about the camera's picture quality. As you've no doubt discovered, those claims are true: This baby can create large, beautiful images. What you may *not* have discovered is that Nikon's default Image Quality setting isn't the highest that the D7100 offers.

Why would Nikon do such a thing? Why not set up the camera to produce the best images right out of the box? The answer is that using the top setting has some downsides. Nikon's default choice represents a compromise between avoiding those disadvantages while still producing images that will please most photographers.

Whether that compromise is right for you, however, depends on your needs. To help you decide, the next several sections of this chapter explain the Image Quality setting, along with the Image Size setting, which is also critical to the quality of images that you print. Just in case you're having quality problems related to other issues, though, the next section provides a defect diagnosis guide.

Diagnosing quality problems

When I say *picture quality,* I'm not talking about the composition, exposure, or other traditional characteristics of a photograph. Instead, I'm referring to how finely the image is rendered in the digital sense. Figure 2-12 illustrates the concept: The first example is a high-quality image with clear details and smooth color transitions. The other examples show five common image defects.

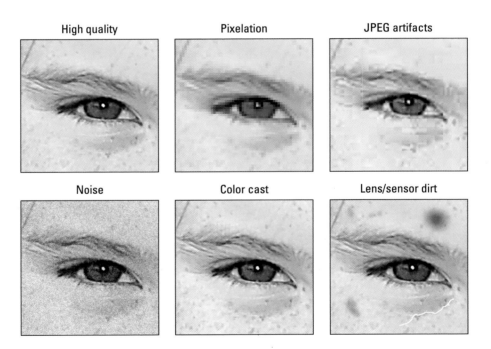

Figure 2-12: Refer to this symptom guide to determine the cause of poor image quality.

Each of these defects is related to a different issue, and only one is affected by the Image Quality setting on your D7100. So if you aren't happy with your image quality, first compare your photos to those in the figure to properly diagnose the problem. Then try these remedies:

- **Pixelation:** When an image doesn't have enough *pixels* (the colored tiles used to create digital images), details aren't clear, and curved and diagonal lines appear jagged. The fix is to increase image resolution, which you do via the Image Size control. See the next section, "Considering image size: How many pixels are enough?" for details.

- **JPEG artifacts:** The "parquet tile" texture and random color defects that mar the third image in Figure 2-12 can occur in photos captured in the JPEG *(jay-peg)* file format, which is why these flaws are referred to as *JPEG artifacts.* This is the defect related to the Image Quality setting; see "Understanding Image Quality options (JPEG or Raw)," later in this chapter, to find out more.

- **Noise:** This defect gives your image a speckled look, as shown in the lower-left example in Figure 2-12. Noise can occur with very long exposure times or when you choose a high ISO Sensitivity setting on your camera. You can explore both issues in Chapter 7.

- **Color cast:** If your colors are seriously out of whack, as shown in the lower-middle example in the figure, try adjusting the camera's White Balance setting. Chapter 8 covers this control and other color issues.

- **Lens/sensor dirt:** A dirty lens is the first possible cause of the kind of defects you see in the last example in the figure. If cleaning your lens doesn't solve the problem, dust or dirt may have made its way onto the camera's image sensor.

    Your D7100 offers an automated sensor-cleaning mechanism (you control its operation via the Clean Image Sensor command on the Setup menu). But if you frequently change lenses or shoot in a dirty environment, the internal cleaning mechanism may not be adequate, in which case a manual sensor cleaning is necessary. You can do this job yourself, but I don't recommend it. Image sensors are delicate beings, and you can easily damage them if you aren't careful. Instead, find a local camera store that offers this service. Sensor cleaning typically costs about $50, but some places offer the service free if you bought the camera there.

 When diagnosing image problems, you may want to open the photos in ViewNX 2 or some other photo software and zoom in for a close-up inspection. Some defects, especially pixelation and JPEG artifacts, have a similar appearance until you see them at a magnified view.

I should also tell you that I exaggerated the flaws in my example images to make the symptoms easier to see. With the exception of an unwanted color cast or a big blob of lens or sensor dirt, these defects may not even be noticeable unless you print or view your image at a very large size. And the subject matter of your image may camouflage some flaws; most people probably wouldn't detect a little JPEG artifacting in a photograph of a densely wooded forest, for example.

In other words, don't consider Figure 2-12 as an indication that your D7100 is suspect in the image quality department. First, *any* digital camera can produce these defects under the right circumstances. Second, by following the guidelines in this chapter and the others mentioned in the preceding list, you can resolve any quality issues that you may encounter.

Considering image size: How many pixels are enough?

Like other digital devices, your D7100 creates pictures out of *pixels,* which is short for *picture elements*. You can see some pixels close up in the right example of Figure 2-13, which shows a greatly magnified view of the eye area in the left image.

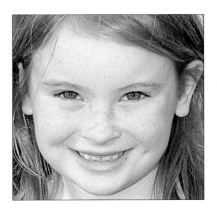 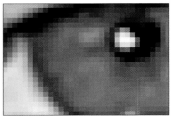

Figure 2-13: Pixels are the building blocks of digital photos.

You can specify the pixel count of your images, also known as the *resolution,* in two ways:

- **Qual button + Sub-command dial:** Hold down the Qual (Quality) button while rotating the Sub-command dial to cycle through the available settings. You can monitor the setting in the Control panel and Information display, in the areas highlighted in Figure 2-14.

- **Shooting menu:** Select the Image Size option and press OK to access the available settings, as shown in Figure 2-15.

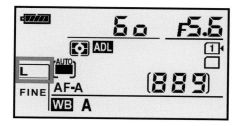
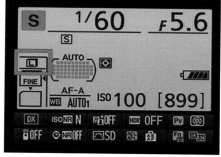

Figure 2-14: The current setting appears in the Control panel and Information display.

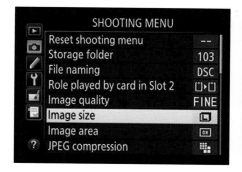
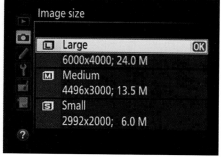

Figure 2-15: You can view the pixel count for each setting in the Shooting menu.

Either way, you can choose from three settings: Large, Medium, and Small. You can view the resulting resolution value for each setting if you adjust the option via the Shooting menu, as shown on the right in Figure 2-15.

The first pair of numbers shown for each setting represents the image *pixel dimensions* — that is, the number of horizontal pixels and the number of vertical pixels. The second value indicates the approximate total resolution, which you get by multiplying the two pixel dimension values. This number is usually stated in megapixels, abbreviated M on the menu screen (but typically abbreviated as MP in other resources, including this book). One megapixel equals 1 million pixels.

Note, however, that if you select Raw (NEF) as your file format, all images are captured at the Large setting. The upcoming section "Understanding Image Quality options (JPEG or Raw)" explains file formats. Also, the numbers you see in Figure 2-15 assume that you use the default setting for the Image Area option, which I explain at the end of this chapter. At the default setting, the camera captures the image using the entire image sensor (the part of the camera on which the image is formed). If you instead use the 1.3x crop setting, which captures the image using only the central portion of the sensor, you get fewer pixels at each Image Size setting, and the menu screen you see on the right in Figure 2-15 reflects those lower values. The Large setting drops to 4800 x 3200 pixels, or 15.4MP; Medium, to 3600 x 2400 pixels, or 8.6MP; and Small, to 2400 x 1600, or 3.8MP.

So how many pixels are enough? To make the call, you need to understand the three ways that pixel count affects your pictures:

- ✓ **Print size:** Pixel count determines the size at which you can produce a high-quality print. If you don't have enough pixels, your prints may exhibit the defects you see in the pixelation example in Figure 2-12, or worse, you may be able to see the individual pixels, as in the right example in Figure 2-13. Depending on your photo printer, you typically need anywhere from 200 to 300 pixels per linear inch, or *ppi,* of the print. To produce an 8 x 10 print at 200 ppi, for example, you need a pixel count of 1600 x 2000, or about 3.2 megapixels.

  Even though many photo-editing programs enable you to add pixels to an existing image, doing so isn't a good idea. For reasons I won't bore you with, adding pixels — known as *upsampling* — doesn't enable you to successfully enlarge your photo. In fact, upsampling typically makes matters worse.

- ✓ **Screen display size:** Resolution doesn't affect the quality of images viewed on a monitor, television, or other screen device the way it does for printed photos. Instead, resolution determines the *size* at which the image appears. This issue is one of the most misunderstood aspects of digital photography, so I explain it thoroughly in Chapter 6. For now, just know that you need *way* fewer pixels for onscreen photos than you do for printed photos. In fact, even the Small resolution setting on your camera creates a picture too big to be viewed in its entirety in most e-mail programs.

- ✓ **File size:** Every additional pixel increases the amount of data required to create a digital picture file. So a higher-resolution image has a larger file size than a low-resolution image.

  Large files present several problems:

  - You can store fewer images on your memory card, on your computer's hard drive, and on removable storage media such as a DVD.

  - When you share photos online, larger files take longer to upload and download.

  - When you edit your photos in your photo software, your computer needs more resources and time to process large files.

As you can see, resolution is a bit of a sticky wicket. What if you aren't sure how large you want to print your images? What if you want to print your photos *and* share them online?

I take the better-safe-than-sorry route, which leads to the following recommendations about which Image Size setting to use:

- **Always shoot at a resolution suitable for print.** You then can create a low-resolution copy of the image in your photo editor for use online. In fact, your camera offers a built-in resizing option; Chapter 6 shows you how to use it.

- **For everyday images, Medium is a good choice.** I find the Large setting (24.0MP) to be overkill for most casual shooting, which means that you're creating huge files for no good reason. Keep in mind that even at the Small setting (2992 x 2000 pixels), you have enough resolution to produce an 8-x-10-inch print at 200 ppi.

- **Choose Large for an image that you plan to crop, print very large, or both.** The benefit of maxing out resolution is that you have the flexibility to crop your photo and still generate a decent-sized print of the remaining image. Figures 2-16 and 2-17 offer an example. When I was shooting this photo, I couldn't get close enough to fill the frame with the main subject of interest, the two juvenile herons in the center. But because I had the resolution cranked up to Large, I could later crop the shot to the composition you see in Figure 2-17 and still produce a great print. In fact, I could've printed the cropped image at a much larger size than fits here.

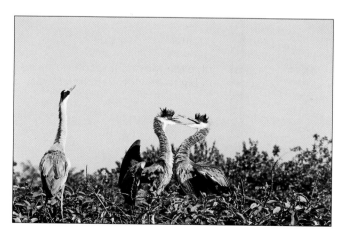

Figure 2-16: I couldn't get close enough to fill the frame with the subject, so I captured this image at the Large resolution setting.

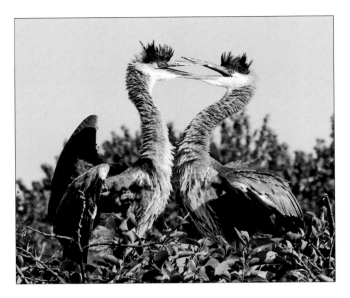

Figure 2-17: A high-resolution original enabled me to crop the photo tightly and still have enough pixels to produce a quality print.

Understanding Image Quality options (JPEG or Raw)

If I had my druthers, the Image Quality option would instead be called File Type because that's what the setting controls.

Here's the deal: The file type, sometimes known as a file *format*, determines how your picture data is recorded and stored. Your choice does impact picture quality, but so do other factors, as outlined earlier in this chapter. In addition, your choice of file type has ramifications beyond picture quality.

At any rate, your D7100 offers two file types: JPEG and Camera Raw, or just Raw for short. You also can choose to record two copies of each picture, one in the Raw format and one in the JPEG format.

You can view the current format in the Control panel and Information display, as shown in Figure 2-18. For JPEG, the displays indicate the JPEG quality level — Fine, Normal, or Basic. (The next section explains these three options.)

In the Information display, the icons used for the Quality setting depend on whether you're using one or two memory cards and how you told the camera to use the card in Slot 2 (done through the Role Played by Card in Slot 2 option on the Shooting menu). In Figure 2-18, the symbol shows that two cards are installed and that the Overflow setting is selected for Slot 2. See the Chapter 1 section related to using two memory cards at the same time for information on how to decode this aspect of the display.

The rest of this chapter explains the pros and cons of each file format to help you decide which one works best for the types of pictures you take. If you already have your mind made up, you can select the format you want to use in two ways:

QUAL

✔ **Qual button + Main command dial:** Hold down the Qual (Quality) button while rotating the Main command dial to cycle through all the format options.

Be sure to spin the Main command dial: Rotating the Sub-command dial while pressing the Qual button adjusts the Image Size (resolution) setting.

✔ **Shooting menu:** You also can set the Image Quality option via the Shooting menu, as shown in Figure 2-19.

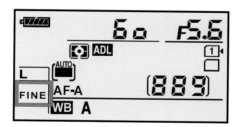 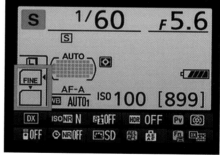

Figure 2-18: The current Image Quality setting appears here.

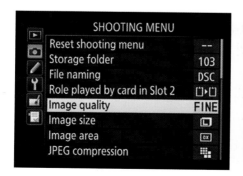 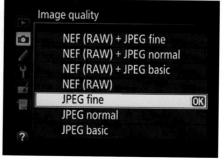

Figure 2-19: The Shooting menu enables you to select the Image Quality setting plus a few related options.

JPEG: The imaging (and web) standard

Pronounced *jay-peg,* the JPEG format is the default setting on your D7100, as it is for most digital cameras. The next two sections tell you what you need to know about JPEG.

JPEG pros and cons

JPEG has become the de facto digital camera file format for two main reasons:

- **Immediate usability:** All web browsers and e-mail programs can display JPEG files, so you can share your pictures online immediately after you shoot them. The same can't be said for Raw (NEF) files, which must be converted to JPEG for online use. You also can print and edit JPEG files immediately, whether you want to use your own software or have pictures printed at a retail site. You can view and print Raw files by using Nikon ViewNX 2, the software that comes with your camera, as well as from some third-party programs. But many programs *can't* open Raw images, and retail printing sites typically don't accept Raw files either. You can read more about the conversion process in the upcoming section "Raw (NEF): The purist's choice."

- **Small files:** JPEG files are much smaller than Raw files. And smaller files consume less room on your camera memory card and in your computer's storage tank.

The downside — you knew there had to be one — is that JPEG creates smaller files by applying *lossy compression.* This process actually throws away some image data. Too much compression leads to the defects you see in the JPEG artifacts example shown earlier in Figure 2-12.

Fortunately, your camera enables you to specify how much compression you're willing to accept, as outlined next.

Customizing your JPEG capture settings

You have two levels of control over how your JPEG images are recorded:

- **Fine, Normal, or Basic:** When choosing the Image Quality setting, you can select from three JPEG options, each of which produces a different level of compression.

    - *JPEG Fine:* At this setting, the compression ratio is 1:4 — that is, the file is four times smaller than it'd otherwise be. In plain English, that means that very little compression is applied, so you shouldn't see many compression artifacts, if any.

- *JPEG Normal:* Switch to Normal, and the compression ratio rises to 1:8. The chance of seeing some artifacting increases as well. This setting is the default option.

- *JPEG Basic:* Shift to this setting, and the compression ratio jumps to 1:16. That's a substantial amount of compression and brings more risk of artifacting.

✓ **Compression priority:** The size of the file produced at any of the three quality levels varies from picture to picture depending on the subject matter. The difference occurs because a picture with lots of detail and a wide color palette can't be as easily compressed as one with large areas of flat color and a limited color spectrum.

By default, the camera applies compression with a goal of producing consistent file sizes, which means that highly detailed photos can take a larger quality hit from compression. But through the JPEG Compression option on the Shooting menu, shown in Figure 2-20, you can tell the camera to instead give priority to producing optimum picture quality when applying compression. To go that route, choose the Optimal Quality setting, as shown in the figure. For the default option, choose Size Priority.

Note that the compression ratios just mentioned for the Fine, Normal, and Basic options assume that you use the Size Priority option. The ratios will vary from picture to picture, as will the picture file sizes, if you select Optimal Quality.

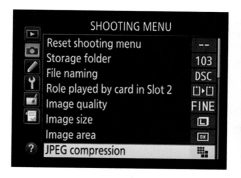 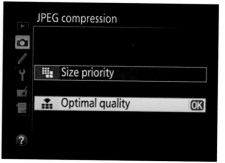

Figure 2-20: Set the JPEG Compression option to Optimal Quality to get the best-looking JPEG pictures.

Even if you choose the Size Priority option and combine it with JPEG Basic — thereby producing the lowest-quality JPEG results — you don't get anywhere near the level of artifacting that you see in my example in Figure 2-12, however. Again, that example is exaggerated to help you be able to recognize artifacting defects and understand how they differ from other image quality issues. In fact, if you keep your image print or display size small, you aren't likely to notice a great deal of quality difference between the compression settings. It's only when you greatly enlarge a photo that the differences become apparent.

Nikon chose the Normal and Size Priority options as the default JPEG settings — in other words, a notch down from the top quality settings. For my money, though, the file-size benefit you gain from dropping the quality down from Fine to Normal and using the Size Priority option instead of Optimal Quality isn't worth even a little quality loss, especially with the price of camera memory cards getting lower every day. You never know when a casual snapshot is going to turn out to be so great that you want to print or display it large enough that even minor quality loss becomes a concern. And of all the defects that you can correct in a photo editor, artifacting is one of the hardest to remove. So if I shoot in the JPEG format, I stick with Fine and set the JPEG Compression option to Optimal Quality.

However, I suggest that you do your own test shots, carefully inspect the results in your photo editor, and make your own judgment about what level of artifacting you can accept. Artifacting is often much easier to spot when you view images onscreen. It's difficult to reproduce artifacting here in print because the print process obscures some of the tiny defects caused by compression.

If you don't want *any* risk of artifacting, bypass JPEG altogether and change the file type to Raw (NEF), explained next.

Raw (NEF): The purist's choice

The second picture file type you can create is Camera Raw, or just *Raw* (as in uncooked) for short.

Each manufacturer has its own flavor of Raw. Nikon's is *NEF* (for Nikon Electronic Format), so you see the three-letter extension NEF at the end of Raw filenames.

Raw pros and cons

Raw is popular with advanced, very demanding photographers for these reasons:

✓ **Greater creative control:** With JPEG, internal camera software tweaks your images, making adjustments to color, exposure, and sharpness as needed to produce the results that Nikon believes its customers prefer. With Raw, the camera simply records the original, unprocessed image data. The photographer then uses a tool known as a *Raw converter* to produce the actual image, making decisions about color, exposure, and so on at that point.

✓ **Higher bit depth:** *Bit depth* is a measure of how many distinct color values an image file can contain. When you choose JPEG as the Image Quality setting, your pictures contain 8 bits each for the red, blue, and green color components, or *channels,* that make up a digital image, for a total of 24 bits. That translates to roughly 16.7 million possible colors.

Choosing the Raw setting delivers a higher bit count. You can set the camera to collect 12 bits per channel or 14 bits per channel. (More about that option and some other Raw-related options momentarily.)

Although jumping from 8 to 14 bits sounds like a huge difference, you may not really ever notice any impact on your photos — that 8-bit palette of 16.7 million values is more than enough for superb images. Where having the extra bits can come in handy is if you really need to adjust exposure, contrast, or color after the shot in your photo-editing program. In cases where you apply extreme adjustments, having the extra original bits sometimes helps avoid a problem known as *banding* or *posterization,* which creates abrupt color breaks where you should see smooth, seamless transitions. (A higher bit depth doesn't always prevent the problem, however, so don't expect miracles.)

✓ **Better picture quality:** Raw doesn't apply the destructive, lossy compression associated with JPEG, so you don't run the risk of the artifacting that can occur with JPEG. On the D7100, you can apply two alternative types of compression to reduce Raw file sizes slightly, but neither impact image quality to the extent of JPEG compression.

As with most things in life, Raw isn't without its disadvantages, however. To wit:

- **You can't do much with your pictures until you process them in a Raw converter.** You can't share them online, for example, or put them into a text document or multimedia presentation. You can print them immediately if you use Nikon ViewNX 2 as well as some advanced photo programs, but most entry-level photo programs require you to convert the Raw files to a standard format such as JPEG or TIFF (a popular format for images destined for professional printing) first.

- **To get the full benefit of Raw, you need software other than Nikon ViewNX 2.** The ViewNX software that ships free with your camera does have a command that enables you to convert Raw files to JPEG or to TIFF. However, this free tool gives you limited control over how your original data is translated in terms of color, exposure, and other characteristics — which defeats one of the primary purposes of shooting Raw.

  A different Nikon program, Nikon Capture NX 2, offers a sophisticated Raw converter, but it costs about $180. You can read more about Capture NX 2 as well as some competing programs in Chapter 6.

  Of course, the D7100 also offers an in-camera Raw converter, which I also cover in Chapter 6. But although it's convenient, this tool isn't the easiest to use because you must rely on the small camera monitor when making judgments about color, exposure, sharpness, and so on. The in-camera tool also doesn't offer the complete cadre of features available in Capture NX 2 and other converter software utilities.

- **Raw files are larger than JPEGs.** The type of file compression that you can enable for Raw files doesn't degrade image quality to the degree you get with JPEG compression, but the tradeoff is a larger file. In addition, Raw files are always captured at the maximum resolution available on the camera, even if you don't really need all those pixels. For both reasons, Raw files are significantly larger than JPEGs, so they take up more room on your memory card and on your computer's hard drive or other picture-storage device.

Whether the upside of Raw outweighs the downside is a decision that you need to ponder based on your photographic needs, your schedule, and your computer-comfort level. If you do decide to try Raw shooting, the next section explains a few Raw setup options.

Customizing your Raw capture settings

If you opt for Raw, you can control three aspects of how your pictures are captured:

- **Raw only or Raw+JPEG:** You can choose to capture the picture in the Raw format or create two files for each shot, one in the Raw format and another in the JPEG format, as shown in Figure 2-21. The figure shows the list of options that appears when you change the Image Quality setting through the Shooting menu; you can select from the same settings when you adjust the option by pressing the Qual button and rotating the Main command dial.

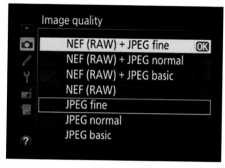

Figure 2-21: You can create two files for each picture, one in the Raw format and a second in the JPEG format.

For Raw+JPEG, you can specify whether you want the JPEG version captured at the Fine, Normal, or Basic quality level, and you can set the resolution of the JPEG file through the Image Size option, explained earlier in this chapter. Again, the Image Size setting doesn't affect the Raw file; the camera always captures the file at the maximum resolution.

I often choose the Raw+JPEG Fine option when I'm shooting pictures I want to share right away with people who don't have software for viewing Raw files. I upload the JPEGs to a photo-sharing site where everyone can view them and order prints, and then I process the Raw versions of my favorite images for my own use when I have time. Having the JPEG version also enables you to display your photos on a DVD player or TV that has a slot for an SD memory card — most can't display Raw files but can handle JPEGs. Ditto for portable media players and digital photo frames.

- **Raw bit depth:** You can specify whether you want a 12-bit Raw file or a 14-bit Raw file. More bits mean a bigger file but a larger spectrum of possible colors, as explained in the preceding section. You make the call through the NEF (Raw) Recording option on the Shooting menu, as shown in Figure 2-22. The default setting is 14 bits.

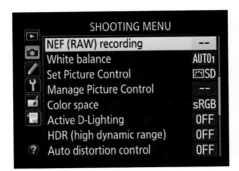 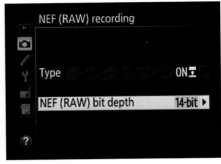

Figure 2-22: Set the file bit depth through this Shooting menu option.

✓ **Raw compression:** By default, the camera applies *lossless compression* to Raw files. As its name implies, this type of compression results in no visible loss of image quality and yet still reduces file sizes by about 20 to 40 percent. In addition, the compression is *reversible,* meaning that any quality loss that does occur through the compression process is reversed at the time you process your Raw images. Technically, some original data may be altered, but you're unlikely to notice the difference in your pictures.

You can change to a setting that delivers a greater degree of file-size savings if you prefer. Again, select the Raw (NEF) Recording option on the Shooting menu, but this time choose Type, as shown on the left in Figure 2-23, and press OK to display the screen shown on the right. Selecting the Compressed setting instead of Lossless Compressed shrinks files by about 35 to 55 percent. Nikon promises that this setting has "almost no effect" on image quality. But the compression in this case is not reversible, so if you do experience some quality loss, there's no going back.

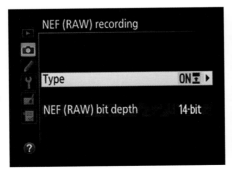 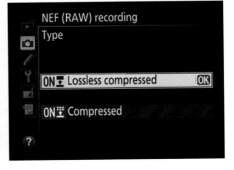

Figure 2-23: To keep Raw file compression to a minimum, select the Lossless Compressed option.

Together, your choices for these three settings make a big difference in the size of your picture files and, thus, your memory card capacity. Most photographers, I think, will be perfectly happy with the settings that produce the smaller Raw files (12-bit, Compressed). And frankly, I doubt that too many people could perceive much difference between a photo captured at that setting and a 14-bit, Lossless Compressed picture. But if you're using your camera for commercial photography — whether you shoot weddings, do high-end studio work, or shoot fine-art photography for sale — you may feel more comfortable knowing that you're capturing files at the absolute maximum quality and bit depth. The higher bit depth also may make sense if you're shooting in really difficult lighting because, again, it gives you the potential of capturing a broader range of colors and tones.

If you choose to create both a Raw and JPEG file, note a couple of things:

- If you're using only one memory card, you see the JPEG version of the photo during playback. However, the Image Quality data that appears with the photo reflects your capture setting (Raw+Basic, for example). The size value relates to the JPEG version; Raw files are always captured at the Large size. To use the in-camera Raw processing option on the Retouch menu, display the JPEG image and then proceed as outlined in Chapter 6.

- If two memory cards are installed, you can choose to send the Raw files to one card and the JPEG files to another by setting the Role Played by Card in Slot 2 option on the Shooting menu to Raw Slot 1 - JPEG Slot 2 setting.

- If both the JPEG and Raw files are stored on the same memory card, deleting the JPEG image also deletes the Raw copy if you use the in-camera delete function. After you transfer the two files to your computer, deleting one doesn't affect the other.

Chapter 5 explains more about viewing and deleting photos. Chapter 1 explains how to configure a two-memory-card setup.

Reducing the Image Area (DX versus 1.3x Crop)

Normally, your D7100 captures photos using the entire *image sensor,* which is the part of the camera on which the picture is formed — similar to the negative in a film camera. However, you have the option of telling the camera to record the picture using a smaller area at the center of the sensor. When you use this alternative setting, the result is the same as if you shot the picture using the entire sensor and then cropped the image by a factor of 1.3.

If you opt for the 1.3x crop setting, framing guidelines appear in the viewfinder to show you the image area that will be captured, as shown in Figure 2-24. You also see a little crop symbol in the upper-right corner of the viewfinder.

1.3x crop framing marks   1.3x symbol

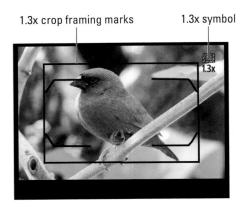

What's the point, you ask? Well, the idea is that you wind up with a picture that has the same angle of view you would get by switching to a lens with a longer focal length. In simplest terms, your subject fills more of the frame, and less background is included. To put it another way, you can think of this option as providing on-the-fly photo cropping.

Figure 2-24: Using the 1.3x crop option captures the scene using a smaller portion of the image sensor.

Of course, because you're using a smaller portion of the image sensor, you're recording the image using fewer pixels, so the resulting image has a lower resolution than one captured using the entire sensor. And as discussed earlier in this chapter, the higher the pixel count, the larger you can print the photo and maintain good print quality. On the flip side, because the camera is working with fewer pixels, the resulting file size is smaller, and it takes less time to record the image to the camera memory card. You also can capture more frames per second when you set the Release mode to the Continuous High or Continuous Low options, as I detail in the earlier section devoted to those two Release modes.

Personally, I prefer to shoot using the entire sensor and then crop the image myself if I deem it necessary. You can even crop the image in the camera, by using the Trim feature that I cover in Chapter 10. And even when I'm shooting fast action, I don't find that the small bump up in the maximum frames per second worth the loss of frame area in most situations.

If you want to try out the 1.3x Image Area option for yourself, you can set things up in several ways:

- ✔ **Information display control strip:** After displaying the Information screen (press the Info button), press the *i* button to activate the control strip at the bottom of the screen. Highlight the Image Area setting, as shown on the left in Figure 2-25, and press OK to reveal the screen shown on the right.

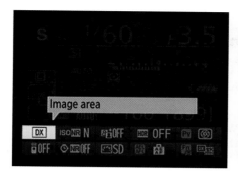
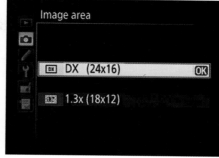

Figure 2-25: You can adjust the Image Area setting by using the Information display control strip.

The whole-sensor setting is the one labeled DX; the cropped setting is named 1.3x. The numbers in parentheses indicate the image sensor size in millimeters: 24 x 16 for the DX setting, and 18 x 12mm for the cropped setting. (*DX* is simply the Nikon name for the size of sensor used in the D7100 and many other Nikon dSLR cameras.)

✔ **Fn button + command dial:** By default, the Fn button is set to provide access to the Image Area setting. Press the button while rotating either command dial to toggle between the DX and 1.3x settings. As you change the setting, the viewfinder display, Information screen, and Control panel display the selected sensor size (24 x 16 or 18 x 12).

✔ **Shooting menu:** You also can adjust the setting via the Image Area option on the Shooting menu, as shown in Figure 2-26.

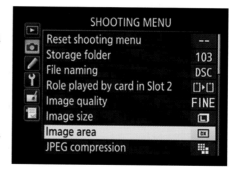

Figure 2-26: You can also look for the option on the Shooting menu.

Taking Great Pictures, Automatically

*A*re you old enough to remember the Certs television commercials from the 1960s and '70s? "It's a candy mint!" declared one actor. "It's a breath mint!" argued another. Then a narrator declared the debate a tie and spoke the famous catchphrase: "It's two, two, two mints in one!"

Well, that's sort of how I see the Nikon D7100. On one hand, it provides a full range of powerful controls, offering just about every feature a serious photographer could want. On the other, it offers automated photography modes that enable people with absolutely no experience to capture beautiful images. "It's a sophisticated photographic tool!" "It's as easy as 'point and shoot!'" "It's two, two, two cameras in one!"

Now, my guess is that you bought this book for help with your camera's advanced side, so that's what other chapters cover. This chapter, however, is devoted to your camera's easiest exposure modes, showing you how to get the best results in the Auto, Auto Flash Off, and Scene modes.

Note: This chapter assumes that you're using the viewfinder to compose your pictures. Things work differently in Live View mode, which enables you to use the monitor instead of the viewfinder, so Chapter 4 concentrates on that option as well as movie recording.

Setting Up for Automatic Success

Your first step in taking advantage of easy-breezy shooting is to set the Mode dial to Auto, as shown in Figure 3-1, or Auto Flash Off or Scene. Remember that you must press and hold the center button in order to rotate the Mode dial.

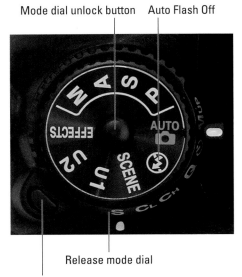

Mode dial unlock button   Auto Flash Off

Release mode dial

Release mode dial unlock button

Figure 3-1: For almost-automatic photography, use the Auto, Auto Flash Off, or Scene modes.

Here's a recap what each setting offers:

- **Auto** is a general purpose, point-and-shoot type of option.

- **Auto Flash Off** does the same thing as Auto but without flash.

- **Scene** gives you access to 16 automatic modes geared to shooting specific types of pictures.

Even in these automatic modes, you have a few ways to control the camera's behavior. The most important settings to check before you compose the photo are the following:

- **Release mode:** This setting, fully detailed in Chapter 2, determines the number of images that are recorded with each press of the shutter button and the timing of each shot. Choose the Release mode via the dial that's directly under the Mode dial, labeled in Figure 3-1. (Don't forget to press the little dial unlock button before moving the dial.)

  For normal shooting, set the dial to the S (Single Frame) position, as shown in the figure; at this setting, you get one picture for each press of the shutter button.

- **Focusing method:** You can enjoy autofocusing, if your lens supports it, or focus manually. On the 18–105mm lens featured in this book, select the lens focus mode via the switch labeled in Figure 3-2. Choose A for autofocusing and M for manual focusing.

  Also, set the camera's Focus mode selector switch to AF for autofocus, as shown in Figure 3-2, or M for manual focusing.

- **Vibration Reduction (VR):** If your lens offers this feature, enabling it helps produce sharper images by compensating for camera movement that can occur when you handhold the camera. On the 18–105 kit lens, turn Vibration Reduction on or off via the switch labeled in Figure 3-2.

Set the switch to Off when you mount the camera on a tripod.

For other lenses, check the lens manual for details about using this feature.

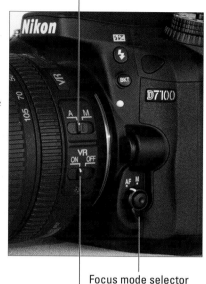

Lens focus-mode switch

Focus mode selector

Vibration Reduction switch

Figure 3-2: You can choose automatic or manual focusing.

✔ **Image Quality and Image Size (Shooting menu):** By default, pictures are recorded at the Large Image Size setting and the Normal Image Quality setting, which creates a JPEG picture file with a moderate amount of compression. Chapter 2 explains both options and offers advice on when you may want to stray from the default settings.

✔ **Image Area (Shooting menu):** By default, the camera uses the DX setting, which records the photo using the entire image sensor. If you switch to the 1.3x crop setting, a smaller area at the center of the sensor is used, giving you the same result as if you shot the picture using the entire sensor and then cropped the photo. Framing guidelines appear in the viewfinder to show you the smaller image area. Stick with the default (DX) until you have time to visit Chapter 2 and digest the implications of using the crop mode.

✔ **Flash mode:** In Auto exposure mode, as well as in many of the Scene modes, the camera automatically raises and fires the built-in flash in dim lighting. In some cases, you can alter the behavior of the flash through the Flash mode setting.

Chapter 7 provides complete details about Flash modes and other flash settings, but here's a look at the basics:

- *Checking the Flash mode:* Symbols representing the current mode appear in the Control panel and Information display, in the areas highlighted in Figure 3-3. (Press the Info button to bring up the Information display.) The Auto Flash mode, whose symbol appears in the figure and the margin here, means that the camera will automatically fire the flash if it thinks the ambient lighting is insufficient. This Flash mode is the default setting.

The *TTL* label that appears with the icon in the Information screen stands for *through-the-lens,* which refers to the way that the camera measures the ambient light when it calculates how much flash power is needed.

Flash mode

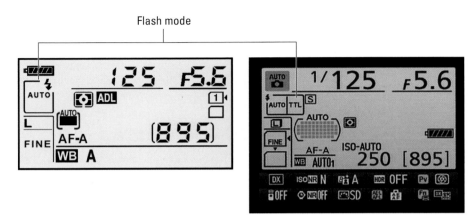

Figure 3-3: These symbols show the current Flash mode.

- *Changing the Flash mode:* Press the Flash button while rotating the Main command dial.

- *Disabling flash:* You can't simply close the flash to disable it — the camera will just raise it again if it thinks extra light is needed. But in some automatic exposure modes, including Auto, you can prevent the flash from firing by choosing Flash Off mode, represented in the displays by the symbol shown in the margin.

- *Using red-eye reduction flash:* Auto mode and some Scene modes also offer this feature, represented in the Flash mode display by the little eye icon shown here. In this Flash mode, the camera emits a burst of light from the AF-assist illuminator lamp on the front of the camera before the flash fires. This light constricts the subject's pupils, which reduces the chances of red-eye.

- *Combining a slow shutter speed with flash:* Some Scene modes combine flash with a slow shutter speed in order to produce brighter backgrounds in dimly lit scenes. The word *Slow* in the Flash mode display indicates that this feature is in force. Because of the slow shutter speed — longer exposure time — use a tripod and ask your subject to remain still during the exposure to avoid a blurry picture.

✔ **ISO Sensitivity:** You have access to one exposure-adjustment option, ISO Sensitivity, which determines how much light is needed to properly expose the image. (Adjust the setting by holding down the ISO button and rotating the Main command dial.) At the default setting, Auto, the camera adjusts the ISO Sensitivity as needed. Stick with this setting until you have time to explore the whys and wherefores of your other options in Chapter 7.

In fact, if you're not up to sorting through any of these choices, ignore everything but the focusing method, Vibration Reduction setting, and the Release mode setting. After all, the default settings are chosen because they're the best solutions for most shooting scenarios. See the end of Chapter 1 to find out how to restore the default settings if you've already played around with them.

As Easy as It Gets: Auto and Auto Flash Off

The following steps walk you through taking a picture in Auto and Auto Flash Off modes. A couple of notes before you start:

- ✔ **The steps show you how to take the picture using autofocusing.** To focus manually, ignore the autofocusing instructions.

- ✔ **Autofocusing information presented here assumes that you're using the viewfinder.** You use a different autofocusing technique in Live View mode, so see Chapter 4 to go that route.

With that preamble done, walk this way to snap a photo:

1. **Set the Mode dial to Auto or Auto Flash Off. (Refer to Figure 3-1.)**

2. **Set the focusing method, Release mode, and other basic settings as outlined in the preceding section.**

3. **Looking through the viewfinder, compose the shot so that your subject is within the autofocus brackets, labeled in Figure 3-4.**

   The camera's autofocusing points are scattered throughout the area indicated by the brackets.

4. **Press and hold the shutter button halfway down.**

   The following occurs:

   - *Exposure metering begins.* The autoexposure meter analyzes the light and selects initial aperture (f-stop) and shutter speed settings, which are two critical exposure controls. These two settings appear in the viewfinder; in Figure 3-5, the shutter speed is 1/125 second, and the f-stop is f/10. (Chapter 7 explains these two options in detail.) The autoexposure meter continues monitoring the light up to the time you take the picture, however, so the f-stop and shutter speed values may change if the lighting conditions change.

Autofocus brackets

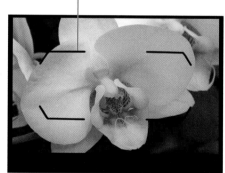

Figure 3-4: Position your subject within the area surrounded by the autofocus brackets.

The shots-remaining area of the viewfinder also changes from showing you how many more pictures can fit on your memory card to how many can fit in the camera's buffer — 28, in Figure 3-5. This number is critical only when you're shooting a burst of images using the Continuous High or Continuous Low Release mode options, so don't worry about it for single-frame shooting. (If the number drops to zero when you're shooting a burst of images, you may need to pause shooting momentarily until the camera can finish writing all the image data to the memory card.)

Selected focus point

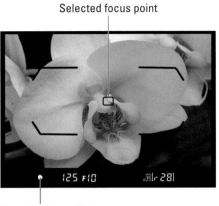

Focus indicator light

Figure 3-5: The round white dot indicates that the camera has locked focus on the objects under the selected focus point.

- *In Auto exposure mode, the built-in flash pops up if the camera thinks additional light is needed.* You can set the Flash mode to auto (normal) or red-eye reduction mode. Or you can disable the flash by changing the Flash mode to Off, as explained in the preceding section.

- *The camera's autofocus system begins to do its thing.* In dim light, the AF-assist lamp on the front of the camera shoots out a beam of light to help the camera find its focusing target.

5. **Check the focus indicators in the viewfinder.**

   When the camera has established focus, one or more little rectangles within the focus brackets flash red for a split second. Those rectangles represent the focus points. Then just a single black focus point remains to show you the final focusing area selected by the camera. For example, in Figure 3-5, the camera selected the center focus point.

   In the display at the bottom of the viewfinder, the round focus indicator, labeled in Figure 3-5, lights to give you further notice that focus has been achieved.

   A triangle to the right or left of the spot where the focus dot should appear means that focus isn't yet spot on. If the triangle is pointing right, as shown in the top image in Figure 3-6, focus is set in front of the subject; if the triangle is points left, focus is set behind the subject. And if both triangles blink, the autofocus system is stymied, so switch to manual focusing or release the shutter button and press halfway again to try refocusing.

6. **Press the shutter button the rest of the way down to record the image.**

I need to add a few important points about working in the Auto and Auto Flash Off exposure modes:

Focus in front of subject

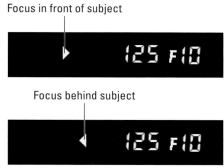

Focus behind subject

Figure 3-6: Triangles in the area where the focus light should appear indicate a focusing problem.

- ✔ **Exposure:** In dim lighting, the camera may need to use a very high ISO setting or very slow shutter speed when the flash is disabled. Unfortunately, a high ISO can create *noise,* a defect that makes your picture look grainy. And a slow shutter speed can produce blur if either the camera or subject moves during the exposure. If you spot either problem, enable flash or add some other light source.

- ✔ **Autofocusing:** Autofocusing behavior is determined by two settings, the AF-area mode and the Autofocus mode. By default, the camera uses the following settings:

    - *AF-area mode:* The Auto Area option is selected, which means that the camera selects which autofocus point to use when establishing focus.

    - *Autofocus mode:* The default setting is AF-A, which stands for *auto-servo autofocus.* If the subject isn't moving, focus remains locked as long as you hold the shutter button halfway down. If the camera detects motion, it continually adjusts focus up to the time you press the button fully to record the picture. (In this situation, the focus indicator light may blink on and off as the camera adjusts focus.) To ensure that focus is correct, you must keep your subject within the area of the viewfinder covered by the focusing brackets.

You can adjust both settings in the Auto and Auto Flash Off modes, but before you do, visit Chapter 8 to find out how the other autofocusing options work.

Taking Advantage of Scene Modes

In Auto and Auto Flash Off exposure modes, the camera tries to figure out what type of picture you want to take by assessing what it sees through the lens. If you don't want to rely on the camera to make that judgment, your D7100 offers *Scene modes,* which are designed to automatically capture specific scenes in ways that are traditionally considered best from a creative standpoint. For example, most people prefer portraits that have softly focused backgrounds. So in Portrait mode, the camera selects settings that can produce that type of background.

Usually, Scene modes also apply color, exposure, contrast, and sharpness adjustments to the picture according to the traditional characteristics of the scene type. Landscape mode typically results in more vibrant colors, especially in the blue-green range, for example, whereas Portrait mode typically produces a softer image with more natural tones.

To access the Scene modes, set the Mode dial to Scene, as shown in Figure 3-7. The following section explains how to select a scene type; following that, you can get brief information about each one.

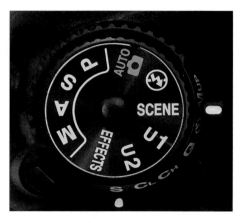

Figure 3-7: Set the Mode dial to Scene to experiment with automatic exposure modes based on different types of photographic scenes.

Before I shoo you off to either section, though, I want to offer a little advice: The Scene modes are a great way to start taking control over your pictures, and if nothing else, they encourage you to think about the characteristics that go into different types of photos. But don't expect miracles, especially if the lighting conditions or subjects are challenging. There's also the whole notion of creative input to consider. Sure, most formal portraits feature a blurred background, but maybe you want to keep the background in focus because the setting is important to the story you're trying to tell — think of a shot of newlyweds standing in front of their very first home, for example. The details of the home likely will be just as important to the couple when they look back on that photo in years to come.

Long story short: Experiment with the Scene modes while you're discovering more about photography. If you're not happy with your results, don't just keep trying over and over with the same Scene mode — you're not going to achieve anything different. Instead, head for Part III of this book, where you can find out how to master the advanced exposure modes and take full control over your pictures.

When you do opt for scene modes, be sure to review the first section of this chapter, "Setting Up for Automatic Success," to set such basic shooting options as the Release mode and focusing method. You have the same control over these options as in the Auto and Auto Flash Off modes.

Scene modes in focus (or not)

When you focus the lens, you determine only the point of sharpest focus. The distance to which that sharp-focus zone extends from that point — what photographers call the *depth of field* — depends in part on the *aperture setting,* or *f-stop,* which is an exposure control. Some Scene modes are designed to choose aperture settings that deliver a certain depth of field.

The Portrait setting, for example, tries to use a wide aperture setting (low f-stop number) because doing so shortens the depth of field, rendering backgrounds softly focused — an artistic choice that most people prefer for those types of shots. On the flip side, the Landscape mode tries to use a small aperture, which produces a large depth of field, keeping both foreground and background objects sharp.

However, the range of apertures the camera can select varies depending on the light. In dim lighting, an open aperture is needed to expose the picture, and in bright light, a small aperture may be required. Additionally, the range of available aperture settings varies from lens to lens. So how much depth of field any Scene mode produces depends on these variables.

Another exposure control, *shutter speed,* also plays a focus role. Moving objects appear blurry at slow shutter speeds; at fast shutter speeds, they appear sharp. In Sports mode, the camera tries to select a shutter speed fast enough to freeze action, but in dim lighting, that may not be possible: The less light, the slower the shutter speed needed to expose the photo. That means that even in Sports mode, a moving subject may appear blurry. Additionally, some Scene modes, such as Night Landscape and Candlelight, choose a slow shutter speed in order to cope with the dark settings. For these modes, it's critical to use a tripod because any camera movement during the exposure can also blur the image.

Selecting a Scene mode

To experiment with Scene modes, follow these steps:

1. Set the Mode dial to Scene.

2. Press the Info button to display the Information screen.

An icon representing the current Scene mode appears in the upper-left corner of the Information display, as shown on the left in Figure 3-8. (This particular icon represents the Portrait mode.) The next section describes each Scene mode.

3. Rotate the Main command dial to choose a different scene.

As soon as you rotate the dial, the display changes to show a scrolling panel of scene types, as shown on the right in Figure 3-8. Keep spinning the dial to cycle through all the options. An example photo appears to give you an idea of what the selected mode produces.

You can also press the WB button to get a text tip that explains more about what the scene type is designed to do.

4. **When you find a Scene mode you like, stop rotating the Main command dial.**

   The camera sets itself up to take the picture.

Current Scene mode

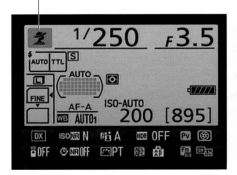
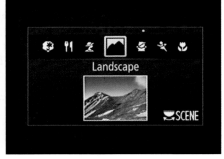

Figure 3-8: Rotate the Main command dial to cycle through the available scene types.

5. **Frame, focus, and shoot.**

   From here on in, everything works as it does for the Auto and Auto Flash Off exposure modes with the exception of your Flash mode choices and the default autofocusing behavior, which vary depending on the scene type you select. (I describe your options in the next section.)

Checking out the Scene (s)

Your camera offers 16 Scene modes, each designed to produce a specific result in terms of lighting, color, and focus. Before you start exploring the Scene choices, note these general pointers:

✔ **Flash:** For modes that permit flash, you may be able to select a different Flash mode; press the Flash button while rotating the Main command dial to cycle through the available settings. (Refer to the first section of this chapter, "Setting Up for Automatic Success," for more details about changing the Flash mode.)

✔ **Autofocus:** For most Scene modes, the default autofocusing settings work as they do when you use the Auto mode. The Autofocus mode is set to AF-A, which means that focus is locked when you depress the shutter button halfway unless the camera senses a moving subject, in which case it adjusts focus until the time you take the picture. And the AF-area mode is set to Auto, meaning that the camera chooses the focus point.

For a few Scene modes, however, the AF-area mode *isn't* set to Auto. Instead, you're involved in choosing the focus point, as follows:

- *Close Up, Candlelight, and Food*: These modes use Single Point AF-area mode. By default, focus is based on a single focus point at the center of the frame. You can use the Multi Selector to move the point to a different position if necessary. (You may need to press the shutter button halfway and then release it to wake up the display first.)

- *Sports and Pet Portrait*: In these modes, the camera sets the AF-area mode to 51-point Dynamic Area. You start by selecting a single focus point, but if the subject leaves that point, the camera looks to other points for focusing information.

Chapter 8 shows you how to make best use of all these focusing options and how to adjust them to suit your subject.

And now without further ado, here's a review of all bazillion Scene modes:

- **Portrait:** Choose this mode to produce the classic portrait look, with the subject set against a softly focused background, as shown in Figure 3-9. Colors are adjusted to produce natural-looking skin tones.

- **Landscape:** In the time-honored tradition of landscape photography, this mode uses settings that keep both foreground and background objects as sharp as possible. It also manipulates the image in a way that produces crisp images with vivid blues and greens to create that bold, vacation-magazine look. (See Figure 3-10.) Flash is disabled.

- **Child:** A variation of Portrait mode, Child mode also aims for a blurry background and natural skin tones. Colors of clothing and other objects, however, are rendered more vividly. I'm not a fan of this mode — I don't want background objects or clothing to take the eye away from the face of my subject.

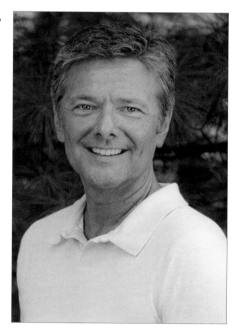

Figure 3-9: Portrait mode produces soft backgrounds to help emphasize your subject.

✔ **Sports:** Select this mode to have a better chance of capturing a moving target without blur, as I did for my romping furboy in Figure 3-11. To accomplish this outcome, the camera selects a fast shutter speed, if possible. In dim lighting, though, it may need to use a slow shutter speed to expose the image — which typically means a shutter speed too low to freeze action. Flash is disabled. Note that in bright lighting, the Pet Portrait mode (see the upcoming bullet on that mode) would produce similar results to what you see in Figure 3-11; that mode is also geared to using a fast shutter speed when possible.

✔ **Close Up:** As with Portrait and Child mode, this mode is designed to produce a blurry background to keep background objects from competing for attention with your subject, as shown in Figure 3-12.

✔ **Night Portrait:** This mode is designed to deliver a better-looking flash portrait at night (or in any dimly lit environment). It does so by constraining your Flash mode choices to Auto Slow-Sync, Auto Slow-Sync with Red-Eye Reduction, or Off. In the first two Flash modes, the camera selects a shutter speed that results in a long exposure time. That slow shutter speed enables the camera to rely more on ambient light and less on the flash to expose the picture, which produces softer, more even lighting. If you disable flash, an even slower shutter speed is used.

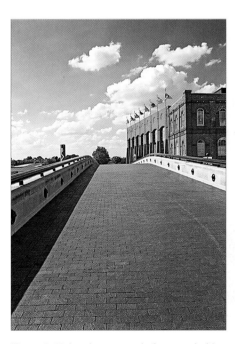 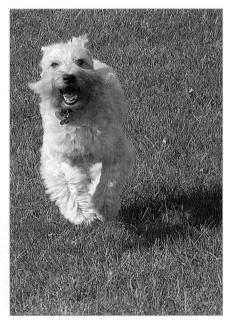

Figure 3-10: Landscape mode features bold colors and a large zone of sharp focus (depth of field).

Figure 3-11: Try Sports mode to capture action.

I cover the issue of long-exposure and slow-sync flash photography in detail in Chapter 7. For now, the critical thing to know is that the slower shutter speed means that you should use a tripod to avoid blur-inducing camera shake. Your subjects also must stay perfectly still during the exposure.

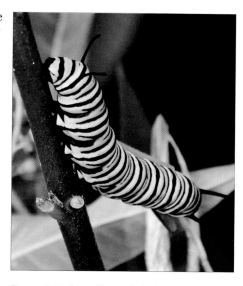

Figure 3-12: Close Up mode helps emphasize the subject by throwing the background out of focus.

✔ **Night Landscape:** This setting uses a slow shutter speed to capture nighttime city scenes, such as the one in Figure 3-13. Because of the long exposure time, use a tripod to avoid camera shake, which can blur the picture. Note that even when the camera remains perfectly still, any moving objects in the scene appear blurry, as does the fountain water in this example. This mode also is designed to reduce noise (a defect that looks like grains of sand) and avoid unnatural colors, both of which are common problems in night landscape shots. Flash is disabled.

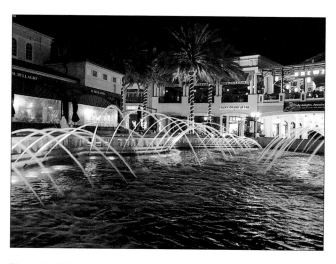

Figure 3-13: To capture this kind of after-dark photo, use Night Landscape mode and a tripod.

- **Party/Indoor:** This mode is designed to capture indoor scenes that are lit by room lighting as well as the flash, using settings that produce a nice balance between the two light sources. If the lighting is very dim, the camera may use a slow shutter speed, so use a tripod to avoid blurring.

- **Beach/Snow:** Use this mode for scenes with lots of bright areas, such as sand or snow, which can fool the camera's autoexposure system into underexposing the image. Flash is disabled.

- **Sunset:** Use this mode when photographing sunsets or sunrises and the sun is in the picture; the camera chooses settings designed to preserve the brilliant colors seen at those times of day. Using a tripod gives you a better chance of producing a sharp shot because the light will be dim and the camera will need to use a slow shutter speed. Flash is disabled.

- **Dusk/Dawn:** Use this mode to better capture the colors of the sky when shooting landscapes just before the sun rises, or just after the sun sets. Flash is disabled. To avoid the possibility of blurry images, use a tripod; this mode may use a slow shutter speed, which can result in blur from camera shake if you handhold the camera.

- **Pet Portrait:** This mode is just like Sports mode except that in dim lighting, the flash fires unless you set the Flash mode to Off. Note that if flash is required, the camera can raise the shutter speed no higher than 1/250 second, by default, which may not be fast enough to capture a speedy animal. See Chapter 7 for details about flash and shutter speed.

- **Candlelight:** Use this mode when shooting subjects lit by candlelight. Flash is disabled, and because the ambient light will be dim, the shutter speed will likely be slow. Again, mount your camera on a tripod to avoid a blurry photo.

- **Blossom:** If you're photographing a field of flowers instead of a single bloom, experiment with this mode. Flash is disabled; again, use a tripod when photographing in low-light situations.

- **Autumn Colors:** This mode applies a color shift that yields pictures with saturated reds and yellows. The built-in flash is disabled. Mount your camera on a tripod in low-light situations.

 - **Food:** This mode increases color saturation to render food more vividly. An important note about flash: Unlike other Scene modes, Food mode requires you to raise the built-in flash yourself if you want to add flash. To do so, press the Flash button; the flash pops up and sets itself to Fill Flash mode, which fires the flash regardless of the ambient light. To go flash free, just close the flash unit. You can't adjust the Flash mode.

4

Exploring Live View Photography and Movie Making

In This Chapter

▶ Getting acquainted with Live View mode

▶ Customizing the Live View display

▶ Exploring Live View and movie focusing options

▶ Taking pictures in Live View mode

▶ Recording, playing, and trimming movies

*L*ike many dSLR cameras, the D7100 offers *Live View,* a feature that enables you to use the monitor instead of the viewfinder to compose photos. Turning on Live View is also the first step in recording a movie; using the viewfinder isn't possible when you shoot movies.

In most respects, the process of shooting pictures in Live View mode is the same as for viewfinder photography. But a few critical steps, including focusing, work very differently. So the first part of this chapter provides a general introduction to Live View shooting and explains everything you need to know about focusing. Following that, you can find details on taking photos in Live View mode and shooting, viewing, and editing movies.

Using Your Monitor as a Viewfinder

The basics of taking advantage of Live View are pretty simple:

✓ **Enabling Live View for photography:** Rotate the Live View switch on the back of the camera to the still photography camera icon, as shown in Figure 4-1, and then press the LV button in the center of the switch.

You hear a clicking sound as the internal mirror that normally sends the image from the lens to the viewfinder flips up, permitting the Live View preview to start. Then your subject appears on the monitor, and you can no longer see anything in the viewfinder. The Information screen, too, is no longer available; instead, settings appear over the live scene, as shown in Figure 4-1. The upcoming section "Customizing the Live View display" shows you how to control what data appears on the monitor.

✔ **Enabling Live View for movie recording:** Set the Live View switch to the movie camera icon and press the LV button to fire up Live View movie mode. The image reflects an aspect ratio of 16:9, the movie aspect ratio, as opposed to the normal 3:2 aspect ratio for still photos.

To start and stop recording, press the red movie record button on top of the camera.

✔ **Exiting Live View mode:** Just press the LV button.

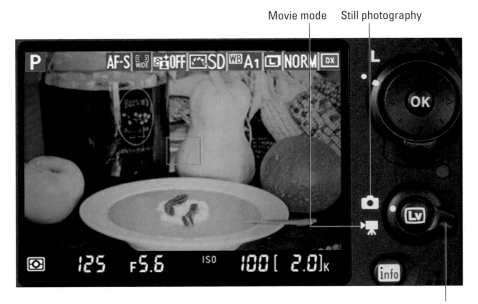

Movie mode   Still photography

Live View switch

Figure 4-1: For still photography, rotate the Live View switch to the camera icon, as shown here; for movie recording, rotate it to the movie-camera icon instead.

As you may have guessed from the fact that I devote a whole chapter to Live View and movie recording, the preceding points are just the start of the story. The next several sections provide additional information that applies to both still photography and movie recording; later sections get into the nitty-gritty of taking pictures and using movie functions.

Live View safety tips

Be aware of the following warnings when you enable Live View:

- ✔ **Cover the viewfinder to prevent light from seeping into the camera and affecting exposure.** The camera ships with a cover for this purpose.

- ✔ **Live View puts additional strain on the battery.** Keep an eye on the battery level to avoid running out of power at a critical moment.

- ✔ **By default, the monitor turns off after ten minutes of inactivity to save battery power.** When 30 seconds remain before monitor shutoff, a countdown timer appears in the upper-left corner of the screen, as shown in Figure 4-2. The warning doesn't appear during playback or when menus are active, however.

Auto shutdown timer

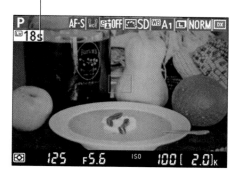

Figure 4-2: This timer appears to alert you to impending monitor shutdown.

You can adjust the shutdown timing via the Monitor Off Delay option, found in the Timers/AE Lock section of the Custom Settings menu and shown on the left in Figure 4-3. Choose the Live View option, as shown on the right, and press the Multi Selector right to reveal the screen where you can change the setting. Options range from 5 to 30 minutes. You also can disable the automatic shutdown by choosing No Limit.

- ✔ **Using Live View for an extended period can harm your pictures and the camera.** In Live View mode, the camera heats up more than usual, and that extra heat can create the right conditions for *noise,* a defect that gives your pictures a speckled look. More important, the increased temperatures can damage the camera. For that reason, Live View is automatically disabled if the camera detects a critical heat level, regardless of the Monitor Off Delay setting.

- ✔ **Aiming the lens at the sun or other bright lights also can damage the camera.** Of course, you can cause problems doing this even during normal shooting, but the possibilities increase when you use Live View.

- ✔ **Some lights interfere with Live View performance.** The operating frequency of some lights, including fluorescent, sodium, and mercury vapor lamps, can create electronic interference that causes the display to flicker or exhibit odd color banding. Usually, the defect appears only on the screen, but in some cases it may also show up in your pictures. Changing the Flicker Reduction option on the Setup menu may resolve this issue. At the default setting, Auto, the camera gauges the light and chooses the right flicker reduction setting for you. You also can choose from two specific frequencies: 50 Hz and 60 Hz. (In the United States and Canada, the standard frequency is 60 Hz; in Europe, it's 50 Hz.)

✓ **The risk of camera shake during handheld shots is increased.** When you use the viewfinder, you can help steady the camera by bracing it against your face. With Live View, you have to hold the camera away from your body to view the monitor, making it harder to keep the camera still. Camera movement during the exposure can blur the shot, so using a tripod is the best course of action. When you do handhold the camera, try enabling Vibration Reduction, if your lens offers it. Detailed in Chapter 1, this option helps compensate for small amounts of camera shake.

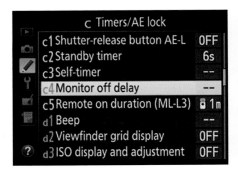 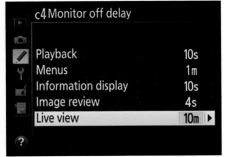

Figure 4-3: Adjust the delay time for automatic monitor shutdown in Live View mode via this menu option.

Customizing the Live View display

For still photography, the display appears by default as shown on the left in Figure 4-4. You can tweak the display in the following ways:

✓ **Change the data display:** You can choose from the following display styles, each of which adds different types of information to the screen. Press the Info button to cycle through the styles.

• *Information on:* This is the default mode, with data similar to what you see in Figure 4-4 appearing for still photography. For movie recording, the display instead shows data related to movie settings.

Later sections of this chapter detail what each of the symbols indicates for still photography and movie recording.

- *Information off:* Press the Info button to view only the major exposure settings, as shown on the right in Figure 4-4.

- *Framing guides:* Press Info once more to display a grid over the scene, as shown on the left in Figure 4-5. The grid is helpful when you need to precisely align objects in your photo.

- *Virtual horizon:* This tool helps you make sure the camera is level to the horizon. A green line through the middle of the display, as shown on the right in Figure 4-5, indicates the level position.

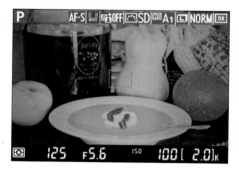 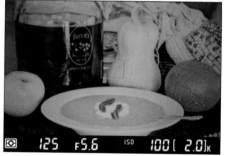

Figure 4-4: Press the Info button to shift from a display showing a bunch of shooting data (left) to only critical picture settings (right).

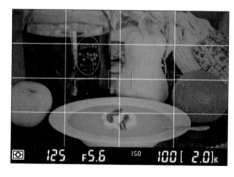 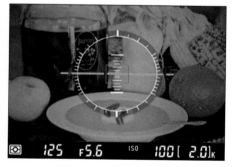

Figure 4-5: The grid (left) and virtual horizon (right) displays are helpful for shots that require precise alignment of objects or of the camera itself.

✔ **Adjusting monitor brightness.**
Press the *i* button to display a
settings control strip on the right
side of the monitor. Highlight the
Monitor Brightness option, as
shown in Figure 4-6, and press OK
to display a screen that contains
a brightness scale. Press the
Multi Selector up or down to
adjust the screen brightness and
then press OK.

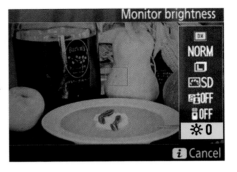

Monitor brightness has *no effect* on
the actual picture brightness. So if
you change the display brightness,
don't use it as a gauge of exposure.
In fact, I suggest that you leave this
option set to the default, 0.

Figure 4-6: To adjust screen brightness, press
the *i* button to display the control strip. Then
choose the Monitor Brightness icon.

Displaying the Live View preview on an HDMI screen

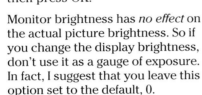

You can connect your camera to an HDMI (High-Definition Multimedia
Interface) device to see the Live View output on that screen. This feature is
often used by studio photographers who want a larger view of their subject
than the camera monitor provides.

A few issues arise when you take advantage of this option:

✔ **You must buy an HDMI type-C mini-pin cable to connect the camera to
the TV.** The cable isn't provided with the camera.

✔ **The on-screen shooting data appears differently than in the figures in
this chapter.** Specifically, camera settings appear along the sides of the
live image instead of atop it. Also, during movie recording, you can't display the virtual horizon tool or show or hide monitor data using the Info
button. Nor does the audio volume meter appear during movie recording.

✔ **You may need to set the Output Resolution option to a setting other
than Auto.** When you connect the camera to an HDTV playback, the
camera automatically adjusts the HDMI output to your HD display. But
when the Live View switch is set to Movie mode, the signal is output
according to the selected movie Frame Rate/Frame Size setting, an
option I cover later in this chapter. If your TV doesn't support your
chosen movie settings, the answer may lie in the HDMI option on the
Setup menu, shown in Figure 4-7. After selecting that option, try changing the Output Resolution to a setting other than Auto. Your movies may
be output to the HD monitor at a frame size smaller than the one you set
for the movie recording, however.

Live View and the Image Area setting

You can set the Image Area option to DX mode or to the 1.3x crop setting for Live View shooting. Chapter 2 explains this setting in detail, but the short story is that at the default setting, DX, the entire image sensor is used to capture a photo. Using the 1.3x crop setting uses a smaller portion of the sensor, with the result the same as if you shot the picture using the entire sensor and then cropped it. For movies, the same reduction in recording area occurs, but both the DX and 1.3x crop frame have a 16:9 aspect ratio, whereas still photos have a 3:2 aspect ratio.

During viewfinder photography, the viewfinder displays a box to indicate the frame area when you set the Image Area option to the 1.3x crop setting. But in Live View mode, the live preview simply updates to show you what portion of the scene will be included in the frame.

You can adjust the Image Area in Live View mode either via the Shooting menu or, when the Live View image is displayed, by pressing the *i* button and then using the control strip that appears on the screen. Select the top option on the strip, press OK, and then select the Image Area option you want to use. Press OK and then press the *i* button again to exit the control strip.

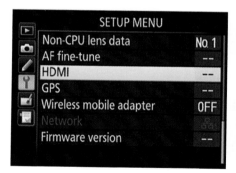 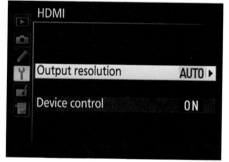

Figure 4-7: When sending the Live View signal to an HDMI display, you may need to adjust these Setup menu options.

✔ **During movie playback, the camera monitor shuts off at some Frame Size/Frame Rate settings.** You can see the movie only on the HD device when you use a frame size of 1920 x 1080 and a frame rate of 60i or 50i or a frame size of 1280 x 720 together with a frame rate of 60p or 50p. (See "Understanding the Frame Size/Frame Rate options," later in this chapter, for an explanation of all these numbers if they're new to you.)

✔ **When you connect the camera to an HDMI-CEC device, set the Device Control option to Off.** That's one of the two options available for the HDMI setting on the Setup menu, shown in Figure 4-7. You can't take pictures or shoot movies when the Device Control option is set to On, as it is by default.

In case you're wondering, CEC stands for Consumer Electronics Control and is a specification that enables you to use your HDMI TV's remote control to operate other devices. For example, if you turn on the Device Control option, you can use the remote to perform the functions of the Multi Selector and OK button during picture playback. The feature just isn't compatible with picture taking and movie recording.

Exploring Live View Focusing

You can opt for autofocusing or manual focusing during Live View shooting, assuming that your lens supports both. If you use the 18–105mm kit lens, set the switch on the lens to the A position for autofocusing and to the M position to focus manually. Also set the Focus mode selector on the camera to AF for autofocusing and M for manual focusing. Figure 4-8 offers a reminder of where to find these two switches.

Remember the following important points about Live View autofocusing:

Lens focus-mode switch   AF-mode button

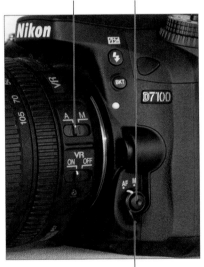

Focus mode selector

Figure 4-8: Use these controls to set the camera and lens to manual or automatic focusing.

- ✓ **Autofocusing typically takes longer in Live View mode.** For fast focusing response, focus manually or exit Live View mode.

- ✓ **Nikon recommends using an AF-S type lens for best results.** The 18–105mm kit lens fits the bill. (AF stands for *autofocus,* and S stands for *silent wave,* a Nikon autofocusing technology.)

- ✓ **You control autofocusing behavior through the Autofocus mode and AF-area mode.** These same settings affect autofocusing for viewfinder photography, but during Live View shooting, the options presented for each setting are different. The next two sections explain the Live View way of the world; Chapter 8 explains how things work when you use the viewfinder. In both cases, though, you adjust the settings the same way:

REMEMBER

- *To set the Autofocus mode:* Press the AF-mode button, labeled in Figure 4-8, while rotating the Main command dial.

- *To set the AF-area mode:* Press the AF-mode button while rotating the Sub-command dial.

You can see the current settings for these two options in the Information display, as shown in Figure 4-9. When you press the AF-mode button, both settings become highlighted, as in the figure, to indicate that they're active and will be adjusted if you rotate the command dials.

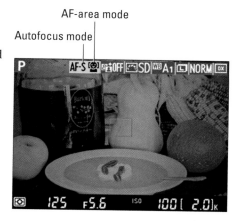

Figure 4-9: Press the AF-mode button to highlight the Autofocus and AF-area mode options; then rotate the command dials to change the settings.

REMEMBER

Choosing an Autofocus mode

The Autofocus setting determines whether the camera locks focus at a specific distance or adjusts focus continuously as your subject moves through the frame (or as you move the camera).

To select the Autofocus mode setting, press and hold the AF-mode button, labeled in Figure 4-8, to highlight the Autofocus mode, labeled in Figure 4-9. Keep the button pressed as you rotate the Main command dial to change the setting. You can choose from two options:

- **AF-S (single-servo autofocus):** The camera sets and locks focus when you press the shutter button halfway. For still photos, just press the button the rest of the way to actually take the picture.

  In movie mode, you can lift your finger off the shutter button after focus is locked; the camera will use the established focusing distance throughout the entire recording unless you press the shutter button halfway to set focus again.

- **AF-F (full-time servo autofocus):** Autofocusing begins as soon as you select this setting — you don't need to press the shutter button halfway — and focusing is adjusted continuously until you *do* press the shutter button halfway. Then focus is locked as long as you keep the button pressed halfway.

The main purpose of this option is to enable continuous focus adjustment during movie recording. Unfortunately, it has a downside: If you use the built-in microphone to record audio, the noise of the autofocus motor is sometimes audible in the soundtrack. The solution is to attach an external microphone and place it far enough away from the camera that it doesn't pick up the focusing sounds.

For still photography, you might find this option helpful when you're not sure where a moving subject will be when you want to snap the picture: As your subject moves or you pan the camera to keep the subject in the frame, autofocus is adjusted so that when the moment comes to take the shot, you just press the shutter button halfway to lock focus and then press the button the rest of the way to take the picture.

Setting the AF-area mode

The AF-area mode setting tells the camera what part of the frame contains your subject so that it can set focusing distance correctly. To adjust the setting, press the AF-mode button, labeled in Figure 4-8, to temporarily highlight the setting icon, labeled in Figure 4-9. While holding the button, rotate the Sub-command dial to cycle through the available settings.

You can choose from the following settings, represented in the display by the icons you see in the margins here:

✔ **Face Priority:** Designed for portrait shooting, this mode attempts to hunt down and focus on faces. Face Detection typically works only when your subjects are facing the camera, however. If the camera can't detect a face, it behaves as if you selected the Wide Area mode, described next.

✔ **Wide Area:** In this mode, you use the Multi Selector to move a focusing frame around the screen to specify your desired focusing spot. It's the most intuitive of the options and the one I rely on most of the time unless I'm shooting a portrait, in which case I prefer Face Priority.

✔ **Normal Area:** This mode works the same way as Wide Area autofocusing but uses a smaller focusing frame. The idea is to enable you to base focus on a very specific area. With such a small focusing frame, however, you can easily miss your focus target when handholding the camera. If you move the camera slightly as you're setting focus and the focusing frame shifts off your subject as a result, focus will be incorrect. For best results, use a tripod in this mode.

✔ **Subject Tracking:** This mode, designed for focusing on a moving subject, tracks a subject as it moves through the frame. Subject Tracking isn't always as successful as you might hope, though. For a subject that occupies a small part of the frame — say, a butterfly flitting through a garden — autofocus may lose its way. Ditto for subjects moving at a fast pace, subjects getting larger or smaller in the frame (when moving toward you and then away from you, for example), or scenes without much contrast between the subject and the background. Oh, and scenes with a great deal of contrast can create problems, too. When the conditions are right, this feature works well, but otherwise, Wide Area gives you a better chance of focusing on a moving subject.

For specifics about setting focus in each of these modes, see the next section.

Stepping through the focusing process

After you explore the Live View autofocusing options detailed in the preceding sections and decide which settings you want to use, follow these steps to set focus:

1. **Choose the Autofocus mode (AF-S or AF-F).**

   Remember, this setting determines whether focus is locked at a specific distance or adjusted continuously as you or your subject move. Use AF-S if you want to lock focus and choose AF-F for continuous autofocusing.

   Dial in the setting by pressing the AF-mode button (see Figure 4-8) while rotating the Main command dial.

   In AF-F mode, the autofocus system perks up and starts hunting for a focus point immediately.

2. **Choose the AF-area mode by pressing the AF mode button while rotating the Sub-command dial.**

   This setting determines what part of the frame the camera considers when establishing focus. Your choices are Face Priority, Wide Area, Normal Area, and Subject Tracking, as outlined in the preceding section.

3. **Locate the focus frame in the Live View display.**

   The appearance of the frame depends on the AF-area mode, as follows:

   - *Wide Area and Normal Area:* You see a red rectangular frame, as shown in Figure 4-10. (The figure shows the frame at the size it appears in Wide Area mode; it's smaller in Normal Area mode.)

   - *Face Priority:* If the camera locates faces, you see a yellow focus frame around each one, as shown on the left in Figure 4-11. In a picture containing multiple faces, one frame has interior corner marks — in

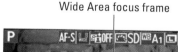

Wide Area focus frame

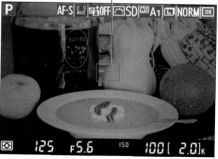

Figure 4-10: The red box represents the focusing frame in Wide Area and Normal Area AF-area mode.

Figure 4-11, see the girl on the right. Those marks indicate the face selected as the one to use to set focusing distance.

If you don't see any yellow boxes but instead see the red frame, the camera can't detect a face and will set focus as it would if you were using Wide Area mode.

- *Subject Tracking:* A white focusing frame like the one shown on the right in Figure 4-11 appears.

In AF-F mode, the frame turns green when the object under the frame is in focus.

Selected face   Subject Tracking focus frame

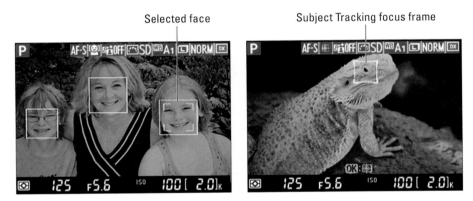

Figure 4-11: The focusing frame appears differently in Face Priority mode (left) and Subject Tracking mode (right).

4. Use the Multi Selector to move the focusing frame over your subject.

For example, I moved the focus frame over the garnish on the soup bowl for my example image, as shown on the left in Figure 4-12.

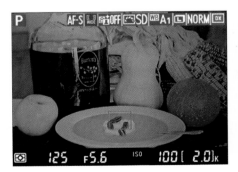
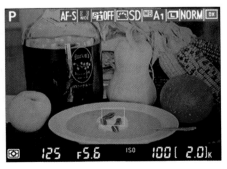

Figure 4-12: Use the Multi Selector to move the frame over your subject (left); the frame turns green when focus is achieved (right).

In Face Priority mode, you can use the Multi Selector to move the box with the corner marks — which indicates the final focusing point — from face to face in a group portrait. In Wide Area and Normal Area modes, press OK to move the focus point to the center of the frame.

5. **In Subject Tracking AF-area mode, press OK to initiate focus tracking.**

   If your subject moves, the focus frame moves with it. To stop tracking, press OK again. (You may need to take this step if your subject leaves the frame — press OK to stop tracking, reframe, and then press OK to start tracking again.)

6. **In AF-S autofocus mode, press and hold the shutter button halfway down to start autofocusing.**

7. **Wait for the focus frame to turn green, as shown on the right in Figure 4-12.**

   What happens next depends on your Autofocus mode:

   - *AF-S mode:* Focus remains locked as long as you keep the shutter button pressed halfway.

   - *AF-F mode:* Focus is adjusted if the subject moves. The focus frame turns red (or yellow or white) if focus is lost; green signals that focus has been achieved again. You can lock focus by pressing the shutter button halfway. (In most cases, the camera will reset focus on your subject when you press the button even if the focus frame is already green.)

QUAL

8. **(Optional) Press the Qual button to magnify the display to double-check focus.**

   Each press gives you a closer look at the subject. A small thumbnail in the corner of the monitor appears, with the yellow highlight box indicating the area that's currently being magnified, as shown in Figure 4-13. Press the Multi Selector to scroll the display if needed.

ISO

   To zoom out, press the ISO button. If you're not using Subject Tracking mode, you can also press OK to quickly return to normal magnification.

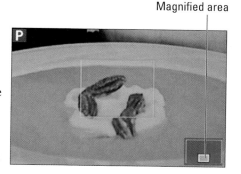

Magnified area

Figure 4-13: Press the Qual button to magnify the display and double-check focus.

Manual focusing in Live View mode

For manual focusing, set the Focus mode selector switch on the front-left side of the camera to M and, if you're using a lens that has a focus method switch, set that switch to M as well. Then turn the lens focusing ring to focus. But note a few quirks:

- ✔ The focusing frame doesn't turn green when you set focus as it does with autofocusing.

- ✔ Even with manual focusing, you still see the focusing frame; its appearance depends on the current AF-area mode setting. In Face Priority mode, the frame automatically jumps into place over a face if it detects one. And if you press OK when Subject Tracking mode is enabled, the camera tries to track the subject under the frame until you press OK again. I find these two behaviors irritating, so I always set the AF-area mode to Wide Area or Normal Area for manual focusing.

- ✔ You can press the Qual button to check focus in manual mode just as you can during autofocusing. After magnifying the scene, press the Multi Selector to scroll the display to view a different area. Press the ISO button to reduce the magnification level.

- ✔ If you're using an AF-S lens, you actually *don't* need to move the camera's Focus mode selector switch to the M position to focus manually — simply setting the lens switch to the M position tells the camera that you're about to focus manually. Just be *sure* that your lens falls in this category, or you can damage the lens and the camera by not adjusting both switches.

Shooting Still Pictures in Live View Mode

After sorting out the focusing options, the rest of the steps involved in taking a picture in Live View mode are essentially the same as for viewfinder photography. But before I walk you through those steps, I want to show you one cool trick for selecting certain picture settings: By pressing the *i* button, you can display a control strip that offers quick access to the settings labeled in Figure 4-14. After you display the strip, use the Multi Selector to highlight the option you want to change and then press OK to display a list of the available options for that setting. Make your choice and press OK again. Press *i* again to exit the control strip.

With that detail out of the way, here are the steps to shoot a photo:

1. **Choose an exposure mode (Auto, P, Scene, and so on).**

   Select this setting via the Mode dial on top of the camera; be sure to press the lock release button in the center of the dial before attempting to turn the dial. Chapter 2 introduces you to all the exposure modes.

The exposure mode determines what picture settings you can control. For full control over all camera options, use the P, S, A, or M mode. (P is the most automatic of these four modes.)

2. **Choose the Release mode via the Release mode dial.**

   The Release mode dial lies underneath the Mode dial; don't forget to press the adjacent button to unlock the dial before trying to rotate it. For normal photography, set the dial to S for Single Frame shooting. You then get one photo for each press of the shutter button. Chapter 2 details all the Release mode options. Note that for remote control shooting with the ML-L3 wireless remote, you must enable the feature via the *i* button control strip or the Shooting menu.

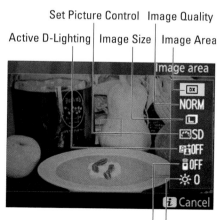

Set Picture Control Image Quality
Active D-Lighting | Image Size | Image Area

ML-L3 Remote Control mode |
Monitor brightness

Figure 4-14: Press the *i* button to display a control strip that provides access to these settings.

3. **Rotate the Live View switch to the still camera position and then press the LV button in the center of the switch.**

   Figure 4-15 reminds you where to find the switch.

4. **Review and adjust other picture settings.**

   At the default Live View display mode, you can view critical shooting settings on the monitor, as shown in Figure 4-16. (Press the Info button to change display modes.) A few side notes:

   - Some settings, such as Exposure Compensation and Flash Compensation, appear only when those features are enabled.

   - If you enable automatic exposure bracketing, you also see a BKT symbol underneath the Image Size/ Quality icon at the top-right corner of the monitor.

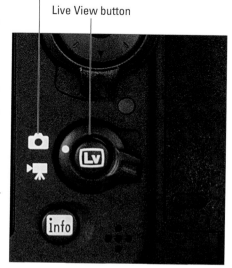

Still photography icon

Live View button

Figure 4-15: For still photography, set the Live View switch to this position and then press the LV button.

- The exposure meter, labeled in Figure 4-16, appears in M (manual exposure mode) to help you gauge whether your exposure settings are on track. In the P, S, and A exposure modes, the meter appears only if the camera anticipates an exposure problem; the meter tells you how far over- or underexposed the image will be. In this regard, the aperture or shutter speed value blinks to indicate an exposure issue. You may also see a blinking flash symbol, which is a suggestion that you use flash. (Just press the Flash button on the side of the camera to raise the flash.)

For details on all these exposure issues, as well as metering mode, ISO, Active D-Lighting, and shutter speed and aperture, head for Chapter 7. Chapter 8 details White Balance and Picture Style, which are color-related settings. If you need help with the Image Size, Image Quality, or Image Area settings, Chapter 2 has the scoop.

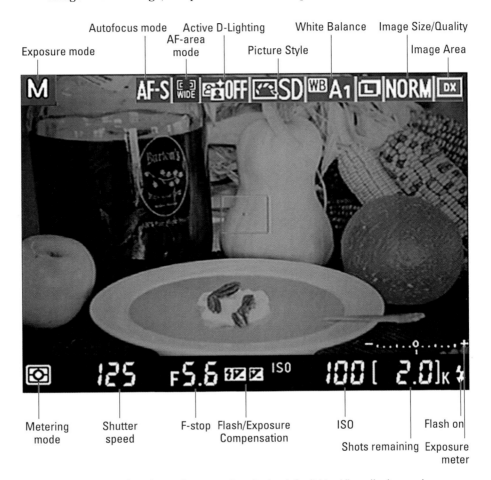

Figure 4-16: You can view these picture settings in the default Live View display mode.

5. **If focusing manually, turn the focusing ring to set focus.**

6. **If using autofocusing, position the focus frame over the subject.**

   And if you're using Subject Tracking autofocus, press OK to initiate tracking.

7. **Press and hold the shutter button halfway down.**

   Exposure metering begins but is adjusted up to the time you take the picture. If you're using Auto exposure mode or certain Scene modes, the built-in flash may pop up in dim lighting.

    You can lock autoexposure by pressing the AE-L/AF-L button; an AE-L symbol then appears next to the Metering mode icon.

   If you're autofocusing, focus locks when the focus frame turns green and remains locked as long as you keep the shutter button pressed halfway.

8. **Press the shutter button the rest of the way to take the picture.**

   If you're shooting in Continuous High or Continuous Low (burst) Release mode, the photos being recorded appear on the monitor in place of the live scene while the shutter button is pressed. In other Release modes, the picture appears briefly on the screen immediately after you take the shot, and then the Live View preview reappears. (Check out Chapter 2 for details on Release modes.)

Shooting Movies

In Live View movie mode, your camera can create stunning high-definition digital movies. The rest of this chapter is devoted to helping you shoot, play, and even edit a movie.

 For more insights into recording movies with your D7100, hop online and check out Nikon Cinema, at www.nikonusa.com/cinema.

Easy-does-it movie recording

Video enthusiasts will appreciate the fact that the D7100 enables you to tweak a variety of movie-recording settings, such as frame size, frame rate, microphone volume, and the like. But if you're not up to sorting through all those options, just record your movies using the default settings. (You can restore the critical defaults by opening the Shooting menu and choosing Reset Shooting Menu.) At the default settings, you get a full HD movie with sound enabled. Microphone volume is adjusted automatically, and the movie file is stored on the memory card in slot 1.

Here's the path I recommend for simple shooting using the defaults:

1. **Set the Mode dial on top of the camera to the P setting.**

In this exposure mode, the camera takes care of movie exposure for you automatically. However, should something appear amiss with exposure or color, you can tweak a setting here and there to resolve the issue — something you can't do in the Auto exposure mode. (See "Exploring other movie options," later in this chapter, for help.)

2. **Set the camera to movie mode by rotating the Live View switch to the movie camera icon, as shown in Figure 4-17.**

3. **Press the LV button to engage the Live View display.**

By default, you see data similar to what you see in Figure 4-18. Press Info to change the display mode. Later sections decode the various bits of data; for now, just pay attention to the available recording time readout, labeled in the figure.

4. **Set focus as outlined earlier in this chapter.**

To take advantage of continuous auto-focusing, set the Autofocus mode to AF-F. (Select this setting by pressing the Focus-mode selector button while rotating the Main command dial.) The camera starts focusing automatically and adjusts focus as necessary throughout the recording. You can lock focus at a specific distance by pressing the shutter button halfway.

If the Autofocus mode is set to AF-S, press the shutter button halfway to set and lock focus. You then can lift your finger off the shutter button; focus remains set unless you press the button halfway to reset focus.

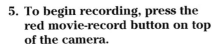

5. **To begin recording, press the red movie-record button on top of the camera.**

Most shooting data disappears from the screen, and a red Rec symbol flashes in the top-left corner, as shown in Figure 4-19. As recording

Live View switch

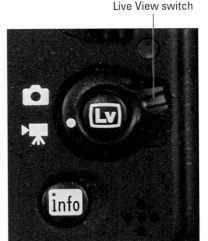

Figure 4-17: After setting the camera to movie mode, press the LV button to engage the Live View display.

Available recording time

Figure 4-18: In the default movie display, you see this assortment of data.

progresses, the area labeled "Time remaining" in the figure shows you how many more seconds of video you can record.

6. **To stop recording, press the movie-record button again.**

   Movies are created in the MOV format, which means you can play them on your computer using most movie-playback programs. You also can view movies in Nikon ViewNX 2, the free software provided with your camera. If you want to view your movies on a TV, see the end of Chapter 5 to find out how to connect your camera to your set.

Recording symbol   Time remaining

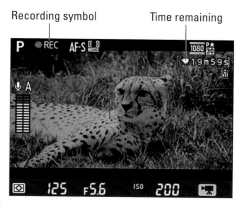

Figure 4-19: The red Rec symbol flashes while recording is in progress.

You can stop your recording and capture a still image in one fell swoop: Just press and hold the shutter button down until you hear the shutter release. But because the camera remains in movie mode until you move the Live View switch to the still photography position, the picture is recorded using the movie frame area and has a 16:9 aspect ratio. The resolution of the picture depends on the Image Size and Image Area settings (detailed in Chapter 2) but varies from a photo taken in still photography mode because of that 16:9 aspect ratio. Flash is disabled as well.

Also be aware that this picture-shooting feature depends on the setting selected for the Assign Shutter Button option, found in the Movie section of the Custom Setting menu. At the default setting, Take Photos, things work as just described. If you change the setting to Record Movies, you can use the shutter button to start and stop recording, but you can no longer take a still picture without shifting out of movie mode. See Chapter 11 for more about this button customization.

Adjusting basic recording settings

When you're interested in taking more control over how your videos are recorded, start by exploring the following basic settings:

- **Frame Size/Frame Rate and Movie Quality:** Together, these settings determine the quality of your video as well as the movie file size.

- **Microphone:** This setting determines how audio is recorded.

- **Destination:** If you have two memory cards installed in the camera, this setting enables you to specify which card gets the movie file.

I detail these options starting with the next section; for now, just familiarize yourself with the process of accessing them. You have two options:

- ✓ **Shooting menu:** You can adjust all four options via the Movie Settings item on the Shooting menu, as shown in Figure 4-20.

- ✓ **Live View control strip:** For even faster access to the settings, set the camera to movie mode and then press the *i* button to display the control strip shown in Figure 4-21. From this screen, you can adjust the four basic recording settings I just mentioned as well as the other settings labeled in the figure. Use the Multi Selector to highlight the option you want to change and press OK to reveal the available settings. Make your choice and press OK; then press the *i* button again to hide the control strip. Note that if you attach headphones to the camera, you can use the Multi Selector to scroll to an additional option that enables you to adjust headphone volume (not shown in the figure).

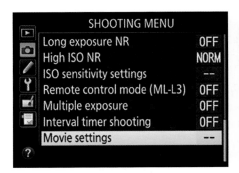
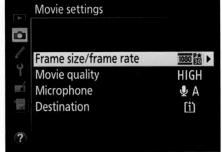

Figure 4-20: The Movie Settings menu item contains the four critical recording settings.

In the default movie display mode, the screen shows you the current settings for each of these options, as shown in Figure 4-22. (Don't see the data? Press the Info button to cycle through the available movie display modes.) To decode what you see and figure out which settings will work best for your next recording, keep reading.

Understanding the Frame Size/Frame Rate options

This setting determines the resolution, or frame size, of your movie, as well as the number of frames per second (fps), both of which affect video quality.

You can access the setting via the Movie Settings option on the Shooting menu (refer to Figure 4-20) or through the control strip (Figure 4-21). If you travel by way of the menu, you're presented with the options shown in Figure 4-23. If you access the setting via the control strip, the options appear superimposed over the live scene, but the available settings are the same.

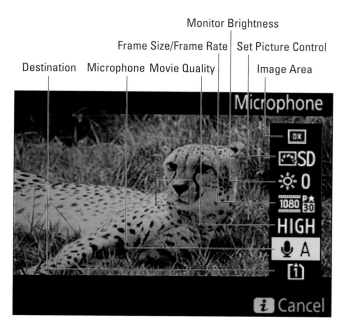

Figure 4-21: Press the *i* button to display the control strip for fast access to these options.

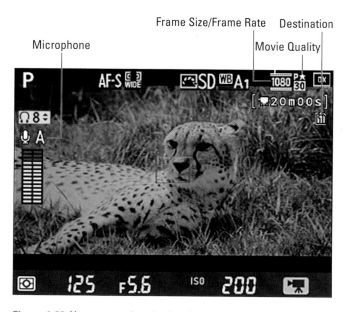

Figure 4-22: You can monitor the four basic recording settings in the display.

If you're a digital video expert, these options probably make perfect sense to you; take your pick and move on. If you're new to video, allow me to present some background that will help you understand this numerical soup.

The first thing you need to know is that which Frame Size/Frame Rate options are available depends on the Image Area setting. I detail this setting in Chapter 2, but here's a quick recap: At the default setting, DX, the camera uses the maximum area of the image sensor to record the image or, in this case, your 16:9 video. The other Image Area option, 1.3x crop, uses a smaller area at the center of the sensor. For movie recording, you can access the first two Frame Size/Frame Rate options *only* when using the 1.3x crop setting; otherwise, they're dimmed, as in Figure 4-23.

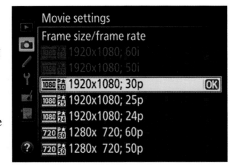

Figure 4-23: These options set the frame size (resolution) and frame rate (frames per second) of your movie.

Okay, now to decipher those Frame Size/Frame rate settings:

- **Frame size:** *Frame size* refers to the number of pixels used to create the movie frame. In the world of HDTV, a frame size of 1920 x 1080 pixels is considered *Full HD* — meaning the best possible (at the moment, anyway) — whereas 1280 x 720 is known as *Standard HD*. The default setting is 1920 x 1080.

- **Frame rate (fps):** This value, stated as *frames per second* (fps), determines the smoothness of the playback. Available frame rates range from 24 to 60 frames per second.

What's the best option? Well, it depends on the visual goal you have for your video. Here are some guidelines to help you achieve that goal:

- *24 fps is the standard for motion pictures.* It gives your videos a softer, more movie-like look.

- *25 fps gives your videos a slightly sharper, more "realistic" look.* This frame rate is the standard for television broadcast in countries that follow the PAL video-signal standard, such as some European countries. If you bought your camera in a PAL part of the world, this setting should be the default.

- *30 fps produces an even crisper picture than 25 fps.* This frame rate is the broadcast video standard for the United States and other countries that use the NTSC signal standard. It's the default setting for cameras bought in those countries, too.

- *50 and 60 fps are often used for recording high-speed action and creating slow-motion footage.* With more frames per second, fast movements are rendered more smoothly, especially if you slow down the movie playback for a slo-mo review of the action.

How about 50 versus 60? You're back to the PAL versus NTSC question: 50 fps is a PAL standard, and 60 is an NTSC standard.

⊩ **P (progressive) versus i (interlaced) video:** Finally, the top two options on the list of Frame Size/Frame Rate settings end with the letter *i,* but the rest are tagged with a *p.* The initials stand for *interlaced* and *progressive,* which refer to two different ways to record the lines of pixels that create a frame of digital video. With interlaced video, a single frame is split into odd and even *fields,* or lines of pixels. The data from the odd lines is recorded first, followed rapidly by the data from the even lines — so rapidly, in fact, that the picture appears seamless during playback. With the second technology, *progressive video,* all the lines are pulled out of the magic video hat in sequential order, in a single pass.

Progressive is the newer technology and tends to deliver smoother, cleaner footage when you're shooting fast motion or panning the camera. But your HDTV should be able to play both types of video. Also, if you plan to combine footage you shoot with your D7100 with existing interlaced footage, it's best to use the interlaced setting so that all your video clips use the same technology.

So summing up, select from one of the following options if you want your movie to adhere to the NTSC video format:

⊩ **1920 x 1080; 60i:** Full HD using 60 interlaced fields to generate a final frame rate of 30 fps. (Remember, an interlaced frame is created by two passes, so your 60 fields combine to produce the 30 fps rate.) At the risk of being repetitive, I remind you that you can't choose this option when the Image Area option is set to DX; you must use the 1.3x crop setting.

⊩ **1920 x 1080; 30p:** Full HD at 30 fps, using progressive video.

⊩ **1920 x 1080; 24p:** Full HD at the movie-like 24 fps progressive video.

⊩ **1280 x 720; 60p:** Standard HD with a frame size of 1280 x 720, a frame rate of 60 frames per second, and progressive video.

For videos that follow the PAL standard, instead select a frame rate of 25, 24, or 50. Again, the 1920 x 1080; 50i setting is available only when you use the 1.3x crop setting for the Image Area option.

One more note before you head out to simpler pastures: See the little symbols appearing to the left of each setting in Figure 4-23? They're simply (yeah, right, "simply") a reminder of what you see on the Live View screen to indicate each setting (take another look at Figure 4-22). The first number specifies the vertical pixel count of the Frame Size; the p or i indicates progressive or interlaced, and the other number tells you the frame rate. Oh, that little star? It means that you selected High as the Movie Quality option, which I describe next. No star means that option is set to Normal.

Selecting the Movie Quality option (bit rate)

Next up on the list of movie settings to digest is Movie Quality, also accessed via the Movie Settings option on the Shooting menu or the Live View control strip. (Refer to Figures 4-20 and 21, respectively.) Remember, you display the control strip by simply pressing the *i* button.

For this option, you can choose from two settings, High and Normal. Your choice determines how much compression is applied to the video file, which in turn affects the *bit rate,* or how much data is used to represent one second of video, measured in Mbps (megabits per second). A higher bit rate means better quality and larger files. On the D7100, High delivers a bit rate of 24 Mbps; Normal, 12 Mbps.

Because bit rate affects the size of the video file, it also determines the maximum length of the video clip you can create each time you press the record button. If you select High as the Movie Quality option, the maximum movie length is 20 minutes. At the Normal setting, you can record 29 minutes and 59 seconds of video at a time.

One last tip about this setting: In the Live View display, a star in the area labeled Movie Quality in Figure 4-22 indicates that the High bit rate is selected. No star means that the option is set to Normal. This same star system reflects the setting in the Frame Size/Frame Rate menu screens, as I outline in excruciating detail at the end of the preceding section.

Controlling audio

You can record sound using the camera's built-in microphone, labeled on the left in Figure 4-24, or you can attach the optional Nikon ME-1 stereo microphone to the jack labeled on the right in the figure. You can even attach headphones via the headphone jack, also labeled in the figure, to monitor sound recording.

One way to adjust audio-recording options is to select Movie Settings from the Shooting menu, press OK, and then select Microphone, as shown on the left in Figure 4-25. Press the Multi Selector right to display the settings shown on the right in the figure. Some of the menu options can be a little intimidating until you know what's what:

- ✔ **Volume meters:** The two bars at the bottom of the screen (labeled "Volume meters" in Figure 4-25) indicate the sound levels being picked up by the microphone. For stereo sound, the top bar represents the left audio channel; the bottom bar, the right channel. For monaural sound, both bars reflect the same data.

  Audio levels are measured in decibels (dB), and levels on the volume meter range from –40 (very, very soft) to 0 (as loud as can be measured digitally). Ideally, sound should peak consistently in the –12 range.

The indicators on the meter turn yellow in this range, as shown in Figure 4-25. If the sound level is too high, the volume meters will peak at 0 and appear red — a warning that audio may be distorted.

Internal microphone   Headphone jack   Microphone jack

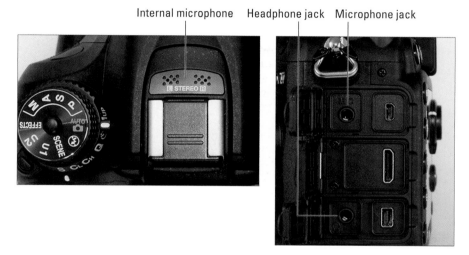

Figure 4-24: You can use the internal microphone (left) or plug in an external microphone and/or headphones (right).

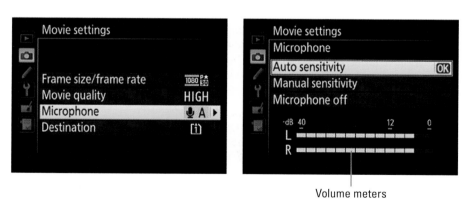

Volume meters

Figure 4-25: Audio recording settings are controlled through the Microphone option.

✔ **Microphone settings:** You can choose from three microphone options:

- *Auto Sensitivity:* The camera automatically adjusts the volume according to the level of the ambient noise. This setting is the default.

- *Manual Sensitivity:* Choose this option and press the Multi Selector right to display the manual sound level control, as shown in Figure 4-26. Press the Multi Selector up and down to adjust the microphone volume; settings range from 1 to 20. Again, the volume meters serve as your guide to the correct microphone sensitivity.

- *Microphone Off:* Choose this setting to record a movie with no sound or when you're using an off-camera microphone and don't want the camera itself to record audio.

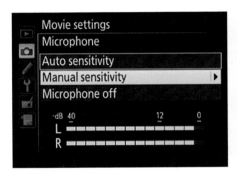 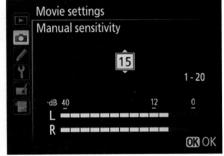

Figure 4-26: To control the microphone sensitivity yourself, choose the Manual Sensitivity option (left); press the Multi Selector up or down to adjust the setting (right).

 After you're familiar with how the audio settings work, you may prefer to adjust them via the movie Live View control strip. Just press the *i* button to display the control strip, highlight the Microphone icon, and press OK to display volume indicators over the screen. Press the Multi Selector up and down to adjust the volume. Move the indicator all the way to the top of the scale to shift to the Auto setting; go all the way to the bottom to turn audio recording off.

If you have headphones attached, you can use the control strip to adjust headphone volume. Scroll to the second screen of the control strip to access the adjustment. (This is one setting you can't control via a menu option.)

 Either way, you must adjust microphone levels and headphone volume *before* starting the recording; you can't change them while recording is in progress.

To see the current settings without going to the menu or control strip, look in the spot labeled Microphone in Figure 4-22, earlier in this chapter. For example, the symbol in the figure shows that the mic is enabled and set to automatic volume adjustment. If you have headphones attached, a headphone volume symbol appears directly above the microphone symbol as shown in the figure.

Choosing a card destination

Finally, a simple option to digest: If you have two memory cards installed in the camera, you can specify which card should hold the video file. Make the call via the Destination option, which you can access via the Movie Settings option on the Shooting menu, as shown in Figure 4-27, or via the control strip, which you display by pressing the *i* button. (Refer to Figure 4-21.)

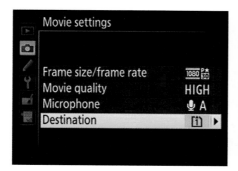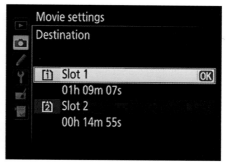

Figure 4-27: You can see which card has the most space and select it to store your video.

By default, movie files are recorded to the memory card in the top card slot (Slot 1). When you choose the Destination option, you can see the length of the movie that will fit on each card at your current recording settings, as shown in Figure 4-27.

Note that the Role Played by Card in Slot 2 option on the Shooting menu, which I detail in Chapter 1, has no effect when you're shooting movies. Regardless of that setting, the entire movie clip goes on the card you select via the Destination option.

Exploring other movie options

In addition to those settings reviewed in the preceding sections, you can control a few other aspects of your cinematic effort:

- **Exposure mode:** You can record movies in any exposure mode (Auto, Scene modes, P, M, and so on). As with still photography, your choice determines which camera settings you can access. The Movie Settings menu options (Frame Size/Frame Rate, Movie Quality, Microphone, and Destination) are available regardless of the exposure mode.

- **Focus options:** Your options are as outlined in the earlier section "Exploring Live View Focusing." As a quick recap, you adjust autofocusing behavior through the Autofocus mode and AF-area mode; look for the current settings in the spots labeled in Figure 4-28.

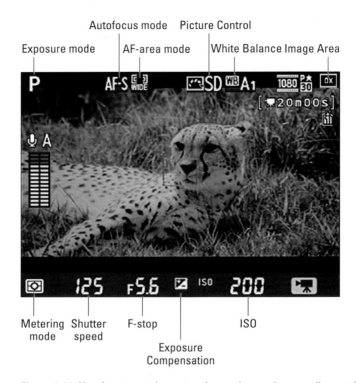

Figure 4-28: Here's your road map to other major movie-recording settings.

- *Autofocus mode:* Choose AF-S to lock focus when you press the shutter button halfway; choose AF-F for continuous autofocusing. Adjust the setting by pressing the AF-mode button (left front side of the camera, in the center of the Focus mode switch) while rotating the Main command dial.

- *AF-area mode:* You can choose from Face Priority, Wide Area, Normal Area, or Subject Tracking. Adjust this setting by pressing the AF-mode button while rotating the Sub-command dial. See the earlier section "Setting the AF-area mode" for the scoop on each of these autofocusing options.

✔ **Image Area:** You can adjust this setting via the Shooting menu or via the movie Live View control strip (press the *i* button); use it to set the imaging area to the DX setting (whole sensor) or 1.3x crop setting. See the sidebar "Live View and the Image Area setting" for details on this particular setting.

✔ **White Balance and Picture Control:** The colors in your movie are rendered according to the current White Balance and Picture Control settings. You have control over these options only when the Mode dial is set to P, S, A, or M:

- *Adjusting White Balance:* Press and hold the WB button while rotating the Main command dial. Look for the setting in the area of the display highlighted in Figure 4-28. You also can adjust this option via the Shooting menu.

- *Adjusting Picture Control:* Select this setting via the Shooting menu or via the movie Live View control strip (press the *i* button to display the strip). Again, Figure 4-28 shows you where in the Live View display to locate the symbol representing the current setting.

Want to record a black-and-white movie? Select Monochrome as the Picture Control. Instant *film noir.*

See Chapter 8 for details about these options.

 Exposure control: Your control over exposure, explained thoroughly in Chapter 7, depends on the exposure mode you select, as follows:

- *Auto, Auto Flash Off, and Scene modes:* The camera sets exposure for you, controlling aperture, shutter speed, and ISO Sensitivity.

- *P, S, and A modes:* In A mode, you can select an f-stop prior to starting recording; in other modes, the aperture is selected for you.

  In all three modes, you can apply Exposure Compensation to tell the camera to produce a brighter or darker picture than its exposure meter thinks is appropriate. Just press the Exposure Compensation button while rotating the Main command dial to adjust the setting. Note, though, that you're limited to an adjustment range of EV +3.0 or –3.0 rather than the usual five steps that are possible during normal photography.

- *M mode:* If you choose M, for manual exposure, you can control aperture, shutter speed, and ISO. You must set the aperture before beginning recording.

  Because this exposure mode is best left for experts and involves more issues than I have room to cover in this book, I opt not to cover it in detail. Your camera instruction manual provides some specific parameters that apply when you shoot movies in the M exposure mode.

Screening Your Movies

To play your movie, press the Playback button. In single-image playback mode, you can spot a movie file by looking for the little movie camera icon in the top-left corner of the screen, as shown in Figure 4-29. You also can view other movie-related data, including the image area, frame size, frame rate, and Movie Quality setting. (Remember: A star means that you set the Movie Quality option to High.) To start playback, press OK.

In the thumbnail and Calendar playback modes, both described in Chapter 5, you see little filmstrip dots along the edges of image thumbnails to represent movie files. This time, press OK twice: once to shift to single-image view and again to start movie playback.

After playback begins, you see the data labeled in Figure 4-30. The progress bar and Time Elapsed value show you how much of the movie has played so far; you can also see the total movie length. The other symbols at the bottom of the screen are there to remind you that you can use various camera buttons to control playback, as follows:

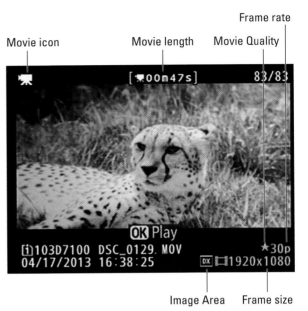

Frame rate

Movie icon   Movie length   Movie Quality

Image Area   Frame size

Figure 4-29: The movie camera symbol tells you you're looking at a movie file.

- ✔ **Stop playback:** Press the Multi Selector up. The white circle labeled "Playback control symbols" in the figure (lower-right) represents the Multi Selector.

- ✔ **Pause/resume playback:** Press down to pause playback; press OK to resume playback.

- ✔ **Fast-forward/rewind:** Press the Multi Selector right or left to fast-forward or rewind the movie, respectively. Press again to double the fast-forward or rewind speed; keep pressing to increase the speed to as fast as 16 times normal. Hold the button down to fast-forward or rewind all the way to the end or beginning of the movie.

- ✔ **Forward/rewind 10 seconds:** Rotate the Main command dial to the right to jump 10 seconds through the movie; rotate to the left to jump back 10 seconds.

- ✔ **Skip to the last frame/first frame:** Rotate the Sub-command dial.

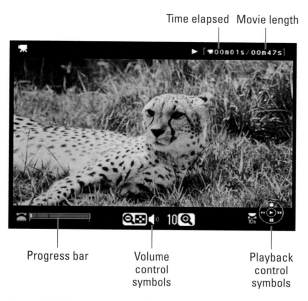

✔ **Advance frame by frame:** First, press the Multi Selector down to pause playback. Then press the Multi Selector right to advance one frame; press left to go back one frame.

✔ **Adjust playback volume:** See the markings labeled "Volume control symbols" in Figure 4-30? They remind you that you can press the Qual button to increase volume and press the ISO button to lower it.

Time elapsed   Movie length

Progress bar   Volume control symbols   Playback control symbols

Figure 4-30: The icons at the bottom of the screen remind you which buttons to use to control playback.

Trimming Movies

You can do some limited movie editing in camera. I emphasize: *limited* editing. You can trim frames from the start of a movie and clip off frames from the end, and that's it.

To eliminate frames from the beginning of the movie, take these steps:

1. **Display your movie in single-image view.**

2. **Press OK to begin playback.**

3. **When you reach the first frame you want to keep, press the Multi Selector down to pause the movie.**

4. **Press the *i* button.**

   You see the menu options shown on the left in Figure 4-31.

5. **Highlight Choose Start/End Point and press OK.**

   You see the options shown on the right in Figure 4-31.

6. **Choose Start Point and press OK.**

   You're returned to the playback screen.

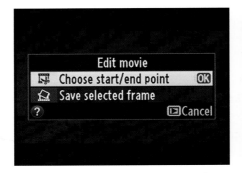 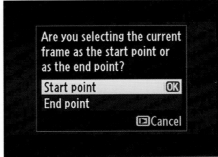

Figure 4-31: With the movie paused, press the *i* button to access the movie-editing screens.

7. **Press the Multi Selector up to lop off all frames that came before the current frame.**

Now you see the options shown in Figure 4-32. To preview the movie, select Preview and press OK; after the preview plays, you're returned to the menu screen.

8. **To preserve your original movie and save the trimmed one as a new file, choose Save as New File and press OK.**

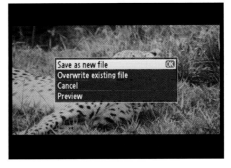

Alternatively, you can opt to overwrite the existing file, but you can't get the original file back if you do.

Figure 4-32: Choose Save as New File to avoid overwriting the original movie file.

A message appears telling you that the trimmed movie is being saved. During playback, edited files are indicated by a little scissors icon that appears in the upper-left corner of the screen.

To instead trim footage from the end of a film, take the same steps, but this time pause playback on the last frame you want to keep in Step 3. Then, in Step 6, select Choose End Point instead of Choose Start Point.

Saving a Movie Frame as a Still Image

You can save a single frame of the movie as a regular image file. Here's how:

1. **Begin playing your movie.**

2. **When you reach the frame you want to capture, press the Multi Selector down to pause playback.**

3. **Press the *i* button to bring up the Edit Movie screen.**

4. **Choose Save Selected Frame and press OK.**

   The frame appears on the monitor.

5. **Press the Multi Selector up.**

6. **On the confirmation screen that appears, select Yes and press OK.**

   Your frame is saved as a JPEG photo.

Remember a few things about pictures you create this way:

- When you view the image, it's marked with a little scissors icon in the upper-left corner.

- The resolution of the picture depends on the resolution of the movie: for example, if the movie resolution is 1920 x 1080, your picture resolution is 1920 x 1080.

- You can't apply editing features from the Retouch menu to the file, and you also can't view all the shooting data that's normally associated with a JPEG picture.

Part II
Working with Picture Files

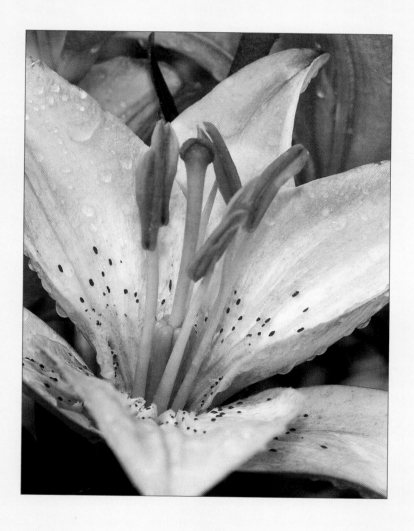

Look for tips about archiving your picture files at www.dummies.com/extras/nikon.

In this part . . .

- ✔ Discover all of your camera's picture-playback features.
- ✔ Erase pictures you don't want and protect the ones you like from being accidentally deleted.
- ✔ Customize the playback screens and get a road map to the playback data.
- ✔ Download pictures from the camera to the computer.
- ✔ Convert Raw (NEF) images using the in-camera converter and the one found in Nikon ViewNX 2.
- ✔ Get help with printing and sharing your photos online.

5

Playback Mode: Viewing, Erasing, and Protecting Photos

In This Chapter

▶ Exploring picture playback functions

▶ Deciphering the picture information displays

▶ Understanding histograms

▶ Deleting and hiding bad pictures and protecting great ones

▶ Creating an in-camera slide show

▶ Viewing pictures on a television set

*W*ithout question, my favorite thing about digital photography is being able to view my pictures the instant after I shoot them. No more guessing whether I captured the image or need to try again, as in the film days; no more wasting money on developing pictures that stink.

Seeing your pictures is just the start of the things you can do when you switch your camera to playback mode, though. You also can review settings you used to take the picture, display graphics that alert you to exposure problems, and add file markers that protect a picture from accidental erasure. This chapter tells you how to use all these playback features and more.

Note: Some information in this chapter applies only to still photographs; if a feature also works for movie files, I spell that out. For help with the basics of movie playback, see the end of Chapter 4.

Customizing Basic Playback Options

 To switch your camera to playback mode, just press the Playback button. Then press the Multi Selector right or left to scroll through your pictures.

Later sections show you how to choose what type of data appears with your pictures and movies, how to display thumbnails of multiple image files at a time, and how to magnify a photo. But first, the next few sections explain options that affect overall playback performance, including how long your pictures appear onscreen and how they're oriented on the monitor.

Adjusting playback timing

You can adjust the length of time that the camera displays photos as follows:

🖊 **Adjust the timing of automatic playback shutoff.** After you press the Playback button, the monitor turns off automatically if 10 seconds elapse without any activity. You can adjust this shutoff timing through the Monitor Off Delay option, found in the Timers/AE Lock section of the Custom Setting menu and shown on the left in Figure 5-1. Choose Playback, as shown on the right, to access the timing options, which range from 4 seconds to 10 minutes. (This setting affects still photos only; movies play in their entirety unless you pause or stop playback.) Remember that the monitor is a big battery drain, so keep the display time as short as you find practical.

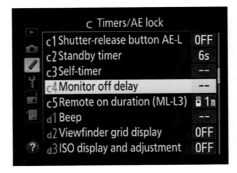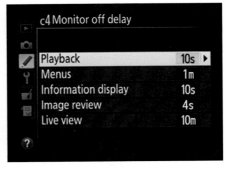

Figure 5-1: You can control how long pictures are displayed before automatic monitor shutdown occurs.

✓ **Enable instant review.** You can tell the camera to display each photo for a quick review immediately after you shoot it. This feature is disabled by default; enable it through the Image Review option on the Playback menu, shown in Figure 5-2. Again, this option has no effect when you're shooting movies; to view a movie, you must set the camera to playback mode and then press the OK button.

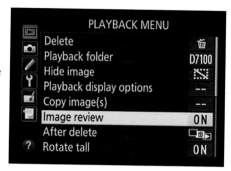

Figure 5-2: Head for the Playback menu to enable instant review.

✓ **Adjust the length of the instant-review period.** By default, the instant-review period lasts 4 seconds, but you can adjust this timing through the Monitor Off Delay option shown in Figure 5-1. Just choose Image Review instead of Playback when you get to the right screen in the figure. Settings range from 2 seconds to 10 minutes.

Enabling automatic picture rotation

When you take a picture, the camera can record the image *orientation* — whether you held the camera normally, creating a horizontally oriented image, or turned the camera on its side to shoot a vertically oriented photo. This orientation data is added to the picture *metadata,* which is hidden data that records various camera settings.

During playback, the camera can read the orientation data and automatically rotate the image so that it appears in the upright position, as shown on the left in Figure 5-3. Or you can disable rotation, in which case vertically oriented pictures appear sideways, as shown on the right in Figure 5-3.

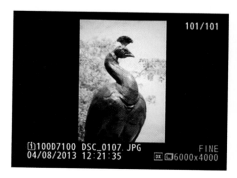 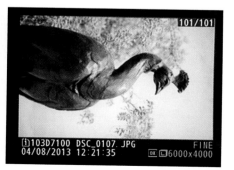

Figure 5-3: You can display vertically oriented pictures in their upright position (left) or sideways (right).

Official photo lingo uses the term *portrait orientation* to refer to vertically oriented pictures and *landscape orientation* to refer to horizontally oriented pictures. The terms stem from the traditional way that people and places are captured in paintings and photographs — portraits, vertically; landscapes, horizontally.

Set your rotation wishes through these menu options, shown in Figure 5-4:

- **Auto Image Rotation:** This option, on the Setup menu, determines whether the orientation data is included in the picture file. The default setting is On; select Off to leave out the data. Note that if you do include the rotation data, the picture is also automatically rotated when you view it in Nikon ViewNX 2, the free software that ships with your camera, and in other photo programs that can read the data.

- **Rotate Tall:** Found on the Playback menu, this option controls whether the camera pays attention to the orientation data. The default setting is On, and vertical pictures are rotated during playback.

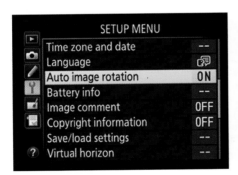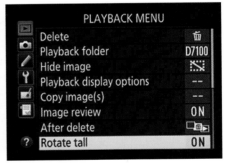

Figure 5-4: Visit the Setup and Playback menus to enable or disable image rotation.

Regardless of these settings, movies aren't rotated, nor are still photos rotated during the instant-review period. Also, be aware that shooting with the lens pointing directly up or down sometimes confuses the camera, causing it to record the wrong orientation data in the file.

Viewing Images in Playback Mode

Here are the basics of playback:

1. Press the Playback button.

You see the last picture you took — or if you just shot a movie, the first frame of that movie.

2. **To scroll through your files, press the Multi Selector right or left.**

   Figure 5-5 reminds you where to find the Multi Selector as well as some other buttons that play a role in picture playback.

   To begin movie playback, press OK. See Chapter 4 for full details on viewing movies.

3. **To return to picture-taking mode, press the Playback button again or press the shutter button halfway and then release it.**

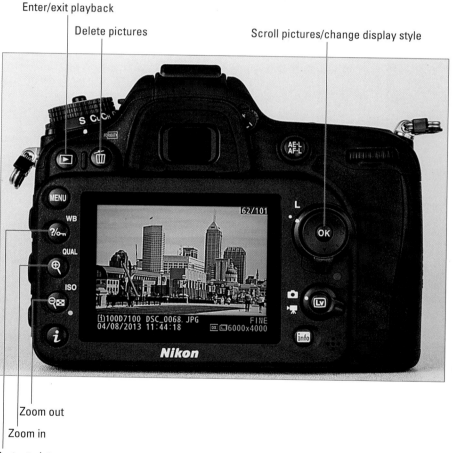

Enter/exit playback

Delete pictures

Scroll pictures/change display style

Zoom out

Zoom in

Protect pictures

Figure 5-5: These buttons play the largest roles in picture playback.

A few tidbits to note:

✔ These steps assume that the camera is set to display a single photo at a time, as shown in Figure 5-5. You can also display multiple images at a time, as explained in the next section.

✔ By default, you see some picture data along with the photo or movie frame, as shown in Figure 5-5. To find out how to interpret the picture information and specify what data you want to see, see the upcoming section "Viewing Picture Data." For now, just remember that you press the Multi Selector up or down to change the display style.

✔ If the camera contains multiple memory cards or storage folders, you can specify which card or folder contains the files you want to view. Skip to the section "Choosing which images to view" to find out how.

✔ Through the Customize Command Dials option on the Custom Setting menu, you can set the Main command dial to scroll through pictures as well as perform some other playback operations. You can set the Sub-command dial to serve some playback duties, too. See Chapter 11 if you're interested.

Viewing multiple images at a time

Instead of displaying each photo or movie file one at a time, you can display 4 or 9 thumbnails, as shown in Figure 5-6, or even a whopping 72 thumbnails. (Movie files are indicated by little sprocket holes along the thumbnail edges.)

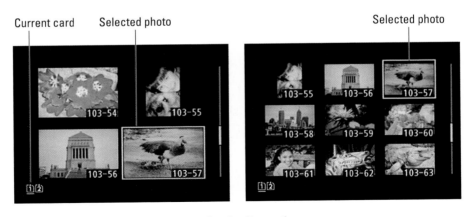

Figure 5-6: You can view multiple image thumbnails at a time.

Here's how things work in thumbnails view:

✔ **Display thumbnails.** Press the ISO button, labeled "Zoom out" in Figure 5-5, to cycle from single-picture view to 4-thumbnail view, press again to shift to 9-picture view, and press once more to bring up those itty-bitty thumbnails featured in 72-image view. One more press takes you to Calendar view, a nifty feature explained in the next section.

✔ **Display fewer thumbnails.** Pressing the Qual button takes you from Calendar view back to the standard thumbnails display or, if you're already in that display, reduces the number of thumbnails so you can see each one at a larger size — hence the "Zoom in" label slapped on the button in Figure 5-5. Again, your first press takes you from 72 thumbnails to 9, your second press to 4 thumbnails, and your third press returns you to single-image view.

Notice the icons on these two buttons: The ISO button sports a magnifying glass with a minus sign, the universal symbol for *zoom out*. And the Qual button's magnifying glass has a plus sign, reminding you that you use this button to *zoom in.*

✔ **Toggle between thumbnails display and full-frame view.** Don't waste time pressing the Qual button repeatedly to zoom back out to the full-frame view: Instead, just press OK. Press OK again to go back to the thumbnails display.

✔ **Scroll the display.** Press the Multi Selector up and down to scroll to the next or previous screen of thumbnails. Remember that this trick is for thumbnails view only; in single-image view, pressing the Multi Selector up or down changes the data display style.

✔ **Select an image.** To perform certain playback functions, such as deleting a photo, you first need to select an image. A yellow box surrounds the selected image, as shown in Figure 5-6. To select a different image, use the Multi Selector to move the highlight box over the image.

If you're using dual memory cards, you can tell which card contains the selected photo by looking at the card icons, labeled in Figure 5-6. The icon for the current card is yellow. See the upcoming section "Choosing which images to view" for a trick you can use to jump immediately to a specific memory card or folder.

Displaying photos in Calendar view

In Calendar display mode, you see a calendar, as shown in Figure 5-7. Select a date, and you can quickly navigate to all pictures you shot that day. A thumbnail image on the calendar indicates that you took pictures on that day.

Selected date   Selected photo

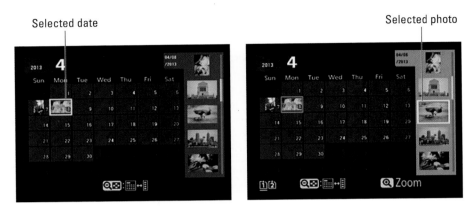

Figure 5-7: Calendar view makes it easy to view all photos shot on a particular day.

The key to navigating Calendar view is the ISO button:

1. **Press the ISO button as needed to cycle through the thumbnail display modes until you reach Calendar view.**

   If you're currently viewing images in full-frame view, for example, you need to press the button four times to get to Calendar view.

2. **Using the Multi Selector, move the yellow highlight box over a date that contains an image.**

   In the left example in Figure 5-7, the 8th of April is selected. (The number of the month appears in the top-left corner of the screen.) After you select a date, the right side of the screen displays thumbnails of pictures taken on that date.

3. **To view all thumbnails from the selected date, press the ISO button again.**

   After you press the button, the vertical thumbnail strip becomes active, as shown on the right in Figure 5-7, and you can scroll through the thumbnails by pressing the Multi Selector up and down. A highlight box appears in the thumbnail strip to indicate the currently selected image.

4. **To temporarily display a larger view of the selected thumbnail, hold down the Qual button.**

   When you release the button, the large preview disappears, and the calendar comes back into view.

5. **To jump back to the calendar and select a different date, press the ISO button again.**

   You can just keep pressing the button to jump between the calendar and the thumbnail strip as much as you want.

6. **To exit Calendar view and return to single-image view, highlight the image you want to view in the thumbnails strip. Then press OK.**

   Press OK again to switch back to Calendar view.

Choosing which images to view

Your camera organizes files into folders that are assigned generic names: 100D7100, 101D7100, and so on. You can see the name of the current folder by looking at the Storage Folder option on the Shooting menu. (The default folder name appears as just 100 on that menu.) You also can create custom-numbered folders through a process outlined in Chapter 11.

During playback, which folder's photos and movies appear depend on the Playback Folder option on the Playback menu, shown in Figure 5-8.

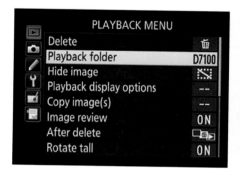 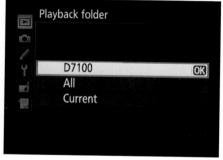

Figure 5-8: Specify which folder you want to view through this option.

You can choose one of three options:

- **D7100 (default setting):** Displays all pictures and movies shot with your camera, regardless of their folder location. If you're using two memory cards, you can access files on both cards.

- **All:** Displays all files in all folders, even those taken with other cameras (as long as they're in a format the camera can display). Again, files from both memory cards are displayed.

- **Current:** Displays files contained in the folder selected as the Storage Folder option on the Shooting menu.

In single-image or thumbnails view (but not Calendar view), you can quickly jump from one memory card or folder to another:

1. **Press and hold the BKT button (on the left side of the camera, just beneath the Flash button).**

2. **Press the Multi Selector up.**

 You see the screen shown on the left in Figure 5-9. You can release the BKT button and Multi Selector at this point.

3. **Highlight a card slot and press right to display a list of folders on that card.**

 The setting of the Playback Folder option on the Playback menu determines which folders appear on the list.

4. **Highlight a folder and press OK.**

 The menu screen disappears, and the first picture or movie in your selected folder appears.

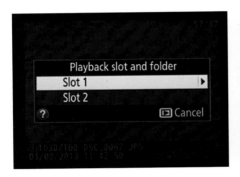 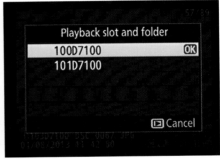

Figure 5-9: During playback, hold down the BKT button and press the Multi Selector up to display this screen and jump to a specific folder.

Magnifying photos during playback

After displaying a photo in single-frame view, as shown on the left in Figure 5-10, you can magnify it, as shown on the right. You can zoom in on still photos only, however; this feature isn't available for movies.

Here's how to use the magnification function:

QUAL

✔ **Zoom in.** Press the Qual button. You can magnify the image to a maximum of 19 to 38 times its original display size, depending on the *resolution* (pixel count) of the photo. Just keep pressing the button until you reach the magnification you want. (Notice the plus-sign magnifying glass symbol on the button, indicating zoom in.)

ISO

✔ **Zoom out.** To zoom out to a reduced magnification, press the ISO button — the one that sports the minus-sign magnifying glass. (That little gridlike thingy next to the magnifying glass reminds you that the button also comes into play when you want to go from full-frame view to one of the thumbnail views.)

Magnified area

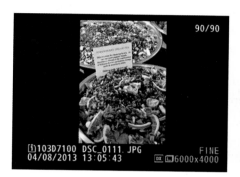 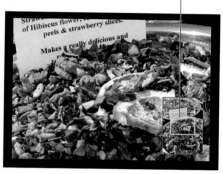

Figure 5-10: Use the Multi Selector to move the yellow outline over the area you want to inspect.

✓ **View another part of the magnified picture.** When an image is magnified, a small thumbnail showing the entire image appears briefly in the lower-right corner of the screen, as shown in Figure 5-10. The yellow outline in this picture-in-picture image indicates the area that's currently consuming the rest of the monitor space. Use the Multi Selector to scroll the yellow box and display a different portion of the image. After a few seconds, the navigation thumbnail disappears; just press the Multi Selector in any direction to redisplay it.

✓ **Inspect faces.** When you magnify portraits, the picture-in-picture thumbnail displays a white border around each face. Rotate the Sub-command dial to examine each face at the magnified view. Unfortunately, the camera sometimes fails to detect faces, especially if the subject isn't looking directly at the camera. When it works correctly, though, this is a pretty great tool for checking for closed eyes, red-eye, and, of course, spinach in the teeth.

✓ **View more images at the same magnification.** While the display is zoomed, you can rotate the Main command dial to display the same area of the next photo at the same magnification.

✓ **Return to full-frame view.** To return to the normal magnification level, you don't need to keep pressing the ISO button until you're all the way zoomed out. Instead, just press OK.

Viewing Picture Data

In single-image picture view, you can choose from a variety of display modes, all shown in Figure 5-11. Each mode presents different shooting data along with the image or movie file.

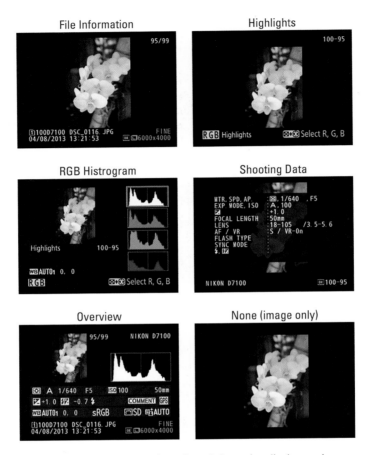

Figure 5-11: You can choose from these information display modes during picture playback.

To change the display mode, press the Multi Selector up or down. When you do this for the first time, only two display modes (File Information and Overview mode), are available, however. The others are hidden by default.

The next section shows you how to choose the display modes you want to use and also how to enable one additional display option that lets you see which focus point was used for the shot. Following that, you can find details about the data you see in each display mode, with the exception of the self-explanatory None (Image Only) mode.

Note: Information and figures in these sections relate to still photography. For help with understanding data that appears during movie playback, see the playback section of Chapter 4. Although you can view the first frame of your movie in any of the standard photo display modes, after you start playback, the movie takes over the whole screen and playback data appears as described in that part of Chapter 4.

Choosing data-display options

By default, only File Information mode and Overview mode are enabled. To access the other modes, along with an option that enables you to view the focus point that the camera used to establish focus, head for the Playback Display Options setting on the Playback menu, as shown in Figure 5-12.

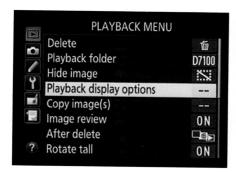
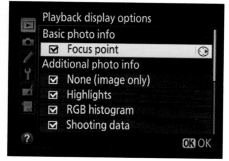

Figure 5-12: These display options are disabled by default.

The menu options work as follows:

▸ **Focus Point:** When this option is turned on, a red rectangle marks the focus point (or points), as shown in Figure 5-13. You also see the same brackets that represent the autofocus area in the viewfinder. These focus indicators appear only when you use the display mode shown in the figure — File Information mode, covered in the next section. They aren't displayed if you focused manually or used the AF-C (continuous-servo) autofocusing mode setting (or the camera chose that setting for you in AF-A mode). I find the focus marks distracting, but make your own call. Chapter 8 explains these autofocusing options.

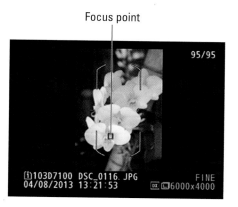

Figure 5-13: You can view the focus point you used when taking the photo.

✔ **Additional Photo Info:** This section of the menu lets you enable and disable all display modes except File Information, which can't be turned off. You have to scroll the menu screen down to access the Overview display mode, not shown in the figure.

A check mark in the box next to an option means that the feature is turned on. To toggle the check mark on and off, highlight the option and then press the Multi Selector right. After turning on the options you want to use, press OK.

The next sections explain what details you can glean from each display mode.

File Information mode

In File Information display mode, the monitor displays the data shown in Figure 5-14. Again, the illustrations here and in the upcoming sections apply to still photos; Chapter 4 helps you sort out movie playback screens.

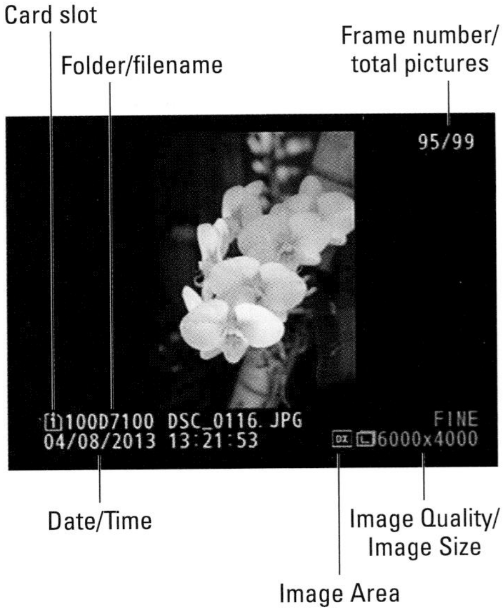

Here's the key to what information appears, starting at the top of the screen and working down:

✔ **Frame Number/Total Pictures:** The first value here indicates the frame number of the currently displayed photo; the second tells you the total number of pictures on the memory card.

✔ **Focus point:** If you enable the Focus Point feature, as outlined in the preceding section, you may see the red focus-point indicator and the autofocus area brackets, as shown in Figure 5-13, depending on the focus settings you used when shooting the picture.

✔ **Card slot:** This value tells you which memory card slot holds the card containing the picture.

✔ **Folder:** Folders are named automatically by the camera unless you create custom folders, an advanced trick you can explore in Chapter 11. The first camera-created folder is named 100D7100. Each folder can contain up to 9,999 images; when you exceed that limit, the camera creates a new folder and assigns the next folder number.

Card slot

Folder/filename

Frame number/ total pictures

95/99

①100D7100 DSC_0116. JPG   FINE
04/08/2013 13:21:53   ☐6000x4000

Date/Time

Image Quality/ Image Size

Image Area

Figure 5-14: In File Information mode, you can view these bits of data.

✔ **Filename:** The camera also automatically names your files. Filenames end with a three-letter code that represents the file format, which is either JPG (for JPEG) or NEF (for Camera Raw) for still photos. Chapter 2 discusses these formats. (If you record a movie, the file extension is MOV, which represents a digital-movie file format.)

The first four characters of filenames also vary. Here's what the two possible codes indicate:

- *DSC_:* This code means you captured the photo at the default Color Space setting, sRGB. You can investigate this option in Chapter 8.
- *_DSC:* If you change the Color Space setting to Adobe RGB, the underscore character comes first.

Each image is also assigned a four-digit file number, starting with 0001. When you reach image 9999, the file numbering restarts at 0001, and the new images go into a new folder to prevent any possibility of overwriting the existing image files. For more information about file numbering, see the section in Chapter 1 that discusses the File Number Sequence option, found on the Custom Setting menu.

✔ **Date and Time:** Just below the folder and filename info, you see the date and time that you took the picture. Of course, the accuracy of this data depends on whether you set the camera's date and time correctly, which you do via the Setup menu.

✔ **Image Area:** This symbol tells you whether the DX or 1.3x crop area of the image sensor was used to record the photo. DX is the default and records the image using the entire sensor. See the last section of Chapter 2 for an explanation of this feature.

✔ **Image Quality:** Here you can see which Image Quality setting you used when taking the picture. Again, Chapter 2 has details, but the short story is this: Fine, Normal, and Basic are the three JPEG recording options, with Fine representing the highest JPEG quality. Raw refers to the Nikon Camera Raw format, NEF.

✔ **Image Size:** This value tells you the image resolution, or pixel count. See Chapter 2 to find out about resolution.

In the top-left corner of the screen, you may see the following two symbols, labeled in Figure 5-15:

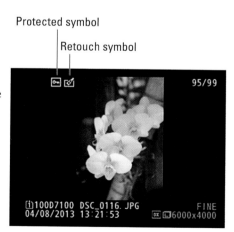

Protected symbol

Retouch symbol

95/99

100D7100 DSC_0116. JPG   FINE
04/08/2013 13:21:53   6000x4000

Figure 5-15: These symbols indicate a protected photo and a retouched photo.

✓ **Protected Status:** A key icon indicates that you used the file-protection feature to prevent the image from being erased when you use the camera's Delete function. See "Protecting Photos," later in this chapter, to find out more. (***Note:*** Formatting your memory card, a topic discussed in Chapter 1, *does* erase even protected pictures.)

✓ **Retouch indicator:** This icon indicates an image that you created by applying Retouch menu options, detailed in Chapter 10, to the original photo.

Highlights display mode

One of the most difficult photo problems to correct in a photo-editing program is known as *blown highlights* in some circles and *clipped highlights* in others. Both terms mean that the brightest areas of the image are so overexposed that areas that should include a variety of light shades are instead totally white.

In Highlights display mode, areas that the camera thinks may be overexposed blink in the camera monitor. To use this mode, you must first enable it by following the instructions in the earlier "Choosing data-display options" section. Then press the Multi Selector down to shift from File Information mode to Highlights mode.

To fully understand all the features of Highlights mode, though, you need to know a little about digital imaging science. First, digital images are called *RGB images* because they're created from the three primary colors of light: red, green, and blue. In Highlights mode, you can display the exposure warning for all three color components — sometimes called color *channels* — combined or view the data for each individual channel.

When you look at the brightness data for a single channel, though, greatly overexposed areas don't translate to white in photos — rather, they result in a solid blob of some other color. I don't have space in this book to provide a full lesson in RGB color theory, but the short story is that when you mix red, green, and blue light, and each component is at maximum brightness, you get white. Zero brightness in all three channels gives you black. If you have maximum red and no blue or green, you have fully saturated red. If you mix two channels at maximum brightness, you also get full saturation. For example, maximum red and blue produce fully saturated magenta. And this is why it matters: Wherever colors are fully saturated, you can lose picture detail. For example, a rose petal that should have a range of tones from light to dark red may instead be bright red throughout.

The moral of the story is that when you view your photo in single-channel display, large areas of blinking highlights in one or two channels indicate that you may be losing color details. Blinking highlights that appear in the same spot in all three channels indicate blown highlights — again, because when you have maximum red, green, and blue, you get white. Either way, you may want to adjust your exposure settings and try again.

Okay, with today's science lesson out of the way, Figure 5-16 displays an image that contains some blown high-lights to show you how things look in Highlights display mode. I captured the screen at the moment the highlight blinkies blinked "off" — the black areas in the figure indicate the blown high-lights. (I labeled a few of them in the figure.) But as this image proves, just because you see the flashing alerts doesn't mean that you should adjust exposure — the decision depends on where the alerts occur and how the rest of the image is exposed. In my candle photo, for example, there are indeed small white areas in the

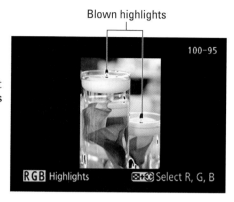

Figure 5-16: In Highlights mode, blinking areas indicate blown highlights.

flames and the glass vase, yet exposure in the majority of the photo is fine. If I reduced exposure to darken those spots, some areas of the flowers would be underexposed. In other words, sometimes you simply can't avoid a few clipped highlights when the scene includes a broad range of brightness values.

In the lower-left corner of the display, the letters that appear highlighted in yellow tell you whether you're looking at a single channel (R, G, or B) or the three-channel, composite display (RGB). The latter is selected in the figure. To cycle between the settings, press the ISO button as you press the Multi Selector right or left.

Along with the blinking highlight warning, Highlights display mode presents the Protect Status and Retouch Indicator icons if you used those features. In the upper-right corner, you see the folder number and the frame number — 100 and 95, respectively, in Figure 5-16. The label "Highlights" also appears to let you know the current display mode.

RGB Histogram mode

From Highlights mode, press the Multi Selector down to get to RGB Histogram mode, which displays your image as shown on the left in Figure 5-17. (**Remember:** You can access this mode only if you enable it via the Playback Display Options setting on the Playback menu.)

The data underneath the thumbnail shows the White Balance settings used for the shot. (White balance is a color feature you can explore in Chapter 8.) The first value tells you the setting (Auto$_1$, in the figure), and the two number values tell you whether you fine-tuned that setting along the amber to blue axis (first value) or green to magenta axis (second value). Zeros, as in the figure, indicate no fine-tuning. You also see the Protect Status key and Retouch Indicator symbol if you use those features on the image.

In addition, you get four charts, called *histograms.* You actually get two types of histograms: The top one is a Brightness histogram and reflects the composite, three-channel image data. The three others represent the data for the single red, green, and blue channels. This trio is sometimes called an *RGB histogram,* thus the display mode name.

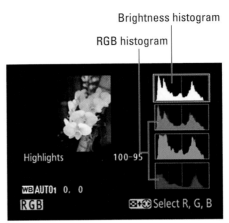

Brightness histogram

RGB histogram

Highlights   100–95

WB AUTO1 0. 0

RGB   Select R, G, B

Figure 5-17: In RGB Histogram mode, you see both a brightness histogram and an RGB histogram.

The next two sections explain what information you can glean from the two types of histograms. But first, here are two quick tips:

- ✔ **Highlights data:** As with Highlights mode, blown highlights blink in the thumbnail, and you can view the warning for either the composite image (RGB) or each individual channel. Press the ISO button as you press the Multi Selector right to cycle between the single-channel and multichannel views. A yellow box also surrounds the histogram representing the active view. For example, the RGB composite view is active in the figure. To get rid of the blinkies, select the Blue channel and then press the Multi Selector right one more time.

- ✔ **Zooming the view:** Press the Qual button to zoom the thumbnail to a magnified view. The histograms then update to reflect only the magnified area of the photo. Press the Multi Selector to scroll the image display. To return to the regular view, press OK.

Reading a Brightness histogram

You can get an idea of image exposure by viewing your photo on the monitor and by looking at the blinkies in Highlights mode, but the Brightness histogram provides a way to gauge exposure that's a little more detailed.

A Brightness histogram indicates the distribution of shadows, highlights, and *midtones* (areas of medium brightness) in your image. Figure 5-18 shows you the histogram for the orchid image featured in Figure 5-17, for example.

Shadows   Highlights

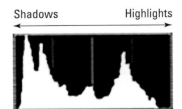

Figure 5-18: The Brightness histogram indicates tonal range, from shadows on the left to highlights on the right.

The horizontal axis of the histogram represents possible brightness values — the maximum *tonal range,* in photography-speak — from the darkest shadows on the left to the brightest highlights on the right. And the vertical axis shows you how many pixels fall at a particular brightness value. A spike indicates a heavy concentration of pixels at that brightness value.

There is no one "perfect" histogram that you should try to achieve. Instead, interpret the histogram with respect to the distribution of shadows, highlights, and midtones that comprise your subject. You wouldn't expect to see lots of shadows, for example, in a photo of a polar bear walking on a snowy landscape. Pay attention, however, if you see a very high concentration of pixels at the far right or left end of the histogram, which can indicate a seriously overexposed or underexposed image, respectively. To find out how to resolve exposure problems, visit Chapter 7.

Understanding RGB histograms

In RGB Histogram display mode, you see two histograms: the Brightness histogram, covered in the preceding section, and an RGB histogram. Figure 5-19 shows you the RGB histogram for the orchid image.

As explained in the earlier section about Highlights mode, digital images are made up of red, green, and blue light. With the RGB histograms, you can view the brightness values for each of those color channels. Again, overexposure in one or two channels can produce oversaturated colors — and thus a loss of picture detail. So, if most of the pixels for one or two channels are clustered toward the right end of the histogram, adjust your exposure settings, as outlined in Chapter 7, and try again.

Photographers schooled in the science of RGB histograms can spot color-balance issues by looking at the pixel values, too. But frankly, color-balance problems are easy to notice just by looking at the image itself on the camera monitor. And understanding how to translate

Less Saturated   More Saturated

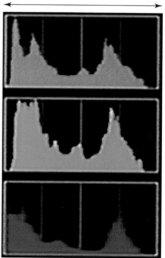

Figure 5-19: The RGB histogram can indicate problems with color saturation.

the histogram data for this purpose requires more knowledge about RGB color theory than I have room to present in this book.

For information about manipulating color, see Chapter 8.

Shooting Data display mode

Before you can access this mode, you must enable it via the Playback Display Options setting option on the Playback menu. See the earlier section, "Choosing data-display options," for details.

In this mode, you can view up to four screens of information, which you toggle among by pressing the Multi Selector up and down. Figure 5-20 shows you the first two screens. The fourth screen appears only if you include copyright data with your picture, a feature you can explore in Chapter 11.

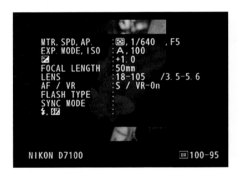 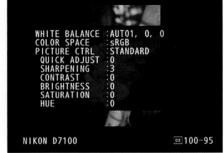

Figure 5-20: You can view the camera settings used to capture the image in Shooting Data display mode.

Most of the data here won't make any sense to you until you explore Chapters 7 and 8, which explain the exposure, color, and other advanced settings available on your camera. Still, I want to call your attention to a couple of data points now:

✔ The top-left corner of the monitor shows the Protected Status key and Retouch Indicator icon, if you used these features. Otherwise, the area is empty, as in the figures. See "Protecting Photos," later in this chapter, for more about that feature; Chapter 10 presents Retouch menu options.

✔ The current folder and frame number appear in the lower-right corner of the display, as does the Image Area setting (DX or 1.3x crop, as explained in Chapter 2).

✔ The Comment item, which is the final item on the third screen, contains a value if you use the Image Comment feature on the Setup menu.

✔ If the ISO value on Shooting Data Page 1 (the first screen in Figure 5-20) appears in red, the camera is letting you know that it overrode the ISO Sensitivity setting that you selected in order to produce a good exposure. This shift occurs only if you enable automatic ISO adjustment in the P, S, A, and M exposure modes; see Chapter 7 for details.

GPS Data mode

This display mode is available only if the image you're viewing was shot with the optional Nikon GPS (Global Positioning System) unit attached. And technically, GPS Data display mode isn't really its own, independent mode, although the camera manual describes it as such. Instead, if you took a picture with the GPS unit enabled, you see an additional screen of data when you set the display mode to Shooting Data (detailed in the preceding section). The data screen shows you the latitude, longitude, and other GPS information recorded with the image file.

Overview mode

Overview mode is the second of the two default photo-information modes — meaning that it's already enabled on the Playback Display Options item on the Playback menu. In this mode, the playback screen contains a small image thumbnail along with scads of shooting data — although not quite as much as Shooting Data mode — plus a Brightness histogram. Figure 5-21 offers a look.

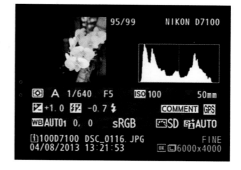

Figure 5-21: In Overview mode, you can view your picture along with the major camera settings you used to take the picture.

The earlier section "Reading a Brightness histogram" tells you what to make of that part of the screen. Just above the histogram, you see the Protected Status key and Retouch Indicator, if you used those features (not shown in the figure). The Frame Number/Total Pictures data appears at the upper-right corner of the image thumbnail. For details on that data, see the earlier section "File Information mode."

To sort out the maze of other information, the following list breaks things down into the five rows that appear under the thumbnail and histogram. In the accompanying figures as well as in Figure 5-21, I include all possible data for the purpose of illustration; if any items don't appear on your screen, it simply means that the relevant feature wasn't enabled when you captured the shot:

- **Row 1:** This row shows the exposure-related settings labeled in Figure 5-22, along with the focal length of the lens you used to take the shot. As in Shooting Data mode, the ISO value appears red if you had auto ISO override enabled in the P, S, A, or M exposure modes and the camera adjusted the ISO for you. Chapter 7 details the exposure settings; Chapter 1 introduces you to focal length.

✓ **Row 2:** This row contains a few additional exposure settings, labeled in Figure 5-23. On the right end of the row, the Comment and GPS labels appear if you took advantage of those options when recording the shot. (You must switch to the Shooting Data mode to view the actual comment and GPS data.)

✓ **Row 3:** The first three items on this row, labeled in Figure 5-24, relate to color options explored in Chapter 8. The second white balance value shows the amount of blue-to-amber fine-tuning adjustment; and the third, the amount of green-to-magenta adjustment (both values are 0 in the figure). The last item indicates the Active D-Lighting setting, another exposure option discussed in Chapter 7.

✓ **Rows 4 and 5:** The final two rows of data (refer to Figure 5-21) show the same information you get in File Information mode, explained earlier in this chapter.

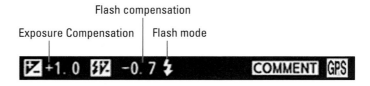

Figure 5-22: Here you can inspect major exposure settings along with the lens focal length.

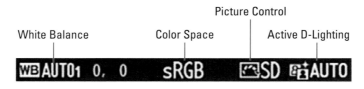

Figure 5-23: This row contains additional exposure information.

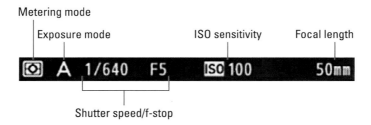

Figure 5-24: Look at this row for details about advanced color settings.

Deleting Photos

You can erase pictures from a memory card when it's in your camera in three ways. The next sections give you the lowdown.

 Regardless of which delete technique you want to use, you can't delete photos that you protected or hid by using the Protect or Hide Image features. Later sections in this chapter explain both features and show you how to unprotect and unhide images so that you can delete them.

Deleting images one at a time

 The Delete button is key to erasing single images, but the process varies depending on which playback display mode you're using, as follows:

- ✔ In single-image view, press the Delete button.

- ✔ In thumbnail view (displaying 4, 9, or 72 thumbnails), use the Multi Selector to highlight the picture you want to erase and then press Delete.

- ✔ In Calendar view, highlight an image in the thumbnail strip and press Delete.

After you press Delete, you see a message asking whether you want to erase the picture. If you do, press the Delete button again. Or, to cancel out of the process, press the Playback button.

If you really want to get down into your camera's customization weeds — and I do believe this is about as weedy as it gets — you can control which picture the camera displays after you delete the current picture. The option — After Delete — lives on the Playback menu. Select the option and press OK to access your choices: Show Next displays the picture after the one you just deleted (the default option); Show Previous displays the one that fell before the one you deleted, and Continue as Before tells the camera to keep going in the same direction you were heading before deleting. For example, if you were scrolling forward through your pictures, the camera continues playback in that direction. Wow, now *that's* control. Have you thought about getting some help for that?

Deleting all photos

Erasing all pictures on a memory card is a five-step process:

1. **Open the Playback menu and select Delete, as shown on the left in Figure 5-25.**

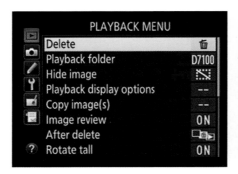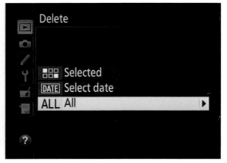

Figure 5-25: You can quickly delete all photos from a memory card.

2. **Press OK to display the right screen in Figure 5-25.**

3. **Highlight All and press the Multi Selector right.**

4. **On the next screen, highlight the memory card that contains the pictures you want to dump and press OK.**

   You then see a screen that asks you to verify that you want to delete all your images.

5. **Highlight Yes and press OK.**

 This step deletes only pictures in the folder that's currently selected via the Playback Folder option on the Playback menu. See the section "Choosing which images to view," earlier in this chapter, for information.

Also remember that deleting photos in this way does not erase any pictures that you protected using the Protect feature or hid from display by using the Hide Image option, both described later in this chapter.

Deleting a batch of selected photos

To erase multiple photos — but not all — display the Playback menu, highlight Delete, and press OK. You see the Delete screen shown on the left in Figure 5-26. You then have two options for specifying which photos to erase:

 ✔ **Select photos one by one.** To go this route, highlight Selected, as shown on the left in Figure 5-26, and press the Multi Selector right to display a screen of thumbnails, as shown on the right. Use the Multi Selector to place the yellow highlight box over the first photo you want to delete and then press the ISO button. A little trash can icon, the universal symbol for delete, appears in the upper-right corner of the thumbnail, as shown in the figure.

Current card/folder   Delete marker

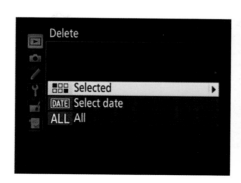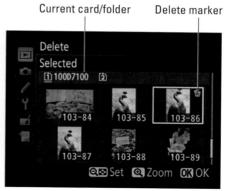

Figure 5-26: Choose this option to tag specific photos for deletion.

If you change your mind, press the ISO button again to remove the Delete tag from the image. To undo deletion for all selected photos, press the Playback button.

A couple of tips to remember:

QUAL

BKT

- For a closer look at the selected image, press and hold the Qual button. When you release the button, the display returns to normal thumbnail view.

- If you have two memory cards installed, the card icon that appears yellow in the upper-left corner of the screen is the selected card. You can use the same technique available during playback to jump between cards and folders: Press the BKT button and press the Multi Selector up to get the screen where you can select a card. Highlight the card, press the Multi Selector right to display the list of folders on the card, and select the one you want to view. Press OK to return to the screen where you tag pictures for deletion. The first photo in your chosen folder is automatically selected. Remember that the folders that appear when you use this option depend on the setting you choose for the Playback Folder option, as covered in the earlier section "Choosing which images to view."

✓ **Erase all photos taken on a specific date.** To dump all pictures you shot on a particular day, choose Select Date from the main Delete screen, as shown on the left in Figure 5-27. Press the Multi Selector right to display a list of dates on which you took the pictures on the memory card, as shown on the right in the figure.

Next, highlight a date and press the Multi Selector right. A little check mark appears in the box next to the date, as shown in Figure 5-27, tagging all images taken on that day for deletion. To remove the check mark and save the photos from the digital dumpster, press the Multi Selector right again.

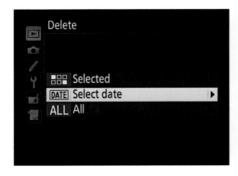 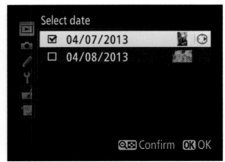

Figure 5-27: With the Select Date option, you can quickly erase all photos taken on a specific date.

Can't remember what photos are associated with the selected date? Try these tricks:

- To display thumbnails of all images taken on the selected date, press the ISO button.

- To temporarily view the selected thumbnail at full-size view, press the Qual button.

- To return to the date list, press the ISO button again.

After tagging individual photos for deletion or specifying a shooting date to delete, press OK to start the Delete process. You see a confirmation screen asking permission to destroy the images; select Yes and press OK. The camera trashes the photos and returns you to the Playback menu.

You have one alternative way to quickly erase all images taken on a specific date: In the Calendar display mode, you can highlight the date in question and then press the Delete button instead of going through the Playback menu. You get the standard confirmation screen asking you whether you want to go forward. Press the Delete button again to dump the files. Visit the section "Displaying photos in Calendar view," earlier in this chapter, for the scoop on that display option.

As with the Delete All option, you can't delete protected or hidden photos using any of these techniques. For more about protecting and hiding photos, see the next two sections.

Hiding Photos during Playback

Suppose that you took 100 pictures — 50 at a business meeting and 50 at the wild after-meeting party. You want to show your boss the photos where you and your co-workers look like responsible adults, but you'd rather not share the ones showing you and your assistant dancing on the conference table. You can always delete the party photos; the preceding section shows you how. But if you want to keep them — you never know when a good blackmail picture will come in handy — you can simply hide the incriminating images during playback.

The key to this trick is the Hide Image option on the Playback menu. After highlighting the option, as shown on the left in Figure 5-28, press OK to display the right screen in the figure.

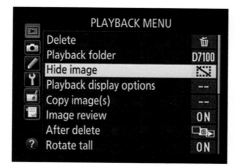 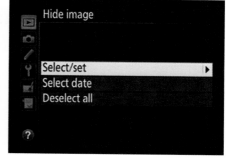

Figure 5-28: The Hide Image function lets you prevent photos from appearing during normal picture playback.

From here, things work pretty much the same as they do for marking a picture for deletion, covered in the preceding section:

✓ **Select and hide photos one by one:** Choose Select/Set, as shown on the right in Figure 5-28, to display thumbnails of your images. Highlight the picture you want to hide and then press the ISO button to tag the photo with the little hide marker, as shown on the left in Figure 5-29.

You can use the same techniques as outlined in the preceding section to jump between memory cards and folders and get a larger view of the selected photo.

After you tag all the images you want to hide, press OK to return to the Playback menu. Your pictures are now hidden.

✓ **Select and hide all photos taken on a specific date:** On the screen shown on the right in Figure 5-28, choose Select Date and press the Multi Selector right. Now you see a list of dates, as shown on the right in Figure 5-29. Highlight the date that contains the photos you want to hide, and then press right to put a check in the box to the left of the date. Again, the tricks that work for deleting photos by date work here, too; see the preceding section for details. Press OK to finalize the process.

Current card/folder   Hide marker

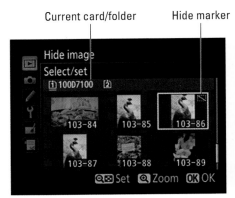
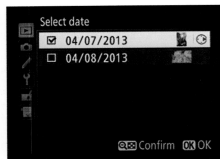

Figure 5-29: You can select photos one by one (left) or by date (right).

A couple of fine points about this feature:

- Hidden images remain viewable from within the Hide Image screens. In other words, if you travel back to the Hide Image menu and choose the Select/Set or Select Date option, you see thumbnails for your hidden images along with those that aren't hidden.

- To redisplay hidden pictures, just reverse the process, removing the hide marker from photos you want to view again. Or, to redisplay all hidden pictures quickly, choose Deselect All from the first Hide Image screen (the right screen in Figure 5-28).

- If you protected a photo before hiding it, redisplaying the picture removes its protected status.

- Before you can delete hidden photos, you first need to remove the Hide Image tags. Or you can format your memory card, which wipes out all photos, hidden or not. To format the card, choose the Format Memory Card option from the Setup menu.

Protecting Photos

You can safeguard pictures from accidental erasure by giving them *protected status.* After you take this step, the camera doesn't allow you to erase a picture by using the Delete button or the Delete option on the Playback menu.

Formatting your memory card, however, *does* erase even protected pictures. In addition, when you protect a picture, it shows up as a read-only file when you transfer it to your computer. Files that have that read-only status can't be altered until you unlock them in your photo software. In Nikon ViewNX 2, the software that ships with your camera, you can do this by clicking the image thumbnail and then choosing File⇨Protect Files⇨Unprotect.

Protecting a picture is easy:

1. **Display or select the picture you want to protect.**

   - *In single-image view,* just display the photo.

   - *In 4/9/72 thumbnail mode,* use the Multi Selector as needed to place the yellow highlight box over the photo.

   - *In Calendar view,* highlight the image in the strip of thumbnails that appears on the right side of the screen. (Press the ISO button to jump between the calendar dates and the thumbnails.)

WB

2. **Press the WB button.**

   See the key symbol on the button? That's your reminder that you use the button to lock a picture. The same symbol appears on protected photos during playback, as shown in Figure 5-30.

3. **To remove protection, display or select the image and then press the WB button again.**

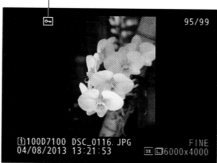

Protect symbol

Figure 5-30: Press the WB button to prevent accidental deletion of the selected image.

Creating a Slide Show

The Slide Show feature sets the camera to automatically display all photos and movies one by one on the camera monitor. Before I show you the steps, note these details:

- ✔ Pictures displayed in the show depend on the setting of the Playback Folder option on the Playback menu. For more about choosing which folder (and which memory card, if you're using two at a time) you want to view, see "Choosing which images to view," earlier in this chapter.

- ✔ Any pictures that you hid through the Hide Image function, also explained earlier in this chapter, do not appear in the show.

To set up and run your show, walk this way:

1. **Display the Playback menu and highlight Slide Show, as shown on the left in Figure 5-31.**

   Scroll to the second screen of the menu to access this option.

2. **Press OK to display the screen shown on the right in Figure 5-31.**

   This screen is where you set the playback options for your show.

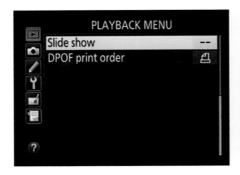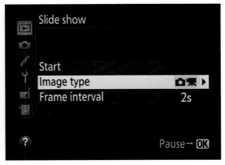

Figure 5-31: Choose Slide Show (left) and press OK to access slide show options (right).

3. Highlight Image Type, as shown on the right in Figure 5-31, and press the Multi Selector right.

You're taken to a screen where you can choose to include both movies and still photos, just movies, or just photos in the show.

4. Select the image types you want to include and press OK.

You return to the slide show setup screen.

5. If you chose Movies Only in Step 4, skip to Step 8.

6. Highlight Frame Interval and press the Multi Selector right.

This option determines how long each photo appears. Intervals range from 2 to 10 seconds. Again, this option doesn't affect movies; the entire movie is always played during the slide show.

7. Highlight the frame interval you want to use and press OK.

Back you go to the slide show setup screen.

8. Highlight Start and press OK.

Your slide show starts playing on the camera monitor.

When the show ends, you see a screen offering four options: You can choose to restart the show, adjust the frame interval, or exit to the Playback menu. Highlight your choice and press OK.

During the show, you can control playback as follows:

✔ **Pause the show.** Press OK. Select Restart and press OK to display pictures again. When you pause the slide show, you also can change the frame interval — a handy option if the pace is too quick or slow — or exit the show. Just highlight your choice and press OK. If you adjust the timing, resume playback by choosing Restart and pressing OK.

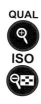

QUAL

ISO

✔ **Adjust movie volume.** If your slide show contains movies with soundtracks, you can use the Zoom In and Zoom Out buttons to adjust the volume:

- *Increase volume.* Press the Qual button.

- *Decrease volume.* Press the ISO button.

✔ **Exit the show.** You have three options:

- *To return to regular playback,* press the Playback button.

- *To return to the Playback menu,* press the Menu button.

- *To return to picture-taking mode,* press the shutter button halfway and release it.

✔ **Skip to the next/previous image manually.** Press the Multi Selector right or left.

✔ **Change the information displayed with the image.** Press the Multi Selector up or down to cycle through the info-display modes. (See the earlier section "Viewing Picture Data" for details on what information is provided in each mode.)

Viewing Your Photos on a Television

You can connect your camera to an HDTV (high-definition television) and view your pictures and movies on that screen. To take advantage of this option, you need a Type C mini-pin HD cable to connect the camera and TV. Before making the connection, visit the Setup menu and explore the HDMI option, shown in Figure 5-32, which offers the following two settings:

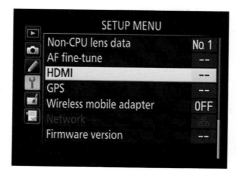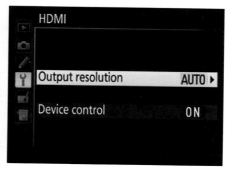

Figure 5-32: Select options for HD playback here.

↙ **Output Resolution:** By default, the camera decides the proper video resolution to send to the TV after you connect the two devices. Through this setting, though, you can choose from five specific output resolutions.

↙ **Device Control:** If your television is compatible with a feature that goes by the name HDMI CEC (Consumer Electronics Control), you can use the buttons on the TV's remote control to perform the functions of the OK button and Multi Selector during full-frame picture playback and slide shows. To make this feature work, set the Device Control option to On.

After you select the necessary HDMI options, grab your video cable, turn off the camera, and then insert the smaller end of the HDMI cable into the HDMI-out port, labeled in Figure 5-33. The port lives under the middle rubber cover on the left side of the camera.

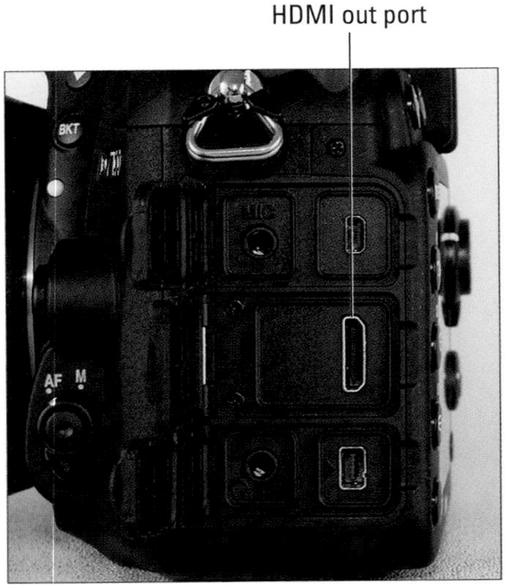

At this point, I need to point you to your TV manual to find out how to connect the other end of the cable to the set itself. You also need to consult your manual to find out which channel to select for playback of signals from auxiliary input devices. Then just turn on your camera to send the signal to the TV set. If you don't have the latest and greatest HDMI CEC capability (or lost your remote), control playback using the same techniques as you normally do to view pictures on your camera monitor. You can also run a slide show by following the steps outlined in the preceding section.

HDMI out port

Figure 5-33: The HDMI port is located under the middle rubber door on the side of the camera.

6

Downloading, Printing, and Sharing Your Photos

In This Chapter

▶ Choosing photo software

▶ Transferring pictures to your computer using Nikon ViewNX 2

▶ Processing Raw (NEF) files

▶ Taking steps to ensure great print quality

▶ Preparing your photos for online sharing

*F*or many digital photographers, moving pictures from the camera to the computer — *downloading,* in geekspeak — is one of the more confusing aspects of the art form. Unfortunately, providing detailed downloading instructions in this book is impossible because the steps vary widely, depending on which computer software you use for the job.

To give you as much help as I can, however, this chapter starts with a quick review of photo software, just in case you aren't happy with your current solution. Following that, you can find information about downloading images, converting pictures that you shoot in the Raw format to a standard format, and preparing your pictures for print and online sharing. I do include specifics for performing some of these critical tasks using Nikon ViewNX 2, which is the free software that ships with your camera.

Choosing the Right Photo Software

Photo programs abound, ranging from inexpensive solutions for beginners to high-end professional options. The good news is that if you don't need serious photo-editing capabilities, you may find a free program that serves your needs. The next section offers a look at a few freebies; following that, I present programs to consider when the free options don't meet your needs.

Three free photo programs

If you don't do much retouching or other manipulation of your photos, one of the following free programs may be a good solution:

✔ **Nikon ViewNX 2:** This program, found on the CD included in your camera box, provides a photo organizer plus a few photo-editing features. You also can use the program to download pictures and to convert Raw files to a standard format. I show you how to accomplish both tasks later in this chapter. Figure 6-1 offers a look at the ViewNX 2 window as it appears when you use Thumbnail Grid view mode, one of three display options available from the View menu.

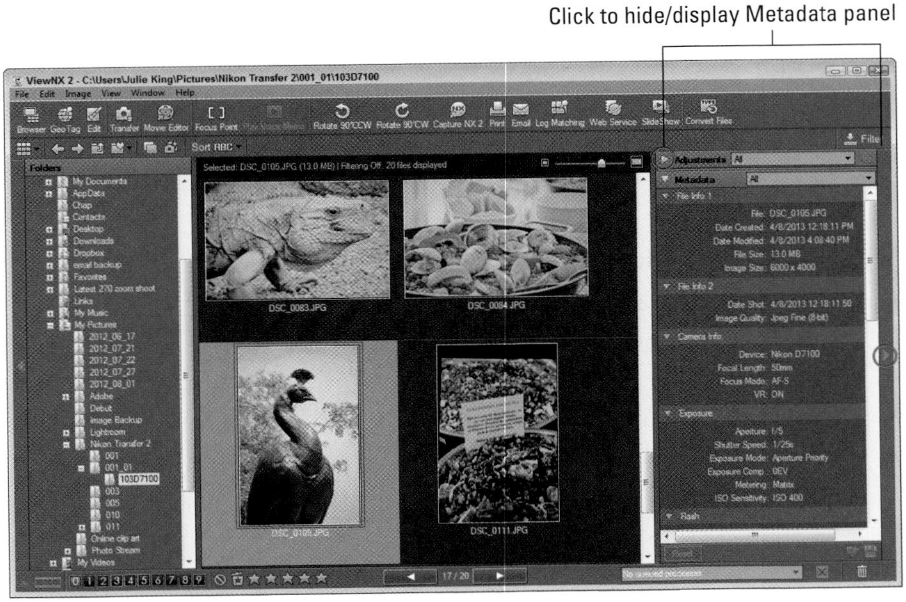

Click to hide/display Metadata panel

Figure 6-1: Nikon ViewNX 2, free with your camera, offers a photo organizer and some photo-editing functions.

One cool feature to note: You can view picture *metadata,* which is hidden data that records the settings you used to take the picture. Just display the Metadata panel, located on the right side of the program window, as shown in Figure 6-1. If the panel is hidden, choose Window⇨ Edit or click the triangle on the far right side of the window and then click the triangle at the top of the panel. (I labeled both controls in the figure.) Many other photo programs also display metadata but sometimes can't reveal data that's very camera-specific.

This book features Nikon ViewNX2 version 2.7.4. To find out which version you have, choose Help⇨About ViewNX 2 in Windows or ViewNX 2⇨ About View NX2 on a Mac. If you own an earlier version, download the updated software from the Nikon website (www.nikon.com). Otherwise, the software may not be fully compatible with files from your D7100.

✔ **Apple iPhoto:** Built into the Mac operating system (OS), this program offers a download tool and organizer plus some basic editing features. Apple provides some great tutorials on using iPhoto at its website (www.apple.com) to help you get started using the program.

✔ **Windows Photo Gallery:** Some versions of Microsoft Windows also offer a free photo downloader and browser, Windows Live Photo Gallery. (The name varies slightly depending on your version of the Windows OS.) Like the other freebies mentioned here, this program offers a few basic retouching tools — again, depending on which version of Windows you use.

Advanced photo programs

For serious retouching or advanced digital-imaging artistry, you need to step up to a full-fledged photo-editing program, such as one of the following:

✔ **Adobe Photoshop Elements (about $100)**

   www.adobe.com/products/photoshop-elements.html

   With a full complement of retouching tools, onscreen guidance for beginners, and templates for creating photo projects such as scrapbooks, Elements offers all the features that most consumers need.

✔ **Nikon Capture NX 2 (about $180)**

   www.capturenx.com/en/index.html

   This Nikon program offers an image browser/organizer plus a wealth of pro-level photo-editing tools, including a sophisticated tool for processing Raw images. Visit its website for tutorials.

✔ **Apple Aperture (about $80 through Mac App store)**

   www.apple.com/aperture

Aperture is geared to shooters who need to organize and process lots of images but typically do only light retouching work — wedding photographers and school portrait photographers, for example.

✔ **Adobe Photoshop Lightroom (about $150, or available as a monthly subscription via Adobe Cloud services)**

www.adobe.com/products/photoshop-lightroom.html

Lightroom is the Adobe counterpart to Aperture. In its latest version, it offers some fairly powerful retouching tools as well.

✔ **Adobe Photoshop (about $700, or available as a monthly subscription via Adobe Cloud services)**

www.photoshop.com

Geared to photo pros, Photoshop offers the industry's most sophisticated retouching tools.

Of these programs, only Elements is designed with the novice in mind, and even using Elements involves a bit of a learning curve. I recommend buying (and reading!) a guidebook or taking some classes to help you maximize your software investment.

Not sure which tool you need, if any? You can download 30-day free trials of all these programs from the manufacturers' websites. One caveat: If you're interested in converting Raw files using the program, make sure that the software supports your D7100. If you own an older version of the program, you may need to update to the latest version in order to work with your camera's Raw files.

Sending Pictures to the Computer

Whatever software you choose, here are the basic ways you can download images to your computer:

✔ **Connect the camera to the computer via a USB cable.** The cable you need is supplied in the camera box.

✔ **Use a memory card reader.** With a card reader, you simply pop the memory card out of your camera and into the card reader instead of hooking the camera to the computer. Many computers and printers now have card readers, and you also can buy standalone readers for less than $30.

✔ **Invest in Eye-Fi memory cards and transfer images via a wireless network.** You can find out more about these special memory cards and how to set up the card to connect with your computer via a wireless network at the manufacturer's website, www.eye.fi. Also check the Eye-Fi details provided in the camera manual; look for the section related to the Eye-Fi Upload option on the Setup menu. I don't cover these cards in this book.

Wireless transfer with the WU-1a

With the optional Nikon WU-1a wireless mobile adapter, which plugs into the camera's USB port, you can transfer photos over a Wi-Fi connection from your camera to some smart phones and tablets. The idea is to make it easy for you to e-mail photos or upload them to Facebook and other social-networking sites without having to bother with downloading the images to your computer first. You also can use the smart phone or device to trigger the camera's shutter button.

At present, this option works only with specific devices; you can get details at the Nikon website (www.nikon.com). The unit costs about $60.

I recommend using a card reader because sending pictures directly from the camera requires that the camera be turned on during the entire download process, wasting battery power. That said, I include information about cable transfer in the next section in case you don't have a card reader. To use a card reader, skip ahead to "Starting the transfer process."

Connecting the camera and computer

With the USB cable that shipped with your camera, you can connect the camera to your computer and then transfer images to the computer's hard drive. The next section explains the actual image-transfer process; the following steps walk you through connecting the two devices:

1. **Check the level of the camera battery.**

   Running out of battery power during downloading can cause problems, including lost picture data. If you purchased the optional AC adapter, use that to power the camera during downloading.

2. **Turn on the computer and turn off the camera.**

3. **Insert the smaller plug on the USB cable into the USB port on the side of the camera, labeled in Figure 6-2.**

4. **Plug the other end of the cable into a USB port on the computer.**

5. **Turn on the camera.**

   What happens now depends on the photo software you have installed on your computer. The next section explains the possibilities and how to proceed with the image transfer process.

6. **When the download is complete, turn off the camera and then disconnect it from the computer.**

Starting the transfer process

After you connect the camera to the computer or insert a memory card into your card reader, your next step depends, again, on the software installed on your computer. Here are the most common possibilities:

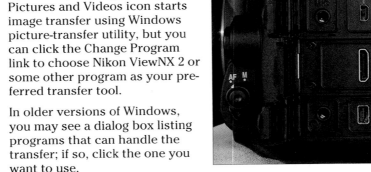

USB port

✓ **On a computer running Windows, a Windows message box similar to the one in Figure 6-3 appears.** The figure shows the dialog box as it appears in Windows 7. By default, clicking the Import Pictures and Videos icon starts image transfer using Windows picture-transfer utility, but you can click the Change Program link to choose Nikon ViewNX 2 or some other program as your preferred transfer tool.

In older versions of Windows, you may see a dialog box listing programs that can handle the transfer; if so, click the one you want to use.

Figure 6-2: The port for connecting the USB cable is hidden under the top rubber door on the left side of the camera.

✓ **A photo program displays a photo-download wizard.** For example, the downloader associated with Nikon ViewNX 2 or some other photo software may leap to the forefront. Usually, the downloader that appears is associated with the software that you most recently installed.

✓ **Nothing happens.** Don't panic; assuming that your card reader or camera is properly connected, all is probably well. Someone simply may have disabled all the automatic downloaders on your system. Just launch your photo software and then transfer your pictures using whatever command starts that process.

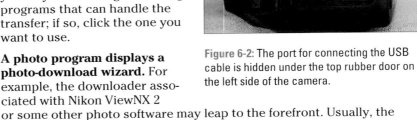

As another option, you can use Windows Explorer or the Mac Finder to drag and drop files from your memory card to your computer's hard drive. You connect the card through a card reader, and the computer sees the card as a drive on the system. Windows Explorer also shows the camera as a storage device when you cable the camera directly to the computer. So the process of transferring files is exactly the same as when you move any other file from a CD, DVD, or other storage device onto your hard drive. (With some versions of the Mac OS, including the most recent ones, the Finder doesn't recognize cameras in this way.)

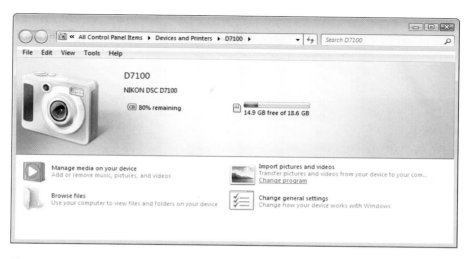

Figure 6-3: Windows 7 may display this initial boxful of transfer options.

In the next section, I provide details on using Nikon ViewNX 2 to download your files. If you use some other software, the concepts are the same, but check your program manual to get the small details. In most programs, you also can find lots of information by simply clicking open the Help menu.

Downloading using ViewNX 2

Built into ViewNX 2 is a handy image-downloading tool called Nikon Transfer 2. Follow these steps to use it:

1. **Attach your camera to the computer or insert a memory card into your card reader.**

   Depending on what software you have installed on your system, you may see a dialog box asking you how to download your photos. If the window that appears is the Nikon Transfer 2 window, as shown in Figure 6-4, skip to Step 3.

   Similarly, if you see a Windows dialog box that contains the Nikon Transfer 2 option, click that option and skip to Step 3.

   If nothing happens, travel to Step 2.

2. **Launch Nikon Transfer 2 (if it isn't already open).**

   Open Nikon ViewNX 2 and then choose File⇨Launch Transfer or click the Transfer button at the top of the window. The window shown in Figure 6-4 appears. (If you use a Mac, the window decor is slightly different, but the main controls and features are the same.)

Click to hide/display options

Select Protected

Select All   Select None

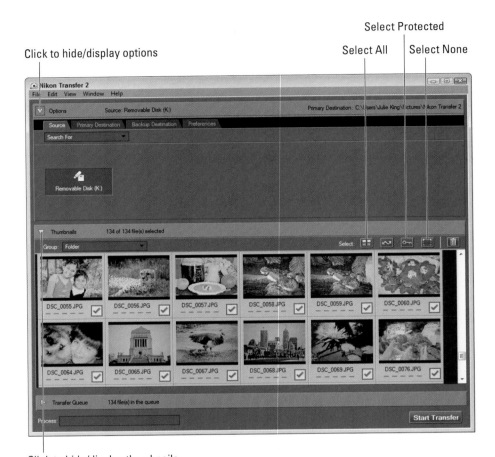

Click to hide/display thumbnails

Figure 6-4: Select the check boxes of the images that you want to download.

3. Display the Source tab to view thumbnails of your pictures, as shown in the figure.

Don't see any tabs? Click the Options triangle, labeled in Figure 6-4, to display them. Then click the Source tab. The icon representing your camera or memory card should be selected. If not, click the icon.

If you have two memory cards in the camera, click the triangle at the bottom-right corner of the camera icon (not shown in the figure). Then choose which card you want to access.

Thumbnails of your images appear in the bottom half of the dialog box. If you don't see the thumbnails, click the Thumbnails arrow, labeled in Figure 6-4, to open the thumbnails area.

4. **Select the images that you want to download.**

   Click a thumbnail to highlight it and then click the box in the lower-right corner of the thumbnail to select that image for downloading.

   Here are a few tips to speed up this process:

   - *Select protected images only.* If you used the in-camera function to protect pictures (see Chapter 5), you can select just those images by clicking the Select Protected icon, labeled in Figure 6-4.

   - *Select all images.* Click the Select All icon, also labeled in the figure.

   - *Select no images.* Click the Select None icon. Use this trick if you accidentally select all photos but don't want to import all of them.

5. **Click the Primary Destination tab at the top of the window.**

   The top of the transfer window now offers options that enable you to specify where and how you want the images to be stored on your computer. Figure 6-5 offers a look.

6. **Choose the folder where you want to store the images from the Primary Destination Folder drop-down list.**

   If the folder you want to use isn't in the list, open the drop-down list, choose Browse from the bottom of the list, and then track down the folder and select it.

   In the center portion of the dialog box, you get a batch of additional storage-folder options. If you're uncertain about which options to choose, the program's Help system spells everything out; choose Help⊅ViewNX 2 Help to access it.

7. **Tell the program whether you want to rename the picture files during the download process.**

   If you do, select the Rename Files during Transfer check box. Then click the Edit button to display a dialog box where you can set up your new filenaming scheme. Click OK after you do so to close the dialog box.

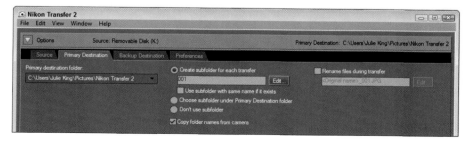

Figure 6-5: Specify the folder where you want to put the downloaded images.

8. (Optional) Set a backup destination.

This option is great if you back up photos to a secondary hard drive. You can download your photos to your primary image-storage drive and to the backup at the same time. To take advantage of this feature, click the Backup Destination tab, select the Backup Files box, and then use the other panel options to specify where you want the files to go.

9. Click the Preferences tab to set the rest of the transfer options.

The tab shown in Figure 6-6 takes over the top of the program window. Here you find a number of options that enable you to control how the program operates. Rather than covering all of them, which are explained quite nicely in the program's Help system (access it via the Help menu), I want to highlight just three of the most helpful and critical options.

- *Transfer New Files Only:* This option, when selected, ensures that you don't waste time downloading images that you've already transferred but are still on the memory card.

- *Delete Original Files after Transfer:* **Turn off this option,** as shown in Figure 6-6. Otherwise, your pictures are automatically erased from your memory card when the transfer is complete. Always make sure the pictures really made it to the computer before you delete them from your memory card. (See Chapter 5 to find out how to use the Delete function on your camera.)

- *Open Destination Folder with the Following Application after Transfer:* You can tell the program to immediately open your photo program after the transfer is complete. Choose ViewNX 2, as shown in the figure, to view, organize, and edit your photos using that program. To choose another program, open the drop-down list, select Browse, and select the program from the dialog box that appears. Click OK after doing so.

Your choices remain in force for any subsequent download sessions, so you don't have to revisit this tab unless you want the program to behave differently.

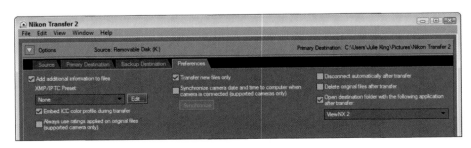

Figure 6-6: Control other aspects of the program's behavior via the Preferences tab.

10. **When you're ready to start the download, click the Start Transfer button.**

    It's located in the lower-right corner of the program window. After you click the button, the Process bar in the lower-left corner indicates how the transfer is progressing. Again, what happens when the transfer completes depends on the choices you made in Step 9; if you selected Nikon ViewNX 2 as the photo program, it opens and displays the folder that contains your just-downloaded images.

Processing Raw (NEF) Files

Chapter 2 introduces you to the Raw file format. The advantage of capturing Raw files — NEF files on Nikon cameras — is that you make the decisions about how to translate the original picture data into an actual photograph. You take this step by using a tool known as a *Raw converter*.

To process your NEF files, you have the following options:

- ✔ **Use the in-camera processing feature.** Through the Retouch menu, you can process your Raw images right in the camera. You can specify only limited image attributes, and you can save the processed files only in the JPEG format, but still, having this option is a nice feature.

- ✔ **Process and convert in ViewNX 2.** ViewNX 2 also offers a Raw processing feature. Again, the controls for setting picture characteristics are a little limited, but you can save the adjusted files in either the JPEG or TIFF format, and TIFF is better at holding onto the original image quality than JPEG.

    TIFF stands for Tagged Image File Format.

- ✔ **Use Nikon Capture NX 2 or a third-party Raw conversion tool.** For the most control over your Raw images, you need to open your wallet and invest in a program that offers a truly sophisticated converter. See the first part of this chapter for a review of Capture NX 2; the other programs mentioned in the same section also offer good Raw converters.

The next two sections show you how to convert Raw files using your camera and ViewNX 2. If you opt for a third-party conversion tool, check the program's Help system for details on how to use the various controls, which vary from program to program.

Processing Raw images in the camera

Through the NEF (RAW) Processing option on the Retouch menu, you can create a JPEG version of a Raw file right in the camera — no computer or other software required. Follow these steps to get the job done:

1. **Press the Playback button to switch to playback mode.**

2. **Display the picture you want to process in the single-image view.**

   If necessary, you can shift from thumbnails view to single-image view by just pressing OK.

3. **Press the *i* button.**

   The Retouch menu appears atop your photo, as shown in Figure 6-7.

4. **Use the Multi Selector to scroll to the NEF (RAW) Processing option, as shown in Figure 6-7.**

5. **Press OK to display your processing options.**

   You see a screen similar to the one in Figure 6-8, which is where you specify what settings you want the camera to use when creating the JPEG version of your Raw image. If you press the Multi Selector down, you scroll to the second page of options, shown in Figure 6-9.

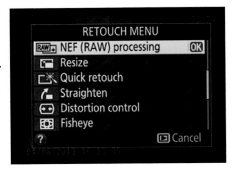

Figure 6-7: In single-image playback mode, press the *i* button to display the Retouch menu.

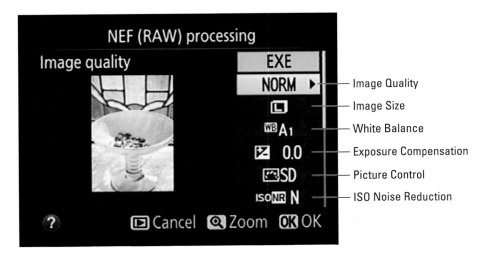

Figure 6-8: These Raw conversion options are on the first page of the menu screen.

6. Set the conversion options.

Along the right side of the screen, you see a vertical column offering the conversion options labeled in Figures 6-8 and 6-9. To establish the setting for an option, highlight it and then press the Multi Selector right. You then see the available settings for the option. Use the Multi Selector to adjust or highlight the setting you want to use and press OK to return to the main Raw conversion screen. Or, if a triangle appears to the right of an option name, you can press the Multi Selector right to uncover additional options.

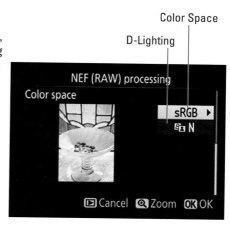

Figure 6-9: Press the Multi Selector down to scroll to the second page of conversion settings.

Rather than detailing all the options here, the following list points you to the chapter where you can explore the settings available for each:

- *Image Quality:* See the Chapter 2 section related to the JPEG format for details on this option. Choose Fine to retain maximum picture quality.

- *Image Size:* Chapter 2 explains this one, too. Choose Large to retain all the original image pixels.

- *White Balance:* Check out Chapter 8 for details about White Balance options, which affect picture colors. Unless colors look off, stick with the default, $Auto_1$ (A1).

- *Exposure Compensation:* With this option, which I cover in Chapter 7, you can adjust image brightness. When using this feature for Raw conversion, you're limited to a range of –2.0 and +2.0; when shooting, you can choose from settings ranging from –5.0 to +5.0.

- *Picture Control:* This option enables you to adjust color saturation, contrast, and image sharpness. For a review of the available settings, see the last part of Chapter 8. Or just experiment with the different settings: The onscreen image preview updates to show you the results of each option.

- *ISO Noise Reduction:* If your picture looks *noisy* — that is, marred by a speckled look — playing with this setting may help eliminate the flaw. See Chapter 7 for an explanation of this feature, which is designed to reduce the amount of noise in pictures shot using a high ISO Sensitivity setting.

- *Color Space:* This setting determines whether the camera sticks with the default color space, sRGB, or the larger Adobe RGB color space when converting your photo. Stick with sRGB until you digest the Chapter 8 section that details this option.

- *D-Lighting:* To brighten the darkest part of your picture without also brightening the lightest areas, try adjusting this setting. It's the post-capture equivalent of the Active D-Lighting feature that's available during shooting; see Chapter 7 for help with the option. To darken shadows, try setting the option to Off.

QUAL

At any time, you can magnify the view of the image by pressing the Qual button. Release the button to return to the normal display.

7. **After setting the conversion options, highlight EXE on the first conversion screen (refer to Figure 6-8) and press OK.**

   The camera records a JPEG copy of your Raw file and displays the copy. The camera assigns the next available file number to the image.

Processing Raw files in ViewNX 2

In Nikon ViewNX 2, you can convert your Raw files to the JPEG format or, for top picture quality, to the TIFF format. Although the ViewNX 2 converter isn't as full-featured as the ones in Nikon Capture NX 2 and some other photo-editing programs, it does enable you to make some adjustments to your Raw images. Follow these steps to try it out:

1. **Open ViewNX 2 and click the thumbnail of the image that you want to process.**

TIP

   You may want to set the program to Image Viewer mode, as shown in Figure 6-10, so that you can see a larger preview of your image. Just choose View⇨Image Viewer to switch to this display mode. To give the photo even more room, also hide the Browser panel, which normally occupies the left third of the window, and the Filmstrip panel that usually runs across the bottom of the window. Choose Window⇨Browser and Window⇨Filmstrip to toggle those window elements on and off.

2. **Display the Adjustments panel.**

   You can see the panel in Figure 6-10. Show and hide this panel and the Metadata panel by choosing Window⇨Edit or by clicking the triangle on the far-right side of the window. You can then display and collapse the individual panels by clicking the triangles to the left of their names. (I labeled the triangles in the figure.) To allow the maximum space for the Raw conversion adjustments, collapse the Metadata panel, as shown in the figure.

3. **To display all available settings, choose All from the Adjustments drop-down list, as shown in Figure 6-10.**

   You may need to use the scroll bar on the right side of the panel to scroll the display to see all the options.

Click to hide/display Adjustments panel

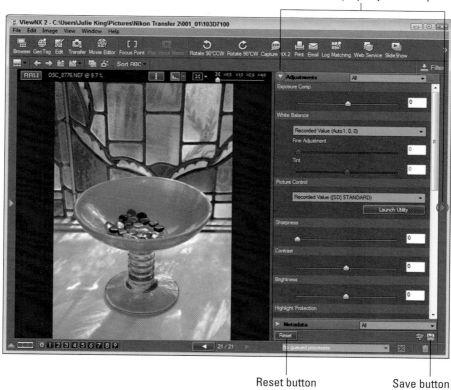

Reset button   Save button

Figure 6-10: Display the Adjustments panel to tweak Raw images before conversion.

4. Use the panel controls to adjust your image.

The preview you see in the image window reflects the default conversion settings chosen by Nikon, but you can play with any of the settings as you see fit. If you need help understanding any of the options, open the built-in help system (via the Help menu), where you can find descriptions of how each adjustment affects your image.

To return to the original image settings, click the Reset button at the bottom of the panel, labeled in Figure 6-10.

5. Click the Save button. (Refer to Figure 6-10.)

This step stores your conversion settings as part of the image file but doesn't actually create your processed image file. Don't worry, though. Your original Raw data remains intact; what's saved with the file is a recipe for processing the image, which you can change at any time.

6. To save the processed file, choose File⇨Convert Files.

You see the Convert Files dialog box, shown in Figure 6-11.

7. Select TIFF(8 Bit) from the File Format drop-down list.

TIFF is the best format because it retains your processed file at the highest image quality. (This format has long been the preferred format for print publication.) Don't choose JPEG; as explained in Chapter 2, the JPEG format applies *lossy compression,* thereby sacrificing some image quality. If you need a JPEG copy of your processed Raw image for online sharing — TIFF files won't work for that use — you can create one by following the steps laid out in the upcoming section "Prepping online photos using ViewNX 2."

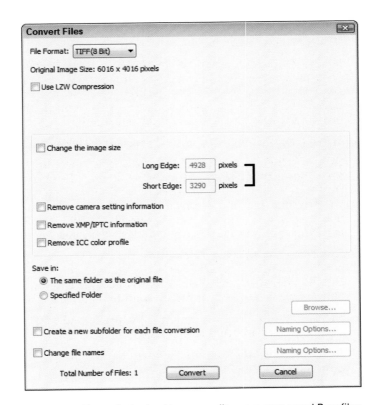

Figure 6-11: To retain the best image quality, save processed Raw files in the TIFF format.

As for the *8 Bit* part of the option name, a *bit* is a unit of computer data; the more bits you have, the more colors your image can contain. Although you can create 16-bit TIFF files in the converter, some photo-editing programs either can't open them or limit you to a few editing tools, so I suggest you stick with the standard, 8-bit image option unless you know your software can handle the larger-bit images.

8. Deselect the Use LZW Compression option.

Although LZW compression reduces the file size somewhat and does not cause any quality loss, some programs can't open files that were saved with this option enabled, so turn it off.

9. Deselect the Change the Image Size check box.

This step ensures that you retain all original pixels in your processed image.

10. Deselect each of the three Remove check boxes.

If you select the check boxes, you strip image *metadata* — the extra text data that's stored by the camera — from the file. Unless you have some specific reason to do so, clear all three check boxes so that you can continue to access the metadata when you view your processed image in programs that know how to display metadata.

11. Select a storage location for the processed TIFF file.

Do this in the Save In area of the dialog box. Select the top option to save your processed file in the same folder as the original file. Or, to put the file in a different folder, select the Specified Folder button. If you do, you see the name of the currently selected alternative folder below the button; change the storage destination by clicking the Browse button and then selecting the drive and folder where you want to put the file.

By selecting the Create a New Subfolder for Each File Conversion check box, you can put your TIFF file into a separate folder within the destination folder. With this check box enabled, click the Naming Options button and then specify how you want to name the subfolder.

12. Specify whether you want to give the processed TIFF a different file-name from the original Raw image.

To do so, select the Change File Names check box, click the Naming Options button, and enter the name you want to use.

If you don't change the filename, the program gives the file the same name as the original Raw file. However, you don't overwrite that Raw file because you're storing the copy in a different file format (TIFF).

13. Click the Convert button.

A window appears to show you the progress of the conversion process. When the window disappears, your TIFF image appears in the storage location you selected in Step 11.

One neat thing about working with Raw images is that you can easily create as many variations of your photo as you want. For example, you might choose one set of options when processing your Raw file the first time and then use an entirely different set to create another version of the photo. Just be sure to give each processed file a unique name so that you don't overwrite the first TIFF file you create with your second version.

Planning for Perfect Prints

Images from your D7100 can produce dynamic prints, but getting the best prints requires a little knowledge and prep work on your part. The next three sections help you avoid the most common printing problems.

Check the pixel count before you print

Resolution — the number of pixels in your digital image — plays a huge role in how large you can print your photos and still maintain good picture quality. You can get the complete story on resolution in Chapter 2, but here's a recap as it relates to printing:

- **Choose the right resolution before you shoot.** Set resolution via the Image Size option on the Shooting menu or by pressing the Qual button while rotating the Sub-command dial. (This option is off-limits if the Image Quality option is set to Raw; all Raw files are captured at the Large Image Size setting.)

- **Aim for a minimum of 200 pixels per inch (ppi).** You'll get a wide range of recommendations on this issue, even among professionals. But in general, if you aim for a resolution in the neighborhood of 200 ppi, you should be pleased with your results. If you want a 4 x 6" print, for example, you need at least 800 x 1200 pixels. When you do the resolution math, remember to take any cropping you plan to do into account.

Depending on your printer, you may get even better results at a slightly lower resolution. On the other hand, some printers do their best work when fed 300 ppi, and a few request 360 ppi as the optimum resolution. However, using a resolution higher than that typically doesn't produce any better prints. Unfortunately, because most printer manuals don't bother to tell you what image resolution produces the best results, finding the right pixel level is a matter of experimentation.

Don't confuse *ppi* with the printer's dpi. *Dots per inch (dpi)* refers to the number of dots of color the printer can lay down per inch; many printers use multiple dots to reproduce one image pixel.

> If you're printing photos at a retail kiosk or at an online site, the software you use to order prints should determine the resolution of your files and then suggest appropriate print sizes. If you're printing on a home printer, though, you need to be the resolution cop.

What do you do if you don't have enough pixels for the print size you have in mind? You have two choices, neither of which provides a good outcome:

- ✔ **Keep the existing pixel count and accept lowered photo quality.** In this case, the pixels get bigger to fill the requested print size. When pixels grow too large, they produce a defect known as *pixelation:* The picture starts to appear jagged, or stairstepped, along curved or oblique lines. Or, at worst, your eye can make out the individual pixels, and your photo begins to look more like a mosaic than, well, like a photograph.

- ✔ **Add more pixels and accept lowered photo quality.** In some photo programs, you can add pixels to an image. (The technical term for this process is *upsampling.*) Some other photo programs even upsample the photo automatically for you, depending on the print settings you choose.

Although adding pixels might sound like a good option, it actually doesn't help in the long run. You're asking the software to make up photo information out of thin air, and the resulting image usually looks worse than the original. You don't see pixelation, but details turn muddy, giving the image a blurry, poorly rendered appearance.

To hammer home the point about the impact of resolution on picture quality, Figures 6-12 through 6-14 show you the same image as it appears at 300 ppi (the resolution required by the publisher of this book), at 50 ppi, and then resampled from 50 ppi to 300 ppi. As you can see, there's just no way around the rule: If you want the best-quality prints, you need the right pixel count from the get-go.

300 ppi

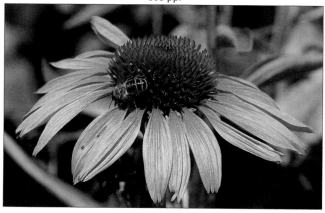

Figure 6-12: A high-quality print depends on a high-resolution original.

50 ppi

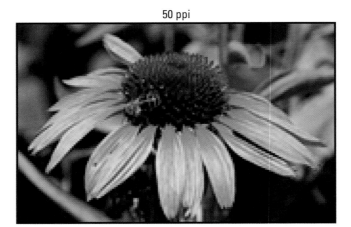

Figure 6-13: At 50 ppi, the image has a jagged, pixelated look.

50 ppi resampled to 300 ppi

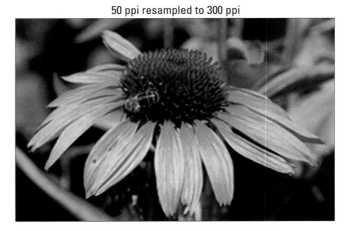

Figure 6-14: Adding pixels in a photo editor doesn't rescue a low-resolution original.

Allow for different print proportions

Your camera produces images that have a 3:2 aspect ratio, which matches the proportions of a 4 x 6" print. To print your photo at other traditional sizes — 5 x 7, 8 x 10, and so on — you need to crop the photo to match those proportions. Alternatively, you can reduce the photo size slightly and leave an empty margin along the edges of the print as needed.

As a point of reference, both images in Figure 6-15 are original, 3:2 images. The red outlines indicate how much of the original can fit within a 5 x 7" frame and an 8 x 10" frame, respectively.

Chapter 10 shows you how to crop your image using the Trim option on the Retouch menu. However, this in-camera tool enables you to crop to only five aspect ratios: 3:2, 4:3, 5:4, 1:1, and 16:9. For other crop proportions, use Nikon ViewNX 2 or some other photo software to do the job. (The crop tool lives on the Adjustments panel in Nikon ViewNX 2.)

You also can usually crop your photo using the software provided at online printing sites and at retail print kiosks. If you plan to simply drop off your memory card for printing at a lab, be sure to find out whether the printer automatically crops the image without your input. If so, use your photo software to crop the photo, save the cropped image to your memory card, and deliver that version of the file to the printer.

 To allow yourself printing flexibility, leave a margin of background around your subject when you shoot. That way, you don't clip off the edges of the subject, no matter what print size you choose. (Some people refer to this margin padding as *head room* when describing portrait composition.)

5 x 7   8 x 10

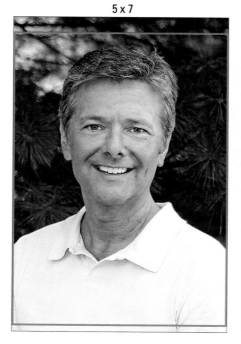 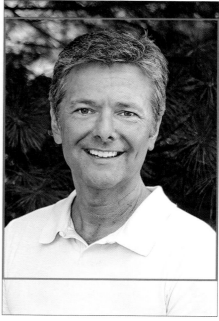

Figure 6-15: Composing your shots with a little head room enables you to crop to different frame sizes.

Get print and monitor colors in sync

Your photo colors look perfect on your computer monitor, but when you print the picture, the image is too red or too green or has another nasty color tint. This problem can occur because of any or all the following factors:

- **Your monitor needs to be calibrated.** If the monitor isn't accurately calibrated, the colors it displays aren't a true reflection of your image. The same caveat applies to monitor brightness: You can't accurately gauge the exposure of a photo if the brightness of the monitor is cranked way up or down. Many monitors sold today are very bright — providing ideal conditions for web browsing and watching movies but not necessarily for photo editing. You may need to turn the brightness way, way down to get to a true indication of image exposure.

  To ensure that your monitor displays photos on a neutral canvas, I recommend that you invest in a monitor calibration tool. These products use a device known as a *colorimeter* to accurately measure display colors. At the end of the calibration process, the tool produces a monitor *profile* that tells your computer how to adjust the display to compensate for any monitor color casts or brightness and contrast issues. Windows or Mac OS X loads this file automatically when you start your computer. Two companies offering this type of tool are Datacolor (`www.datacolor.com`) and X-rite (`www.xrite.com`).

- **One of your printer cartridges is empty or clogged.** If your prints look great one day but are way off the next, the number-one suspect is an empty ink cartridge or a clogged print nozzle or head. Check your manual to find out how to perform the necessary maintenance to keep the nozzles or print heads in good shape.

- **You chose the wrong paper setting in your printer software.** When you set up a print job, be sure to select the right setting from the paper type option — glossy or matte, for example. This setting affects how the printer lays down ink on the paper.

- **Your photo paper is low quality.** Sad but true: Cheap, store-brand papers usually don't render colors as well as name-brand papers.

  Some paper manufacturers, especially those that sell fine-art papers, offer downloadable *printer profiles,* which are data files that tell your printer how to manage color for the paper. Refer to the manufacturer's website for information on how to install and use the profiles.

- **Your printer and photo software fight over color management duties.** Some photo programs offer color management tools, which enable you to control how colors are handled as an image passes from camera to monitor to printer. Most printer software also offers color management features. The problem is that if you enable the color management controls in both your photo software and printer software, you can create conflicts that lead to wacky colors. Check your photo software and printer manuals for color management options and ways to turn them on and off.

Exploring two special printing options

Your camera has two features that enable you to print directly from the camera or memory card:

- **DPOF (Digital Print Order Format):** With this option, accessed via the DPOF Print Order option on the Playback menu, you select pictures from your memory card and then specify how many copies you want of each image. Then, if your photo printer has a memory card slot compatible with your camera's cards and supports DPOF, you pop the card into that slot. The printer reads your "print order" and outputs the requested prints. (You use the printer's own controls to set paper size, print orientation, and other print settings.)

- **PictBridge:** If you have a PictBridge-enabled photo printer, you can connect the camera to the printer by using a USB cable. A PictBridge interface appears on the camera monitor, and you use camera controls to select pictures to print as well as to specify print options such as page size.

If you're interested in exploring either printing feature, look for details in your camera manual.

Even if all these issues are resolved, however, don't expect perfect color matching between printer and monitor. Printers simply can't reproduce the entire spectrum of colors that a monitor can display. In addition, monitor colors always appear brighter because they are, after all, generated with light.

Finally, be sure to evaluate print colors and monitor colors in the same ambient light — daylight, office light, whatever — because that light source has its own influence on the colors you see. Also allow your prints to dry for 15 minutes or so before you make any final judgments.

Preparing Pictures for Online Use

Have you ever received an e-mail containing a photo so large that you can't view the whole thing on your monitor without scrolling the e-mail window? This annoyance occurs because monitors can display only a limited number of pixels. The exact number depends on the screen resolution setting, but suffice it to say that today's digital cameras produce photos with pixel counts in excess of what the monitor can handle.

Thankfully, the newest e-mail programs incorporate features that automatically shrink the photo to a viewable size. That doesn't change the fact that a large photo file means longer downloading times, though — and if recipients choose to hold onto the picture, a big storage hit on their hard drives. And some mail programs limit the size of files you can send, so you may not even be able to ship your high-resolution pictures through them.

Sending a high-resolution photo *is* the thing to do if you want the recipient to be able to generate a good print. However, it's polite practice to ask people if they *want* to print 11 x 14 glossies of your puppy before you send them a dozen 24 megapixel (MP) shots.

For simple onscreen viewing, I suggest limiting your photos to fewer than 1000 pixels on the longest side of the image. That ensures that people who use an e-mail program that doesn't offer the latest photo-viewing tools can see the entire picture without scrolling the viewer window.

This size recommendation means that even if you shoot at your camera's lowest Image Size setting (2992 x 2000), you wind up with more pixels than you need for onscreen viewing. Some new e-mail programs have a photo-upload feature that creates a temporary low-res version for you, but if not, creating your own copy is easy. (If you're posting to a photo-sharing site, you may be able to upload all your original pixels, but many sites have resolution limits.)

In addition to resizing high-res images, check their file types; if photos are in the Raw (NEF) or TIFF format, you need to create a JPEG copy for online use. Web browsers and e-mail programs can't display Raw or TIFF files. You can tackle both bits of photo prep in ViewNX 2 or by using the Resize option in your camera. The next sections explain both methods.

Prepping online photos using ViewNX 2

For pictures already on your computer, you can create small-sized JPEG copies for online sharing using ViewNX 2. Just click the image thumbnail and then choose the Convert Files command, found on the File menu. When the Convert Files dialog box appears (see Figure 6-16), set up things as follows:

- ✓ **Select JPEG as the file format.** Make your selection from the File Format drop-down list.

- ✓ **Set the picture-quality level.** Use the Quality slider, labeled in Figure 6-16, to set the picture quality, which is controlled by how much JPEG compression is applied when the file is saved. For best quality, drag the slider all the way to the right, but remember the tradeoff: As you raise the quality, less compression occurs, which results in a larger file size. (See Chapter 2 for more information about JPEG compression.)

- ✓ **Set the image size (number of pixels).** To resize the photo, select the Change the Image Size check box and then enter a value (in pixels) for the longest dimension of the photo. The program automatically fills in the other value.

- ✓ **Select all three Remove check boxes, as shown in Figure 6-16.** Selecting these options removes unnecessary camera metadata, which reduces image file size.

The rest of the options work just as they do during Raw conversion; see "Processing Raw files in ViewNX 2," earlier in this chapter, for details.

Quality slider

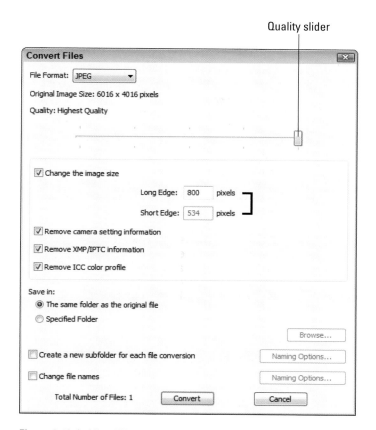

Figure 6-16: In ViewNX 2, select the Convert Files option to create a web-friendly version of a photo.

If you're resizing a JPEG original, be sure to give the small version a new name to avoid overwriting that original.

Creating screen-friendly copies in the camera

The in-camera Resize tool is found on the Retouch menu; the next two sections provide details on how to use it. Your resized images are saved in the JPEG format, which is the web-friendly format. Resized JPEG files are saved using the same Image Quality setting (Fine, Normal, or Basic) as the original. Raw originals are saved as JPEG Fine images. Either way, your original picture file remains untouched.

One tip before you dig in: Although you can use the tool on Raw images as well as JPEG images, I prefer to convert my Raw photos to JPEGs first. That way, I can adjust the picture qualities as I see fit before making the small copy. For details, see "Processing Raw images in the camera," earlier in this chapter. Then I use the converted photo as the basis for my online copy.

Resizing a single photo

To create a small copy of just one image, take these steps:

1. **Press the Playback button to set your camera to playback mode.**

2. **Display the picture in single-image view.**

   If the monitor currently displays multiple thumbnails, just press OK to switch to single-image view.

3. **Press the *i* button to display the Retouch menu over your image, as shown on the left in Figure 6-17.**

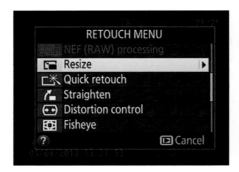 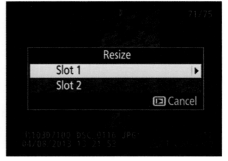

Figure 6-17: The Resize feature creates a low-res, e-mail–friendly copy of a photo.

4. **Highlight Resize and then press OK or press the Multi Selector right.**

   You see the screen shown on the right in the figure.

5. **If two memory cards are installed, highlight the card where you want to store the small copy.**

6. **Press the Multi Selector right.**

   The screen shown in Figure 6-18 appears, offering the list of size options (stated in pixels) avail-

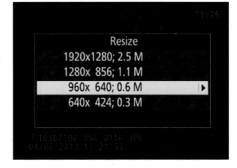

Figure 6-18: The size values are stated in pixels.

able for your small copy. The second value stated for each option is the megapixel count — total pixels, with one megapixel equal to 1 million pixels.

7. **Highlight the size you want to use for your copy.**

8. **Press the Multi Selector right to display a confirmation screen.**

9. **Highlight Yes and then press OK.**

   The camera duplicates the selected image and *downsamples* (eliminates pixels from) the copy to achieve the size you specify in Step 7.

When you view your small-size copies on the camera monitor, they appear with a Retouch icon at the top of the screen and a Resize icon at the bottom, as shown in Figure 6-19.

Retouch symbol

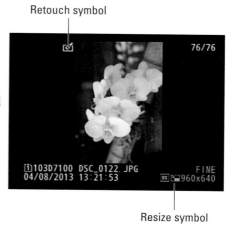

Resize symbol

Figure 6-19: The Resize icon indicates a small-size copy.

Resizing a batch of images

To create small copies of several photos on your memory card, use the following alternative in-camera resizing process:

1. **Press the Menu button and then display the Retouch menu.**

2. **Select the Resize option, as shown on the left in Figure 6-20, and then press OK.**

   You see the screen shown on the right in Figure 6-20.

3. **If two memory cards are installed, select Choose Destination and then select which card you want to use to store the resized images.**

4. **Select Choose Size to choose the size for the small copies.**

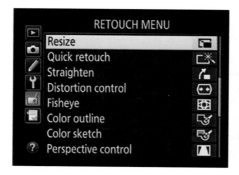
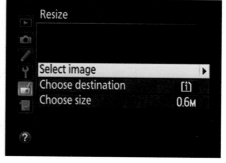

Figure 6-20: Start directly from the Retouch menu to resize a bunch of pictures at the same time.

5. **Choose Select Image and then press OK to display thumbnails of all your pictures, as shown in Figure 6-21.**

An X over a thumbnail means that the picture can't be resized. You can't resize movie files, for example, or already resized images.

6. **Move the yellow highlight box over a thumbnail and press the ISO button to tag the photo for resizing.**

You see a resize icon in the top-right corner of the thumbnail, as shown in Figure 6-21. Press the button again to remove the tag.

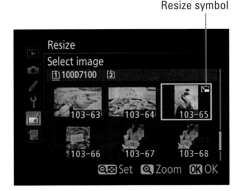

Resize symbol

Figure 6-21: Press the ISO button to tag a picture for resizing.

7. **After selecting all your pictures, press OK.**

8. **Highlight Yes and press OK once more.**

Again, resized photos appear with the Retouch and Resize symbols, as shown earlier in Figure 6-19.

Copying Files from One Card to Another

When you have two memory cards installed in the camera, you can use the Copy Image(s) option on the Playback menu to copy pictures from one card to the other. Follow these steps:

1. **On the Playback menu, choose Copy Image(s) and press OK.**

2. **Highlight Select Source and press the Multi Selector right.**

You see a screen listing both memory cards (Slot 1 and Slot 2).

3. **Highlight the memory card that contains the pictures you want to copy and press OK.**

You return to the main Copy Image(s) screen.

4. **Highlight Select Image(s) and press the Multi Selector right.**

You see a screen listing all folders on the selected card.

5. **Highlight the folder that contains your pictures and press the Multi Selector right.**

You see a screen with three options: Select All Images, Select Protected Images, and Deselect All.

6. Choose an initial picture-selection option.

Choose Select All Images to copy every picture on the card; choose Select Protected Images to copy just photos that you tagged with the Protect feature, covered in Chapter 5.

The third option, Deselect All, is a little counterintuitive: The camera initially assumes that you want to copy every picture on the card, so it tries to help by automatically preselecting all them. You can later deselect the ones you don't want to copy, but if you're copying just a few pictures out of a large group, it's faster to choose Deselect All so that you start out with no pictures selected. Then you don't have to waste time "untagging" all the ones you don't want to copy.

7. Press OK to display thumbnails of your photos.

Check marks appear with any photos currently selected for copying. In Figure 6-22, for example, the top, right photo is selected.

8. Press the ISO button to add or remove a photo from the selection.

Pressing the button toggles the check mark on and off.

9. After selecting the photos you want to copy, press OK.

Now you see the screen shown on the right in Figure 6-22.

10. Choose the Select Destination Folder option and press the Multi Selector right.

You see a screen offering two options: The first, Select Folder by Number, enables you to specify a three-digit folder number. (Press the Multi Selector left or right to highlight a value, and press up or down to change the number.) The second option, Select Folder from List, displays all available folders. After choosing a folder number or folder, press OK.

Selected symbol

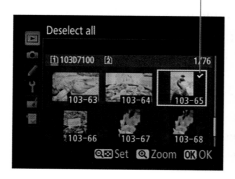
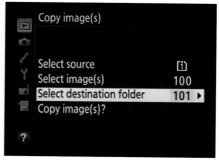

Figure 6-22: Press the ISO button to tag photos for copying (left); then set the Destination folder for the copies (right).

11. **Choose the Copy Image(s)? option and press OK.**

12. **Highlight Yes and press OK to copy the photos.**

When you use this feature, remember these final pointers:

- ✔ If the destination card doesn't have enough space for all the selected images, the camera alerts you that all images may not be copied. You can choose to go forward or cancel the operation and install a card that has more free space.

- ✔ If the destination card contains an image that has the same filename as one you select for copying, the camera gives you the option to overwrite the existing file, overwrite all existing files without any further confirmation notices, skip copying that file, or cancel the copy operation.

- ✔ When you copy a protected picture, both the copy and the original remain protected. See Chapter 5 for details about protecting images.

Part III
Taking Creative Control

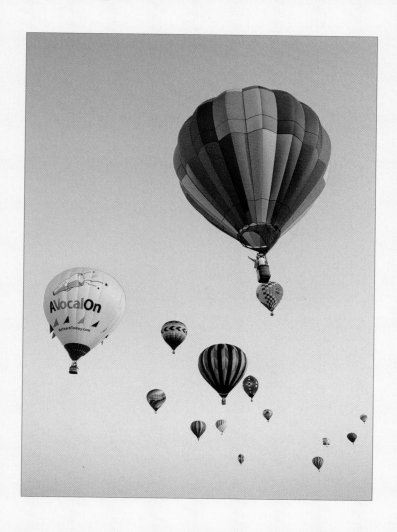

Discover five easy composition tricks you can use to shoot more captivating photos at
www.dummies.com/extras/nikon.

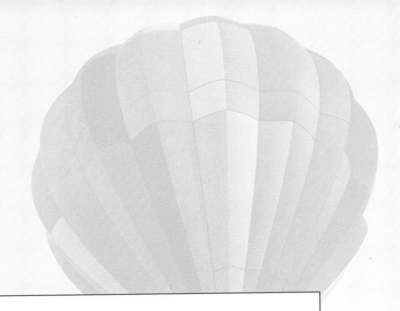
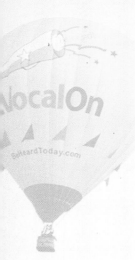

In this part . . .

- Explore the advanced exposure modes: P, S, A, and M.
- Tweak autoexposure results using Exposure Compensation, Active D-Lighting, and HDR.
- Get tips for producing better flash pictures.
- Master the autofocusing system and get help with manual focusing.
- Understand how to control depth of field (the distance over which focus remains sharp).
- Manipulate color by using White Balance and other color options.

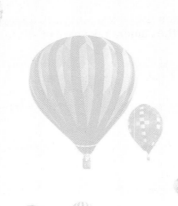

7

Getting Creative with Exposure and Lighting

In This Chapter

▶ Understanding the basics of exposure

▶ Choosing the right exposure mode: P, S, A, or M?

▶ Reading meters and other exposure cues

▶ Solving exposure problems

▶ Getting better flash results

▶ Creating a safety net with automatic exposure bracketing

*U*nderstanding exposure is one of the most intimidating challenges for a new photographer. Discussions of the topic are loaded with technical terms — *aperture, metering, shutter speed, ISO,* and the like. Add the fact that your camera offers many exposure controls, all sporting equally foreign names, and it's no wonder that most people throw up their hands and decide that their best option is to stick with the Auto exposure mode and let the camera take care of all exposure decisions.

You can, of course, turn out good shots in Auto mode, and I fully relate to the confusion you may be feeling — I've been there. But I can also promise that when you take things nice and slow, digesting the exposure pie a piece at a time, the topic is not as complicated as it seems on the surface. I guarantee that the payoff will be well worth your time and brain energy, too. You'll not only gain the know-how to solve just about any exposure problem but also discover ways to use exposure to put your creative stamp on a scene.

To that end, this chapter provides everything you need to know to really exploit your camera's exposure options, from a primer in exposure science (it's not as bad as it sounds) to explanations of all exposure controls, including those related to flash. In addition, because some controls aren't accessible in the fully automatic exposure modes covered in Chapter 3, this chapter provides more details about the four advanced modes, P, S, A, and M.

Introducing the Exposure Trio: Aperture, Shutter Speed, and ISO

Any photograph, whether taken with a film or digital camera, is created by focusing light through a lens onto a light-sensitive recording medium. In a film camera, the film negative serves as that medium; in a digital camera, it's the image sensor, which is an array of light-responsive computer chips.

Between the lens and the sensor are two barriers — the aperture and shutter — which work in concert to control how much light makes its way to the sensor of a digital camera. The actual design and arrangement of the aperture, shutter, and sensor vary depending on the camera, but Figure 7-1 offers an illustration of the basic concept.

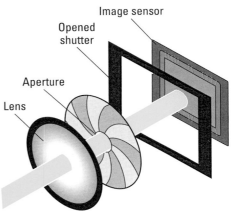

Figure 7-1: Aperture size and shutter speed determine how much light strikes the image sensor.

The aperture and shutter, along with a third feature — ISO — determine *exposure,* which is basically the picture's overall brightness and contrast. This three-part exposure formula works as follows:

➤ **Aperture (controls amount of light):** The *aperture* is an adjustable hole in a diaphragm inside the lens. You change the aperture size to control the size of the light beam that can enter the camera.

Aperture settings are stated as *f-stop numbers,* or simply *f-stops,* and are expressed with the letter *f* followed by a number: f/2, f/5.6, f/16, and so on. The lower the f-stop number, the larger the aperture, and the more light is permitted into the camera, as illustrated by Figure 7-2. (If it seems backward to use a higher number for a smaller aperture, think of it this way: A higher value creates a bigger light barrier.)

✔ **Shutter speed (controls duration of light):** The shutter works something like, er, the shutters on a window. The camera's shutter stays closed, preventing light from striking the image sensor (just as closed window shutters prevent sunlight from entering a room) until you press the shutter button. Then, the shutter opens briefly to allow light that passes

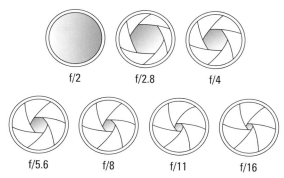

f/2   f/2.8   f/4

f/5.6   f/8   f/11   f/16

Figure 7-2: A lower f-stop number means a larger aperture, allowing more light into the camera.

through the aperture to hit the sensor. The exception to this scenario is when you compose in Live View mode: When you enable Live View, the shutter opens and remains open so that your image can form on the sensor and be displayed on the monitor. When you press the shutter button, the shutter first closes and then reopens for the exposure.

Either way, the length of time that the shutter is open is the *shutter speed,* which is measured in seconds: 1/60 second, 1/250 second, 2 seconds, and so on.

✔ **ISO (controls light sensitivity):** *ISO,* which is a digital function rather than a mechanical structure on the camera, enables you to adjust how responsive the image sensor is to light.

The term *ISO* is a holdover from film days, when an international standards organization rated each film stock according to light sensitivity: ISO 200, ISO 400, ISO 800, and so on.

On a digital camera, the sensor itself doesn't actually get more or less sensitive when you change the ISO. Instead, the light "signal" that hits the sensor is either amplified or dampened through electronics wizardry, sort of like how raising the volume on a radio boosts the audio signal. The upshot is the same as changing to a more light-reactive film stock: Using a higher ISO means that less light is needed to produce the image, enabling you to use a smaller aperture, faster shutter speed, or both. In other words, just remember that ISO equals light sensitivity.

Distilled to its essence, the image-exposure formula is this simple:

✔ Together, aperture and shutter speed determine how much light strikes the image sensor.

✔ ISO determines how much the sensor reacts to that light and thus how much light is needed to expose the picture.

The tricky part of the equation is that aperture, shutter speed, and ISO settings affect your pictures in ways that go beyond exposure. You need to be aware of these side effects, explained in the next sections, to determine which combination of the three exposure settings will work best for your picture.

Understanding exposure-setting side effects

You can create the same exposure with many combinations of aperture, shutter speed, and ISO, but the settings you select affect your image beyond exposure, as follows:

- ✓ Aperture affects *depth of field,* or the distance over which focus remains acceptably sharp.
- ✓ Shutter speed determines whether moving objects appear blurry or sharply focused.
- ✓ ISO affects the amount of image *noise,* which is a defect that looks like specks of sand.

As you can imagine, understanding how aperture, shutter speed, and ISO affect your image enables you to have much more creative control over your photographs — and, in the case of ISO, to also ensure the quality of your images. The next three sections explore these exposure side effects in detail.

Aperture affects depth of field

Depth of field refers to the distance over which focus appears acceptably sharp in a photograph. With a shallow depth of field, your subject appears more sharply focused than faraway objects; with a large depth of field, the sharp-focus zone spreads over a greater distance.

As you reduce the aperture size by choosing a higher f-stop number — *stop-down the aperture,* in photo lingo — you increase depth of field. As an example, see Figure 7-3. For both shots, I established focus on the fountain statue. Notice that the background in the first image, taken at f/13, is sharper than in the right example, taken at f/5.6.

One way to remember the relationship between f-stop and depth of field is to think of the *f* as standing for *focus.* A higher f-stop number produces a larger depth of field, so if you want to extend the zone of sharp focus to cover a greater distance from your subject, you set the aperture to a higher f-stop. Higher *f*-stop number, greater zone of sharp *focus.* (Please *don't* share this tip with photography elites, who will roll their eyes and inform you that the *f* in *f-stop* most certainly does *not* stand for focus but for the ratio between the aperture size and lens focal length — as if *that's* helpful to know if you're not an optical engineer.)

It's also important to understand that aperture is just one contributor to depth of field; other factors include the focal length of your lens and the distance between that lens and your subject. Chapter 8 has the complete story, but the short version is that depth of field decreases as you increase focal length or get closer to your subject. For example, if you shoot a subject close-up using a telephoto lens, you wind up with a much shorter depth of field than if you use a wide-angle lens and stand at a distance from the subject. I shot both example images in Figure 7-3 using the same focal length and from the same distance, so the only variable was the f-stop.

Shutter speed affects motion blur

At a slow shutter speed, moving objects appear blurry, whereas a fast shutter speed captures motion cleanly. This phenomenon has nothing to do with the focus point of the camera but rather on the movement occurring — and being recorded — during the time when the shutter is open.

Compare the photos in Figure 7-3, for example. The static elements are perfectly focused in both images although the background in the left photo appears sharper because I shot that image using a higher f-stop, increasing the depth of field. But how the camera rendered the moving portion of the scene — the fountain water — was determined by the shutter speed. At a shutter speed of 1/25 second (left photo), the water blurs, giving it a misty look. At 1/125 second (right photo), the droplets appear more sharply focused, almost frozen in mid-air. How high of a shutter speed you need to freeze action depends on the speed of your subject.

f/13, 1/25 second, ISO 200   f/5.6, 1/125 second, ISO 200

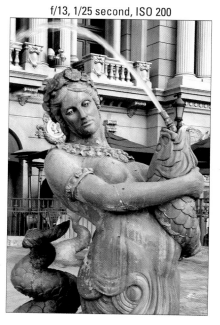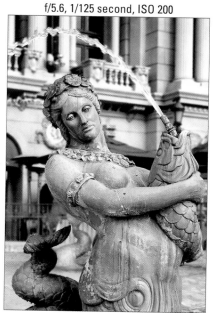

Figure 7-3: Widening the aperture (choosing a lower f-stop number) decreases depth of field.

If your picture suffers from overall blur, as in Figure 7-4, the camera moved during the exposure, which is always a danger when you handhold a camera. The slower the shutter speed, the longer the exposure time and the longer you have to hold the camera still to avoid the blur that's caused by camera shake. How slow you can go and successfully hand-hold the camera varies from person to person, so do your own tests to see where your handheld threshold lies. Or, to avoid the issue altogether, use a tripod.

Freezing action isn't the only way to use shutter speed to creative effect. When shooting waterfalls, for example, most photographers use a very slow shutter speed to give the water even more of a flowing, romantic look than you see in my fountain example. With colorful moving subjects, a slow shutter can produce some cool abstract effects and create a heightened sense of motion. Chapter 9 offers examples of both effects.

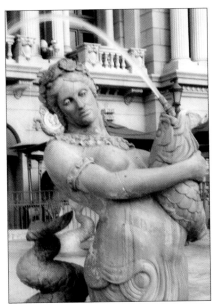

Figure 7-4: If both stationary and moving objects are blurry, camera shake is the usual cause.

ISO affects image noise

As ISO increases, making the image sensor more reactive to light, you increase the risk of producing noise. *Noise* is a defect that looks like sprinkles of sand and is similar in appearance to film *grain,* a defect that often mars pictures taken with high ISO film. Figure 7-5 offers an example.

Ideally, then, you should always use the lowest ISO setting on your camera to ensure top image quality. Sometimes, though, the lighting conditions simply don't permit you to do so and still use the aperture and shutter speeds you need. Take my rose image as an example. When I shot these pictures, I didn't have a tripod, so I needed a shutter speed fast enough to allow a sharp hand-held image. I opened the aperture to f/6.3, which was the maximum on the lens I was using, to allow as much light as possible into the camera. At ISO 100, I needed a shutter speed of 1/40 second to expose the picture, and that shutter speed wasn't fast enough for a successful handheld shot. You see the blurred result on the left in Figure 7-6. By raising the ISO to 200, I was able to use a shutter speed of 1/80 second, which enabled me to capture the flower cleanly, as shown on the right in the figure.

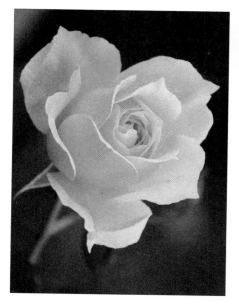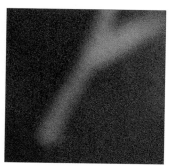

Figure 7-5: Caused by a very high ISO or long exposure time, noise becomes more visible as you enlarge the image.

Fortunately, you don't encounter serious noise on the D7100 until you really crank up the ISO. In fact, you may even be able to get away with a fairly high ISO if you keep your print or display size small. Some people probably wouldn't even notice the noise in the left image in Figure 7-5 unless they were looking for it, for example. But as with other image defects, noise becomes more apparent as you enlarge the photo, as shown on the right in that same figure. Noise is also easier to spot in shadow areas of your picture and in large areas of solid color.

How much noise is acceptable — and, therefore, how high of an ISO is safe — is your choice. Even a little noise isn't acceptable for pictures that require the highest quality, such as images for a product catalog or a travel shot that you want to blow up to poster size.

A high ISO isn't the only cause of noise: A long exposure time (slow shutter speed) can also produce the defect. So, how high you can raise the ISO before the image gets ugly varies, depending on shutter speed.

ISO 100, f/6.3, 1/40 second

ISO 200, f/6.3, 1/80 second

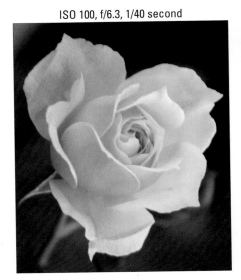 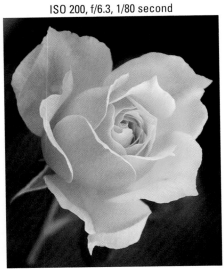

Figure 7-6: For this image, raising the ISO allowed me to bump up shutter speed enough to capture a blur-free shot while handholding the camera.

Doing the exposure balancing act

As you change any of the three exposure settings — aperture, shutter speed, and ISO — one or both of the others must also shift to maintain the same image brightness. Say that you're shooting a soccer game, for example, and you notice that although the overall exposure looks great, the players appear slightly blurry at your current shutter speed. If you raise the shutter speed, you have to compensate with a larger aperture (to allow in more light during the shorter exposure) or a higher ISO setting (to make the camera more sensitive to the light) — or both.

Again, changing these settings impacts your image in ways beyond exposure:

- ✔ Aperture affects depth of field, with a higher f-stop number increasing the distance over which objects appear sharp.
- ✔ Shutter speed affects whether motion of the subject or camera results in a blurry photo. A faster shutter "freezes" action and also helps safeguard against all-over blur that can result from camera shake.
- ✔ ISO affects the camera's sensitivity to light. A higher ISO makes the camera more responsive to light but increases the chance of image noise.

So when you boost that shutter speed to capture your soccer subjects, you have to decide whether you prefer the shorter depth of field that comes with a larger aperture or the increased risk of noise that accompanies a higher ISO.

Everyone has their own approach to finding the right combination of aperture, shutter speed, and ISO, and you'll no doubt develop your own system as you become more practiced at using the advanced exposure modes. In the meantime, here's how I handle things on the D7100:

- ✔ I use ISO 100, the lowest ISO setting on the camera, unless the lighting conditions are so poor that I can't use the aperture and shutter speed I want without raising the ISO.

- ✔ If my subject is moving, I give shutter speed the next highest priority in my exposure decision. I might choose a fast shutter speed to ensure a blur-free photo or, on the flip side, select a slow shutter to intentionally blur the subject, an effect that can create a heightened sense of motion.

- ✔ For stationary subjects, I make aperture a priority over shutter speed, setting the aperture according to the depth of field I have in mind.

Keeping all this straight is a little overwhelming at first, but the more you work with your camera, the more the whole exposure equation will make sense to you. In the meantime, keep moving through this chapter for details on how to actually adjust aperture, shutter speed, and ISO settings and for help with solving exposure problems.

Exploring the Advanced Exposure Modes

In the automatic modes I describe in Chapter 3, you have little control over exposure. You may be able to choose from one or two Flash modes, and you can adjust ISO. To gain full control over exposure, set the Mode dial to one of the advanced modes highlighted in Figure 7-7: P, S, A, or M. You also need to use these modes to take advantage of many other camera features.

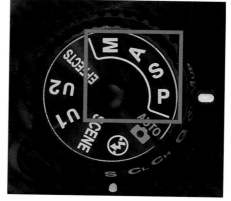

The difference among the four modes is the level of control over aperture and shutter speed, as follows:

Figure 7-7: You can control exposure and certain other picture properties fully only in P, S, A, or M mode.

✔ **P (programmed autoexposure):** In this mode, the camera selects both aperture and shutter speed, but you can choose from different combinations of the two for creative flexibility.

✔ **S (shutter-priority autoexposure):** In this mode, you select a shutter speed, and the camera chooses the aperture setting that produces a good exposure at your selected ISO setting.

✔ **A (aperture-priority autoexposure):** The opposite of shutter-priority autoexposure, this mode asks you to select the aperture setting. The camera then selects the appropriate shutter speed.

✔ **M (manual exposure):** You specify both shutter speed and aperture.

To sum up, the first three modes are semi-automatic exposure modes that are designed to help you get a good exposure while still providing you with some photographic flexibility. Note one important point about the semi-auto modes, however: In extreme lighting conditions, the camera may not be able to select settings that will produce a good exposure, and it doesn't stop you from taking a poorly exposed photo. You may be able to solve the problem by using features designed to modify the autoexposure results, such as Exposure Compensation (explained later in this chapter), but there are no guarantees.

Manual mode puts all exposure control in your hands. If you're a longtime photographer who comes from the days when manual exposure was the only game in town, you may prefer to stick with this mode. If it ain't broke, don't fix it, as they say. And in some ways, manual mode is simpler than the semi-auto modes because if you're not happy with the exposure, you just change the aperture, shutter speed, or ISO setting and shoot again. You don't have to fiddle with features that enable you to modify your autoexposure results.

My personal choice is to use aperture-priority autoexposure when I'm shooting still subjects and want to control depth of field — aperture is my *priority* — and to switch to shutter-priority autoexposure when I'm shooting a moving subject and am most concerned with controlling shutter speed. Frankly, my brain is taxed enough by all the other issues involved in taking pictures — what my Release mode setting is, what resolution I need, where I'm going for lunch as soon as I make this shot work — that I appreciate having the camera do some of the exposure lifting.

However, when I know exactly what aperture and shutter speed I want to use, or I'm after an out-of-the-ordinary exposure, I use manual exposure. For example, sometimes when I'm doing a still life in my studio, I want to create a certain mood by underexposing a subject or even shooting it in silhouette. The camera is always going to fight you on that result in the P, S, and A modes because it so dearly wants to provide a good exposure. Rather than dialing in all the autoexposure tweaks that could eventually force the result I want, I simply set the mode to M, adjust the shutter speed and aperture directly, and give the autoexposure system the afternoon off.

But even in manual mode, you're never really flying without a net: The camera assists you by displaying the exposure meter, explained next.

Reading (And Adjusting) the Meter

To help you determine whether your exposure settings are on cue in M (manual) exposure mode, the camera displays an exposure meter in the viewfinder and Information display. You can see a close-up look at how the meter looks in the viewfinder in Figure 7-8; Figure 7-9 shows you where to find the meter in the Information display. To activate the meter displays, just press the shutter button halfway and then release it.

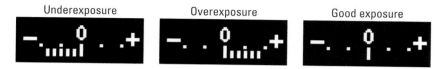

Underexposure   Overexposure   Good exposure

Figure 7-8: The meter indicates whether your exposure settings are on target.

The minus-sign end of the meter represents underexposure; the plus sign, overexposure. So if the little notches on the meter fall to the left of 0, as shown in the first example in Figure 7-8, the image will be underexposed. If the indicator moves to the right of 0, as shown in the second example, the image will be overexposed. The farther the indicator moves toward the plus or minus sign, the greater the potential problem. When the meter shows a balanced exposure, as in the third example, you're good to go.

Exposure meter

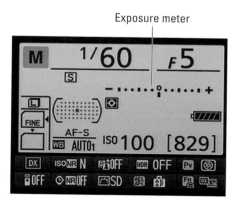

Figure 7-9: In M exposure mode, the exposure meter appears in the Information display.

In the other exposure modes, the meter appears if the camera anticipates an exposure problem. Notches under the meter indicate the extent of the exposure problem, just as in manual mode. In dim lighting, you may also see a blinking flash symbol, which is a not-so-subtle suggestion to add some light to the scene. (You can disable the flash alert through the Flash Warning option on the Custom Setting menu if you like; look for the option in the Shooting/Display section of the menu.)

Keep in mind, too, that the meter's suggestion on exposure may not always be the one you want to follow. For example, you may want to shoot a backlit subject in silhouette, in which case you *want* that subject to be underexposed.

In other words, the meter is a guide, not a dictator. In addition, remember that the exposure information the meter reports is based on the *exposure metering mode,* which determines which part of the frame the camera considers when calculating exposure. At the default setting, exposure is based on the entire frame, but you can select two other metering modes. See the upcoming section "Choosing an Exposure Metering Mode" for details.

If you're so inclined, you can customize the meter in the following ways:

- ✓ **Adjust the meter shutoff timing.** The meter turns on anytime you press the shutter button halfway, but then it turns off automatically if you don't press the button again for a period of time — 6 seconds, by default. You can adjust the shutoff timing through the Standby Timer option, found on the Timers/AE Lock submenu of the Custom Setting menu and shown on the left in Figure 7-10. Choices range from 4 seconds to 30 minutes. You can also disable the auto meter shutdown by choosing No Limit, but remember that the metering system uses battery power, so keeping it active for long periods of time isn't a good move.

- ✓ **Reverse the meter orientation.** For photographers used to a camera that orients the meter with the positive (overexposure) side appearing on the left and the negative (underexposure) side on the right, the D7100 offers the option to flip the meter to that orientation. This option also lies on the Custom Setting menu, on the Controls submenu. Hunt down the Reverse Indicators option, as shown on the right in Figure 7-10. (The setting shown in the figure is the default.)

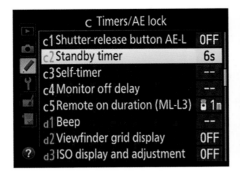
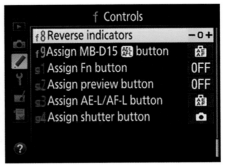

Figure 7-10: You can customize the behavior of the exposure meter.

Setting Aperture, Shutter Speed, and ISO

The next sections detail how to view and adjust these critical exposure settings. For a review of how each setting affects your pictures, check out the first part of this chapter.

Exposure stops: How many do you want to see?

A *stop* is an increment of exposure. To increase exposure by one stop means to adjust the aperture or shutter speed to allow twice as much light into the camera as the current settings permit. To reduce exposure by one stop, you use settings that allow half as much light. Doubling or halving the ISO value also adjusts exposure by one stop.

By default, major exposure settings on the D7100 are based on one-third stop adjustments. For example, when you adjust the Exposure Compensation value, a feature that enables you to request a brighter or darker picture than the camera's autoexposure system thinks is correct, you can choose settings of EV 0.0 (no adjustment), +0.3, +0.7, and +1.0 (one full stop of adjustment).

If you prefer, you can tell the camera to present exposure adjustments in half-stop increments so that you don't have to cycle through as many settings each time you want to make a change.

Make your preferences known through these two options, found in the Metering/Exposure section of the Custom Setting menu. (The menu uses the term *step* instead of *stop*, but the results are the same.) The two settings affect specific exposure components:

- **ISO Sensitivity Step Value:** Affects ISO settings only.
- **EV Steps for Exposure Cntrl (Control):** Affects shutter speed, aperture, Exposure Compensation, Flash Compensation, and exposure bracketing settings. Also determines the increment used to indicate the amount of under- or overexposure in the meter.

The default setting, 1/3 stop, provides the greatest degree of exposure fine-tuning, so I stick with that option. In this book, all instructions assume that you're using the defaults as well.

Adjusting aperture and shutter speed

You can view the current aperture (f-stop) and shutter speed in the Control panel, viewfinder, and Information display, as shown in Figure 7-11. If you don't see the values, the exposure meter isn't awake; to bring it out of its slumber, press the shutter button halfway.

Shutter speed   Aperture (f-stop)

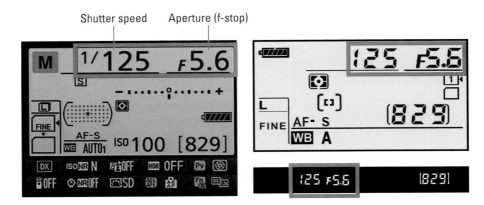

Figure 7-11: You can view the f-stop and shutter speed setting in all three displays.

Before I explain how to select the f-stop and shutter speed, I need to share a few notes about the latter setting:

- **Shutter speeds are presented in the viewfinder and Control panel as whole numbers, even if the shutter speed is set to a fraction of a second.** For example, the number 125 indicates a shutter speed of 1/125 second. When the shutter speed slows to 1 second or longer, quote marks appear after the number — 1" indicates a shutter speed of 1 second, 4" means 4 seconds, and so on.

- **In M (manual) exposure mode, you can access two shutter speed options not available in other modes:**

  - *Bulb:* At this setting, which you access by going one step past the slowest shutter speed (30 seconds), the shutter remains open as long as you hold down the shutter button. Again, you can shoot bulb exposures only in the M (manual) exposure mode. And if you select the bulb setting in M mode and then change to the S (shutter-priority auto) mode, the word *Bulb* flashes in the display to remind you to change to manual exposure. Well, to remind you that something's amiss, anyway.

  - *Time:* This setting, represented by two dashes (- -) in the displays, is related to the ML-L3 wireless remote control. The shutter opens when you press the remote's shutter-release button and stays open for 30 minutes or until you press the button a second time. Remember that to use the remote control, you must set the Remote Control Mode (ML-L3) option on the Shooting menu to On. (You also can enable the option via the Information display control strip.) See Chapter 2 for more about remote-control shooting.

✔ In M and S (shutter-priority autoexposure mode), you also see one shutter speed marked with an x, which indicates the *flash sync speed.* This setting indicates the fastest shutter speed that works with flash. The default flash sync speed is 1/250 second, but you can set another speed through a Custom Setting option. See the later section "Enabling high-speed flash (Auto FP)" for details. If you want to use 1/250 second as your shutter speed, you can select either the x250 setting or the plain ol' 1/250 setting. (The x250 setting appears one setting below the 30 second setting in S mode and one notch below the Time setting in M mode.)

With those tidbits out of the way, the following list tells you how to select the aperture and shutter speed in each exposure mode:

✔ **P (programmed auto):** The camera shows you its recommended f-stop and shutter speed when you press the shutter button halfway, but you can rotate the Main command dial to select a different combination of settings. The number of possible combinations depends upon the aperture settings and shutter speeds the camera can select, which in turn depend on the lighting conditions, your lens, and the ISO setting.

An asterisk (*) appears next to the P symbol in the Information display after you rotate the Main command dial. You also see a P* symbol in the Control panel. These symbols indicate that you adjusted the aperture/shutter speed settings from those the camera initially suggested. To get back to the initial combo of shutter speed and aperture, rotate the Main command dial until the asterisk disappears from the Information display and the P* symbol vanishes from the Control panel.

✔ **S (shutter-priority autoexposure):** Rotate the Main dial to change the shutter speed. As you do, the camera adjusts the aperture as needed to maintain what it considers the proper exposure.

Remember that as the aperture shifts, so does depth of field. So even though you're working in shutter-priority mode, keep an eye on the f-stop, too, if depth of field is important to your photo. Also note that in extreme lighting conditions, the camera may not be able to adjust the aperture enough to produce a good exposure at your current shutter speed — again, possible aperture settings depend on your lens. You may need to compromise on shutter speed or ISO.

✔ **A (aperture-priority autoexposure):** In this mode, you control aperture, and the camera adjusts shutter speed automatically. To set the aperture (f-stop), rotate the Sub-command dial.

When you stop-down the aperture (raise the f-stop value), be careful that the shutter speed doesn't drop so low that you run the risk of camera shake if you're handholding the camera. And if your scene contains moving objects, make sure that the shutter speed that the camera selects is fast enough to stop action (or slow enough to blur it, if that's your creative goal). These same warnings apply when you use P mode.

✔ **M (manual exposure):** In this mode, you select both aperture and shutter speed, like so:

- *To adjust shutter speed:* Rotate the Main command dial.

- *To adjust aperture:* Rotate the Sub-command dial.

If you don't like the exposure that the camera produces in P, S, or A modes, you have two ways to produce a different result:

✔ **Apply Exposure Compensation.** This option tells the camera to produce a darker or lighter exposure on your next shot. See "Applying Exposure Compensation," later in this chapter, for details.

✔ **Select a different metering mode.** The Metering mode setting tells the camera which part of the frame to consider when setting exposure; by default, the entire frame is used. I explain this option a couple sections down the road, too.

Of course, you can always simply switch to M mode and dial in the f-stop and shutter speed that deliver the exposure you want, too. Also check out the later sections related to Active D-Lighting and HDR mode for some exposure-tweaking features designed for shooting high-contrast subjects; these features work for M mode as well as P, S, and A modes.

Controlling ISO

The ISO Sensitivity setting determines how much the image sensor reacts to light and, therefore, how much light you need to expose the picture. At a higher ISO, you can use a faster shutter speed or a smaller aperture (higher f-stop number) because less light is needed. A higher ISO also increases the possibility of noise, though, as illustrated earlier in Figure 7-5.

You can choose ISO values ranging from 100 to 6400 plus several additional settings at the upper limit: Hi 0.3, Hi 0.7, Hi 1, and Hi 2; which translate to ISO values ranging from 8000 to 25600. At the Hi settings, of course, you can expect increased image noise, so avoid using those settings unless you have no other way to get the shot.

In addition to selecting a specific ISO setting, you have the option of choosing Auto ISO. At this setting, the camera selects the ISO needed to expose the picture at the current shutter speed and aperture.

You can view the ISO setting in the Information display, as shown on the left in Figure 7-12. But the Control panel and viewfinder show the ISO setting *only* when Auto ISO is enabled. At other settings, press the ISO button to hide all other data but the ISO value in the Control panel and to replace the shots remaining value with the ISO setting, as shown on the right in the figure.

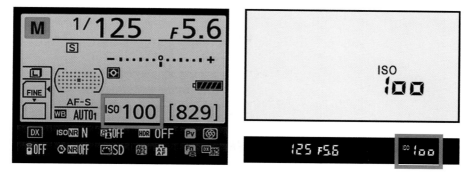

Figure 7-12: Press the ISO button while rotating the Main command dial to adjust ISO.

You can adjust the setting in two ways:

- **ISO button:** While pressing the button, use these techniques to select a setting, depending on your exposure mode:

  - *Auto, Auto Flash Off, Scene, and Effects modes:* Rotate the Main command dial.

  - *P, S, A, and M modes:* Rotate the Main command dial to select any ISO setting but Auto; rotate the Sub-command dial to toggle Auto ISO on and off.

- **Shooting menu:** Select ISO Sensitivity Settings, as shown on the left in Figure 7-13, and then choose ISO Sensitivity, as shown on the right. Again, things work differently depending on your exposure mode; the settings shown on the second screen of the figure are available in the P, S, A, and M modes only. In other modes, the ISO Sensitivity option is available but the others are off-limits.

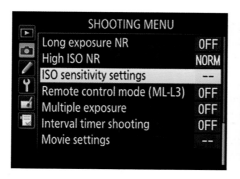 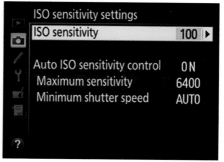

Figure 7-13: You can access additional ISO options through the Shooting menu.

A few fine points about using Auto ISO:

- ✏ **Auto ISO in the fully automatic exposure modes:** In Auto, Auto Flash Off, Scene, and Effects modes, the camera selects the ISO for you.

- ✏ **Auto ISO in P, S, A, and M modes:** In these modes, you can enable Auto ISO as sort of a safety net. Here's how it works: You dial in a specific ISO setting — say, ISO 100. If the camera decides that it can't expose the image at that ISO given your current aperture and shutter speed, it automatically adjusts ISO as necessary.

Even better, you can tell the camera exactly when and how it should step in and offer ISO assistance. Put in your order via the ISO Sensitivity Settings option on the Shooting menu. First turn Auto ISO Sensitivity Control to On, as shown in Figure 7-14. You can then gain access to the two options that set the Auto ISO limits, which work as follows:

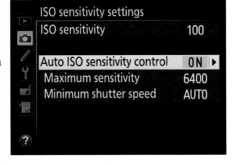

Figure 7-14: In P, S, A, and M modes, you can set limits for Auto ISO override.

- • *Maximum Sensitivity:* Specify the highest ISO setting the camera may select when it overrides your ISO decision.

- • *Minimum Shutter Speed:* Set the minimum shutter speed at which the ISO override engages. At the Auto setting, the camera selects the minimum shutter speed for override based on the focal length of your lens, the idea being that with a longer lens, you need a faster shutter speed to avoid the blur that camera shake can cause when you handhold the camera. However, exposure is given priority over camera-shake considerations, so if the camera can't expose the picture at what it thinks is a safe shutter speed for the lens focal length, it will use a slower speed.

If the camera is about to override your ISO setting, it alerts you by blinking an ISO-Auto label in the displays. And in playback mode, the ISO value appears in red if you view your photos in a display mode that includes the ISO value. (Chapter 5 has details.)

You'd think that with a setting as seemingly simple as ISO, that would be the end of your options, but there's actually one more: ISO Display and Adjustment, found in the Shooting/Display section of the Custom Setting menu and shown in Figure 7-15. This option affects the display of the ISO setting in the Control panel.

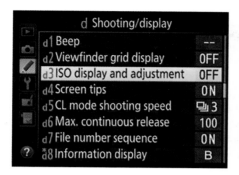
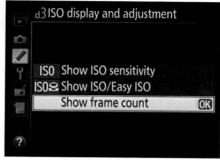

Figure 7-15: This option lets you replace the shots remaining value in the Control panel with the current ISO setting.

The options work as follows:

- ✓ **Show ISO Sensitivity:** The ISO setting takes the place of the shots remaining value in the Control panel so that you can view the ISO setting without pressing the ISO button. Of course, then you have to look at the Information display or viewfinder to see the shots remaining value — not, in my opinion, a good tradeoff.

- ✓ **Show ISO/Easy ISO:** The ISO setting takes the place of the shots remaining value in the Control panel, as with menu option 1. The Easy ISO part of the name means that you can adjust ISO in P and S exposure modes by simply rotating the Sub-command dial and in A mode by rotating the Main command dial. You don't have to press the ISO button to change the setting. Again, not a great choice, in my opinion: It's too easy to forget that this function is enabled and accidentally change the ISO setting without realizing it.

- ✓ **Show Frame Count:** This setting is the default (and I recommend sticking with it). The shots remaining value tells you how many more pictures will fit on your memory card, and you press the ISO button to display the ISO value in the Control panel.

Choosing an Exposure Metering Mode

To fully interpret what your exposure meter tells you, you need to know which *metering mode* is active. The metering mode determines which part of the frame the camera analyzes to calculate the proper exposure. The metering mode affects more than the meter, however: It also determines the exposure settings that the camera selects for you when you shoot in the P, S, and A exposure modes as well as in the fully automatic exposure modes.

Dampening noise

High ISO settings and long exposure times can result in *noise,* the digital defect that gives your pictures a speckled look. (Refer to Figure 7-5.) To help solve the problem, your camera offers two noise-removal filters:

✔ **High ISO Noise Reduction** is designed to reduce the appearance of ISO-related noise.

✔ **Long Exposure Noise Reduction** dampens noise that occurs during long exposures.

You can enable both filters through the Information display strip, as shown on the left in the figure here. (To activate the strip, press the *i* button.) In the figure, the Long Exposure Noise Reduction filter is active; the High ISO Noise Reduction filter lives directly upstairs. You also can access both filters via the Shooting menu, as shown in the right figure here.

If you turn on Long Exposure Noise Reduction, noise removal is applied to pictures taken at shutter speeds of longer than 1 second. For High ISO Noise Reduction, you can choose from four settings: the High, Normal, and Low

settings let you control the strength of the noise-removal effect; at the fourth setting, Off, the camera actually still applies a tiny amount of noise removal, but only at ISO 1250 or higher.

Be aware that both features have a few disadvantages. First, the filters are applied after you take the picture, as the camera processes the image data. While the Long Exposure Noise Reduction filter is being applied, the message *Job Nr* appears in the viewfinder and Control panel. The time needed to apply this filter can significantly slow down your shooting speed — in fact, it can double the time the camera needs to record the file to the memory card.

Second, although filters that go after long-exposure noise work fairly well, those that attack high ISO noise work primarily by applying a slight blur to the image. Don't expect this process to totally eliminate noise, and do expect some resulting image softness. You may be able to get better results by using the blur tools or noise-removal filters found in many photo editors because you can retouch just the areas where noise is most noticeable.

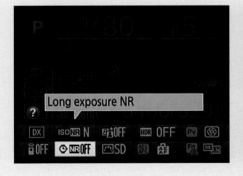

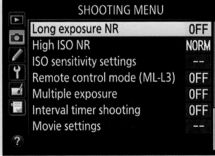

In the P, S, A, and M modes, you can adjust the metering mode by pressing the Metering button (top of the camera) while rotating the Main command dial. An icon representing the current metering mode appears in the Information display and Control panel, as shown in Figure 7-16.

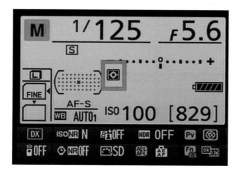 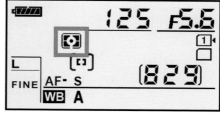

Figure 7-16: This symbol represents the matrix metering mode.

Your camera offers three metering modes, represented by the icons you see in the margins here:

 ✔ **Matrix:** The camera bases exposure on the entire frame. This setting is the default for the P, S, A, and M exposure modes and is the only option when you shoot in any other exposure mode (Auto, Scene, and so on).

 ✔ **Spot:** In this mode, the camera bases exposure on a circular area about 3.5mm in diameter. Exactly which part of the frame that circle covers depends on focus settings that I detail in Chapter 8:

- • If you use autofocusing and set the AF-area mode to Auto Area, in which the camera chooses the focus point for you, exposure is based on the center focus point.

- • When you use the other AF-area mode settings or manual focusing, you use the Multi Selector to select a focus point, and the camera bases metering on that point.

 ✔ **Center-weighted:** A blend of matrix and spot metering, this mode bases exposure on the entire frame but puts extra emphasis — or *weight* — on the center of the frame.

Normally, the area that's given priority in this mode is about 8mm in diameter. You can alter the critical metering area through the Center-Weighted Area option, found in the Metering/Exposure section of the Custom Setting menu and shown in Figure 7-17. You can change the size of the metering circle to 6mm, 10mm, 13mm. (The menu option is available only when the Mode dial is set to P, S, A, or M.)

The Center-Weighted Area option also offers an Avg setting, which tells the camera to take a reading of the entire frame and then base exposure on the average brightness values it sees. The difference between this option and the Matrix setting is that Matrix is based on a newer, more capable technology, whereas Avg is based on a system used in earlier Nikon cameras. Longtime Nikon shooters who are familiar with this metering option may appreciate its inclusion, but the matrix system typically delivers a better exposure if you're concerned about objects throughout the frame, so I suggest that you stick with that when you want to expose the photo with the entire frame in mind.

b Metering/exposure	
b1 ISO sensitivity step value	1/3
b2 EV steps for exposure cntrl	1/3
b3 Easy exposure compensation	OFF
b4 Center-weighted area	(•) 8
b5 Fine-tune optimal exposure	--
c1 Shutter-release button AE-L	OFF
c2 Standby timer	6s
c3 Self-timer	--

Figure 7-17: You can customize the center-weighted metering area.

As an example of how metering mode affects exposure, Figure 7-18 shows the same image captured at each mode. In the matrix example, the bright background caused the camera to select an exposure that left the statue quite dark. Switching to center-weighted metering helped somewhat but didn't quite bring the statue out of the shadows. Spot metering produced the best result as far as the statue goes, although the resulting increase in exposure left the sky and background monument a little washed out.

Matrix metering   Center-weighted metering   Spot metering

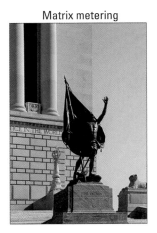 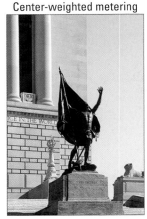 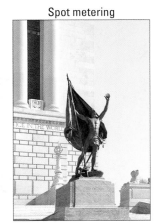

Figure 7-18: Spot and center-weighted metering can produce a better exposure of backlit subjects.

In theory, the best practice is to check the metering mode before you shoot and choose the one that best matches your exposure goals. But that's a pain, not just in terms of having to adjust yet one more setting but in terms of having to *remember* to adjust one more setting. So until you're comfortable with all the other exposure controls on your camera, just stick with matrix metering. If your subject turns out to be under- or overexposed, you can try again using spot or center-weighted metering or, as an alternative, stick with matrix metering and instead use Exposure Compensation and the other options that I outline in the next section to tweak exposure.

One final point about metering: The FineTune Optimal Exposure option, found on the Metering/Exposure submenu of the Custom Setting menu, enables you to fiddle with the metering system beyond just specifying the size of the center-weighted metering area. For each metering mode, you can specify that you always want a brighter or darker exposure than what Nikon's engineers determined to be optimal when developing the camera. In essence, you're recalibrating the meter. Although it's nice to have this level of control, I advise against making this adjustment. It's sort of like reengineering your oven so that it heats to 300 degrees when the dial is set to 325 degrees — it's easy to forget that you made the shift and not be able to figure out why your exposure settings aren't delivering the results you expected. If your camera consistently under- or overexposes your pictures when you use the semi-automatic exposure modes (P, S, or A) or fully auto modes, it may be time for a service check at your local camera-repair shop.

Sorting through Your Camera's Exposure-Correction Tools

In addition to the normal controls over aperture, shutter speed, ISO, and metering mode, your camera offers tools that enable you to solve exposure problems. The next several sections introduce you to these features.

Applying Exposure Compensation

When you shoot in the P, S, or A modes, the camera automatically selects settings that it thinks will produce a proper exposure. If you don't agree with the result, you can force a darker or brighter exposure on your next shot by using *Exposure Compensation.* As an example, see the first image in Figure 7-19. The initial exposure selected by the camera left the balloon too dark; I used Exposure Compensation to produce the brighter exposure on the right.

EV 0.0 EV +1.0

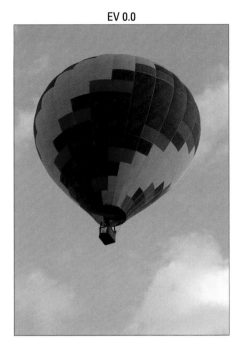 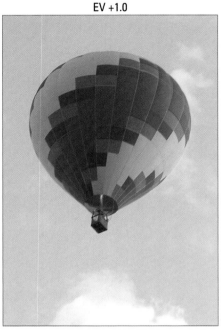

Figure 7-19: For a brighter exposure, raise the Exposure Compensation value.

 To apply Exposure Compensation, hold down the Exposure Compensation button, found near the shutter button. All data except the Exposure Compensation value disappears from the Control panel and is dimmed in the Information display. In the viewfinder, the Shots Remaining value is replaced by the Exposure Compensation value. While holding the button, rotate the Main command dial to adjust the value. The exposure meter reflects your change as you adjust the value.

Here's what you need to know to make sense of the numbers:

- Exposure Compensation settings are stated in terms of EV values, as in EV +2.0. Possible values range from EV +5.0 to EV –5.0. (*EV* stands for *exposure value.*)

    Each full number on the EV scale represents an exposure shift of one stop. See the earlier sidebar "Exposure stops: How many do you want to see?" to see how you can tweak the increments of EV adjustment the camera offers.

- A setting of EV 0.0 results in no exposure adjustment.

- For a brighter image, raise the EV value; for a darker image, lower the EV value.

After you release the Exposure Compensation button, the 0 on the meter blinks to remind you that Exposure Compensation is active, and the meter indicates the amount of compensation in force. For example, in the left screen in Figure 7-20, the meter indicates an adjustment of EV +1.0. (If you have difficulty making out the meter reading, press the Exposure Compensation button again to view the numerical value in the displays.) You also see a little plus/minus symbol (the same one that decorates the Exposure Compensation button) in the Control panel and Information display, labeled in the figure.

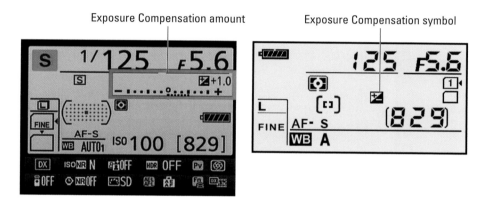

Figure 7-20: The plus/minus symbol tells you that Exposure Compensation is being applied.

Your Exposure Compensation setting remains in force until you change it, even if you power off the camera, so you may want to make a habit of checking the setting before each shoot or always setting the value back to EV 0.0 after taking the last shot for which you want to apply compensation.

A few other tips about using Exposure Compensation:

✔ How the camera arrives at the brighter or darker image depends on the exposure mode:

- *In A (aperture-priority autoexposure) mode,* the camera adjusts the shutter speed but leaves your selected f-stop in force.

- *In S (shutter-priority autoexposure) mode,* the opposite occurs: The camera opens or stops down the aperture, leaving your selected shutter speed alone.

- *In P (programmed autoexposure) mode,* the camera decides whether to adjust aperture, shutter speed, or both.

- *In all three modes,* the camera may also adjust ISO if you have Auto ISO Sensitivity Control enabled.

Don't forget that the camera can adjust f-stop only so much, according to the aperture range of your lens. And the range of shutter speeds, too, is limited by the camera itself, although you're not likely to reach those limits on the D7100, which offers speeds from 30 seconds to 1/8000 second. If you hit the aperture or shutter speed wall, you either have to compromise on shutter speed or aperture or adjust ISO.

✔ When you use flash, the Exposure Compensation setting affects both background brightness and flash power by default, but you have the option to disable the setting's effect on flash. Pull up the Bracketing/ Flash section of the Custom Setting menu and look for the Exposure Comp for Flash setting, shown in Figure 7-21. If you don't want flash output to be affected by the Exposure Compensation setting, choose Background Only as the setting. You can then adjust flash power if needed via the Flash Compensation setting, explained in the upcoming section "Adjusting flash output."

✔ The Metering/Exposure section of the Custom Setting menu contains an Easy Exposure Compensation option. If you enable this feature, you can adjust the Exposure Compensation setting in the P and S exposure modes simply by rotating the Sub-command dial. In A exposure mode, you use the Main command dial instead of the Sub-command dial (because you use the Sub-command dial in A mode to adjust the f-stop). I don't recommend enabling this feature: You can easily rotate the dials by mistake and not realize that you adjusted the setting.

✔ If you don't want to fiddle with Exposure Compensation, just switch to manual exposure mode and select whatever aperture and shutter speed settings produce the exposure you're after. Start with the settings selected by the camera in the autoexposure mode you were using and then just go from there. Exposure Compensation has no effect on manual exposures; again, that adjustment is made only in the P, S, and A modes.

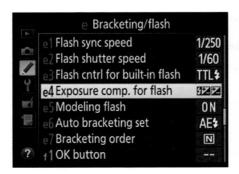
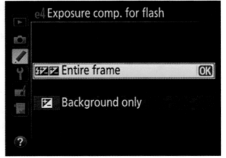

Figure 7-21: This setting determines whether Exposure Compensation affects flash output in flash photos.

Although the camera doesn't change your selected exposure settings in manual mode if Exposure Compensation is enabled, the exposure meter is affected by the current setting, which can lead to some confusion. The meter indicates whether your shot will be properly exposed based on the Exposure Compensation setting. So if you don't realize that Exposure Compensation is enabled, you may mistakenly adjust your exposure settings when they're actually on target for your subject. This is yet another reason why it's best to always reset the Exposure Compensation setting back to EV 0.0 after you're done using that feature.

Using Autoexposure Lock

To help ensure a proper exposure, your camera continually meters the light in a scene until the moment you depress the shutter button fully and capture the image. In autoexposure modes — that is, any mode but M — it also keeps adjusting exposure settings as needed to maintain a good exposure.

For most situations, this approach works great, resulting in the right settings for the light that's striking your subject at the moment you capture the image. On occasion, though, you may want to lock in exposure settings. For example, perhaps you want your subject to appear at the far edge of the frame. If you were to use the normal shooting technique, you'd place the subject under a focus point, press the shutter button halfway to lock focus and set the initial exposure, and then reframe to your desired composition to take the shot. The problem is that exposure is then recalculated based on the new framing, which can leave your subject under- or overexposed.

The easiest way to lock exposure settings is to switch to M (manual) exposure mode and use the f-stop, shutter speed, and ISO settings that work best for your subject. If you prefer to stay in P, S, or A mode, you can press the AE-L/AF-L button to lock exposure and focus before you reframe. By keeping the button pressed between shots, you can even keep using the same exposure and focus for a series of photographs. Here's the technique I recommend:

1. **Set the metering mode to spot metering.**

   Press the Metering button while rotating the Main command dial to change the setting.

2. **If autofocusing, set the Autofocus mode to AF-S and the AF-area mode to Single Point.**

   Press the AF-mode button and rotate the Main command dial to change the Autofocus mode; press the button while spinning the Sub-command dial to change the AF-area mode. (The AF-mode button is the unmarked button at the center of the Focus-mode selector on the left front side of the camera.)

   When using these autofocus settings or manual focusing, you see a single focus point in the viewfinder.

3. **Use the Multi Selector to move the focus point over your subject.**

You may need to press the shutter button halfway and release it to activate the exposure meters before you can do so. Also, be sure that the Focus Selector Lock switch on back of the camera is set to the white dot and not the L position. Otherwise, you can't adjust the focus point.

In spot-metering mode, the focus point determines the area used to calculate exposure, so this step is critical whether you use autofocusing or manual focusing.

4. **Press the shutter button halfway.**

The camera sets the initial exposure settings. If you're using autofocusing, focus is also set at this point. For manual focusing, turn the focusing ring on the lens to bring the subject into focus.

5. **Press and hold the AE-L/AF-L button.**

This button sits just to the right of the viewfinder. While the button is pressed, the letters AE-L appear at the left end of the viewfinder.

By default, focus is locked at the same time if you're using autofocusing. You can change this behavior by customizing the AE-L/AF-L button function, as outlined in Chapter 11.

6. **Reframe the shot if desired and take the photo.**

Be sure to keep holding the AE-L/AF-L button until you release the shutter button! And if you want to use the same focus and exposure settings for your next shot, just keep the AE-L/AF-L button pressed.

Expanding tonal range with Active D-Lighting

A scene like the one in Figure 7-22 presents a classic challenge: Choosing exposure settings that capture the darkest parts of the subject appropriately causes the brightest areas to be overexposed. And if you instead *expose for the highlights* — that is, set the exposure settings to capture the brightest regions properly — the darker areas are underexposed.

In the past, you had to choose between favoring the highlights or the shadows. But thanks to Active D-Lighting, you have a better chance of keeping your highlights intact while better exposing the darkest areas. To put it another way, you can expand the *tonal range,* or *dynamic range,* of the image, which are two different terms used to describe the range of brightness values in an image.

Active D-Lighting off

Active D-Lighting Auto

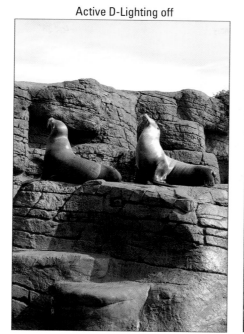 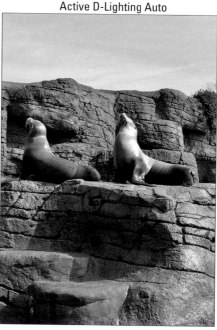

Figure 7-22: Active D-Lighting captured the shadows without blowing out the highlights.

In my seal scene, turning on Active D-Lighting produced a brighter rendition of the darkest parts of the rocks and the seals, for example, and yet the color in the sky didn't get blown out as it did when I captured the image with Active D-Lighting turned off. The highlights in the seal and in the rocks on the lower-right corner of the image also are toned down a tad in the Active D-Lighting version.

Active D-Lighting does its thing in two stages. First, it selects exposure settings that result in a slightly darker exposure than normal. This half of the equation guarantees that you retain details in your highlights. After you snap the photo, the camera brightens the darkest areas of the image. This adjustment rescues shadow detail.

In Auto, Auto Flash Off, Scene, and Effects modes, the camera decides how much Active D-Lighting adjustment is needed. In the P, S, A, and M modes, you can specify the amount of adjustment in two ways:

✔ **Information display control strip:** Press the I button to activate the control strip. Then use the Multi Selector to highlight the Active D-Lighting icon, as shown in Figure 7-23, and press OK.

✔ **Shooting menu:** Select Active D-Lighting from the Shooting menu, as shown on the left in Figure 7-24. Press OK.

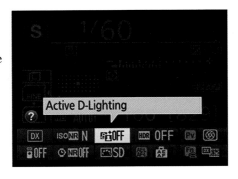

Figure 7-23: The fastest route to the Active D-Lighting option is via the Information display control strip.

Either way, you're taken to the screen shown on the right in Figure 7-24, where you can set the adjustment level. At the Auto setting, the camera determines how much adjustment is needed. I used this setting for the seal photo in Figure 7-22. If you prefer to take control, you can select from Extra High, High, Normal, and Low. Choose Off to disable the adjustment.

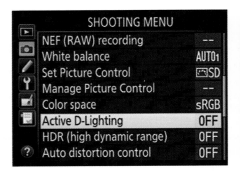
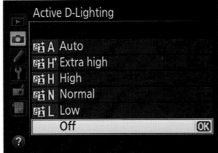

Figure 7-24: At the Auto setting, the camera automatically applies the amount of Active D-Lighting adjustment as it sees fit.

Off is the default setting for the P, S, A, and M modes, and that's the option I recommend. I prefer to decide for each subject whether I want any adjustment rather than having the camera apply it to every shot. And even with a high-contrast scene that's designed for the Active D-Lighting feature, you may prefer the contrasty look that results from disabling the option.

A few other pointers:

✔ The Active D-Lighting symbol in the control strip shows you the current setting. In the Control panel, you see the letters ADL next to the metering mode symbol at any setting but Off, but the symbol doesn't tell you what setting is in force (Auto, High, and so on).

- You get the best Active D-Lighting results in matrix metering mode.

- In the M exposure mode, the camera doesn't change your shutter speed or f-stop to achieve the darker exposure it needs for Active D-Lighting to work; instead, the meter readout guides you to select the right settings unless you have automatic ISO override enabled. In that case, the camera may instead adjust ISO to manipulate the exposure.

- You can't use Active D-Lighting at ISO Hi 0.3 or above or when shooting movies.

- If you're not sure how much adjustment to apply, try Active D-Lighting bracketing, which automatically records the scene using different adjustment levels. See the last section in this chapter for details.

- The Retouch menu offers a D-Lighting filter that applies a similar adjustment to existing pictures. (See Chapter 10 for help.) Some photo-editing programs, including Nikon ViewNX 2, which ships with your camera, also have good shadow and highlight recovery filters. In either case, when you shoot with Active D-Lighting disabled, you're better off choosing exposure settings that will record the highlights as you want them. It's difficult to bring back lost highlight detail after the fact, but you typically can unearth at least a little detail from the shadows.

Exploring high dynamic range (HDR) photography

In the past few years, many photographers have been experimenting with a technology called high dynamic range (HDR) photography. *Dynamic range* refers to the spectrum of brightness values that a camera or other imaging device can record. The idea behind HDR is to capture the same shot multiple times, using different exposure settings for each image. You then use special imaging software — *tone-mapping* software — to combine the exposures in a way that uses specific brightness values from each shot to create a merged image with a much higher dynamic range than the camera can capture in a single frame.

 Your camera offers an HDR option designed to let you enjoy HDR photography without having to mess with any special software. When you enable the feature, the camera automatically records two images, each at different exposure settings, and then does the tone-mapping manipulation for you to produce a single HDR image.

So how is HDR different from Active D-Lighting, other than the fact that it records two photos instead of manipulating a single capture? Well, with the HDR feature, you can request an exposure shift of up to three stops between the two photos. That enables you to create an image that has a broader dynamic range than you can get with Active D-Lighting.

Figure 7-25 shows an example of the type of results you can expect. In this scene, half of the area is in bright sunshine, and the other is in shadow. For the top-left photo in the figure, I exposed for the highlights, which left the right side of the scene too dark. For the top-right image, I set exposure for the shaded area, which blew out the highlights in the sunny areas. When snapping the third image, I enabled the HDR feature, setting the option to a three-stop adjustment. The shadows aren't completely eliminated, and some parts of the rose bush on the left side of the shot are a little brighter than I want, but on the whole, the camera balanced out the exposure fairly well.

Before you get too excited about the HDR feature, however, note these points:

- ✔ Because the camera records and merges two photos, the feature works well only on stationary subjects. If the subject is moving, it will appear as two translucent forms in different areas in the merged frame.

- ✔ Use a tripod to make sure that you don't move the camera between shots.

- ✔ You can't use the HDR feature if you set the Image Quality option to Raw (NEF) or Raw+JPEG. It works only for JPEG photos.

- ✔ The following features also are incompatible with HDR: flash, autobracketing, movie recording, bulb and time shutter speeds, multiple exposure, and time-lapse photography.

Exposed for highlights

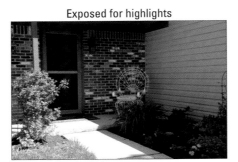

Exposed for shadows

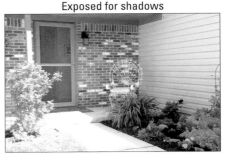

HDR, Extra High

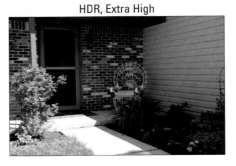

Figure 7-25: HDR enables you to produce an image with an even greater tonal range than Active D-Lighting.

More critically, if you want to do "real" HDR imagery — and by that, I mean the type you see in photography and art magazines — you need to go beyond the two-frame, three-stop limitations of the in-camera HDR feature. Just to give you a point of comparison, Figure 7-26 shows an example that I created by blending five frames with a variation of five stops between frames. The first two images show you the brightest and darkest exposures; the bottom image shows the HDR composite.

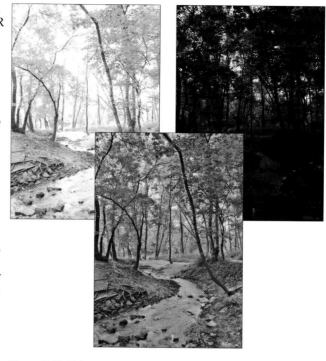

Figure 7-26: Using HDR software tools, I merged the brightest and darkest exposures (top) along with several intermediate exposures, to produce the composite image (bottom).

On the other hand, the effect created by the camera's HDR tool looks more realistic than the one in Figure 7-26 because the tonal range isn't stretched to such an extent. When applied to its extreme limits, HDR produces images that have something of a graphic-novel look. My example in Figure 7-26 is pretty tame; some people might not even realize that any digital trickery has been involved. To me, it has the look of a hand-tinted photo.

And of course, even though the in-camera HDR tool may not be enough to produce the surreal HDR look that's all the rage these days, you can still use your camera for HDR work — you just have to adjust the exposure settings yourself between shots and then merge the frames using your own HDR software. Shoot the images in the Raw format because HDR tone-mapping tools work best on Raw images, which contain more bits of picture data than JPEG files.

To try out the version of HDR on the D7100, take these steps:

1. **Access the HDR feature using one of these techniques:**

   - Press the *i* button to activate the Information display control strip and then highlight the HDR option, as shown on the left in Figure 7-27.

   - Open the Shooting menu and highlight the HDR option, as shown on the right in the figure.

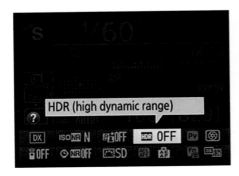

Figure 7-27: You can access the HDR feature from the control strip (left) or Shooting menu (right).

2. **Press OK to display the screen shown in Figure 7-28.**

3. **Select your HDR settings, as follows:**

   - *HDR Mode:* Select On (Series) to enable HDR for all shots until you disable the feature. Choose On (Single Photo) to enable the option for just your next shot. Choose Off to disable the feature.

   - *HDR Strength:* You can choose from four levels of HDR exposure shift: Low, Normal, High, or Extra High. Choose Extra High for the 3-stop exposure maximum. I used this setting to produce the image in Figure 7-25. At the Auto setting, the camera chooses what it considers the best adjustment. However, when a metering mode other than Matrix is in effect, choosing Auto results in the same adjustment you get at the Normal setting.

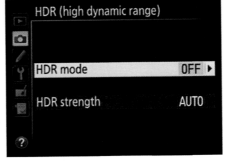

Figure 7-28: Set up your HDR session via these menu options.

4. **Press the shutter button halfway and release it to exit the menu screen.**

   The letters *HDR* appear in the Control panel, and if you press the shutter button halfway, they appear in the shots remaining area of the viewfinder. The Information display indicates the HDR Strength setting.

5. **Select the exposure settings and other picture settings as usual.**

6. **Frame, focus, and shoot.**

   Frame your subject a little loosely; the camera may need to trim the edges of the frame to perfectly align the two shots in the HDR image.

   The camera records two frames in quick succession and then creates the merged HDR image.

Working with Flash

Sometimes, no amount of fiddling with aperture, shutter speed, and ISO produces a bright-enough exposure — in which case, you simply have to add light. Your camera's built-in flash offers the most convenient solution, but you can also attach an external flash to the camera's hot shoe, labeled in Figure 7-29. (When you first take the camera out of the box, the contacts on the shoe are protected by a little cover; remove the cover to attach a flash.)

How much flash control you have depends on your exposure mode:

Flash button   Hot shoe

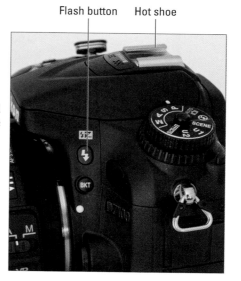

Figure 7-29: Press the Flash button to pop up the built-in flash in the P, S, A, and M exposure modes.

✔ **Auto, Scene, and Effects modes:** With one exception, the Food Scene mode, these modes all feature automatic flash, meaning that in dim lighting, the camera automatically raises and fires the built-in flash (assuming that an external flash isn't attached, in which case popping up the built-in flash would deliver a nasty punch in the nose). Regardless of whether you're relying on the onboard flash or an external unit, you may be able to choose from a couple of Flash modes, but other flash controls are roped off. And certain Scene and Effects modes disable flash.

✔ **P, S, A, and M modes and the Food Scene mode:** In these modes, you take total control over flash. If you want to use the built-in flash, press the Flash button, also labeled in Figure 7-29. To go flash-free, just press the top of the flash unit gently down to close it.

Even in these modes, however, the camera displays a blinking flash (lightning bolt) symbol in the viewfinder if it thinks you're off your rocker not to use flash. Find that feature annoying? You can disable it via the Flash Warning option on the Custom Setting menu. Look for the option in the Shooting/Display section of the menu. (You have to set the Mode dial to P, S, A, or M to access the setting.)

Chapter 3 offers help with using the flash in the Auto and Scene modes; the rest of this chapter digs into features available in the P, S, A, and M modes.

Setting the Flash mode

Whether you're using the built-in flash or an external flash, you can choose from several Flash modes. This setting determines the timing of the flash and also affects how much of the picture is exposed by ambient light and how much is lit by the flash.

To set the mode, press the Flash button while rotating the Main command dial. As soon as you press the button, the Information display and Control panel change to show an icon representing the Flash mode and, in P, S, A, and M exposure modes, the Flash Compensation value, as shown in Figure 7-30. (Flash Compensation enables you to adjust flash power; look for details later in this chapter.) In the viewfinder, you see the Flash Compensation value plus a lightning bolt icon indicating that flash is ready to fire.

Flash mode   Flash Compensation setting

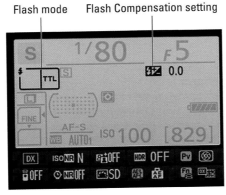

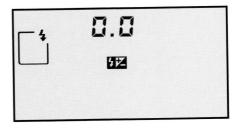

Figure 7-30: Press the Flash button while rotating the Main command dial to change the Flash mode.

Finding more flashes of inspiration

Although this book gets you started with flash photography, there's much more to the topic than I have room to cover. Here are my favorite resources for delving more deeply into the topic:

✔ The Nikon United States website (www.nikonusa.com) offers great tutorials on flash photography. Start in the Learn & Explore section of the site.

✔ At Strobist online, a website completely dedicated to flash photography, www.strobist.blogspot.com,

you can learn from and share with other photographers.

✔ You can find several good books detailing the entire Nikon flash system, which it calls the Creative Lighting System (CLS, for short). This system is designed to enable you to light subjects with multiple flash heads and then control all the flashes with one main unit. The built-in flash on your camera can serve as the CLS controller; see the upcoming section, "Enabling manual, repeating, or commander-mode flash," for details.

The Flash mode icon shown in the Information display in Figure 7-30 reflects the current setting of the Flash Cntrl for Built-in Flash menu option, shown in Figure 7-31. The option lives in the Bracketing/Flash suburb of the Custom Setting menu. For normal flash, stick with the default setting, TTL, as shown in the figure. TTL — *through-the-lens* — refers to the fact that the camera bases the necessary flash power on the amount of light actually coming through the lens. For a look at what the other options do, see the upcoming section "Enabling manual, repeating, or commander-mode flash."

e Bracketing/flash	
e1 Flash sync speed	1/250
e2 Flash shutter speed	1/60
e3 Flash cntrl for built-in flash	TTL⚡
e4 Exposure comp. for flash	⚡🔲
e5 Modeling flash	ON
e6 Auto bracketing set	AE⚡
e7 Bracketing order	N
f1 OK button	--

Figure 7-31: For normal flash operation, set this menu item to TTL.

In the P, S, A, and M exposure modes, your Flash mode choices break down into three basic categories, described in the next sections: normal flash; Red-Eye Reduction flash; and the special-purpose sync modes, Slow-Sync and Rear-Sync. In the Auto exposure mode, you have access to the first two flash options although they go by different names (Auto and Auto with Red-Eye Reduction), and the camera fires the flash only if the ambient light is sufficiently dim. In the Scene and Effects modes, flash choices depend on the scene or effect you choose, so see Chapters 3 and 10, respectively, for details.

Normal flash (Front-Curtain Sync)

For normal flash, select the setting represented in the Control panel by the symbol you see in the margin here. The symbol looks nearly the same in the Information display, but includes the letters TTL. (Refer to Figure 7-30).

This mode is officially named *Front-Curtain Sync,* which refers to how the flash is synchronized with the opening of the shutter. Here's the deal: The D7100 uses a type of shutter that involves two curtains moving across the frame each time you press and release the shutter button. When you press the shutter button, the first curtain opens, allowing light through to the sensor. At the end of the exposure, the second curtain draws across the frame to once again shield the sensor from light. With Front-Curtain Sync, the flash fires when the front curtain opens. This arrangement produces normal flash exposures. *Rear-Curtain Sync,* in which the flash fires at the end of the exposure, is a special-effects Flash mode, as illustrated later in this chapter.

Although most people think of flash as a tool to use only in dim lighting, it can improve outdoor photos taken in strong daylight, too. After all, your main light source — the sun — is overhead, so although the top of the subject may be adequately lit, the front typically needs some additional illumination. As an example, Figure 7-32 shows a floral image taken both with and without a flash. For outdoor portraits, a flash is even more important, especially if your subject is wearing a hat, which throws shade on the face. (See Chapter 9 for more tips on using flash for portraits.)

A few complications arise when you use flash in bright light, however:

> ✔ **You may need to stop-down the aperture or lower ISO to avoid overexposing the photo.** Because of how the camera needs to synchronize the firing of the flash with the opening of the shutter, the fastest shutter speed you can use with the built-in flash by default is 1/250 second. The upcoming section "Enabling high-speed flash (Auto FP)" explains how you can raise the top shutter speed to 1/320 for the built-in flash, but even so, you may need to stop-down the aperture significantly or lower the ISO setting to avoid overexposing the image when shooting in bright sun. When you use some external flash units, you can set the flash to sync at any shutter speed.
>
> As another option, you can place a neutral density filter over your lens; this accessory reduces the light that comes through the lens without affecting colors. Of course, if possible, you can simply move your subject into the shade.

No flash

With flash

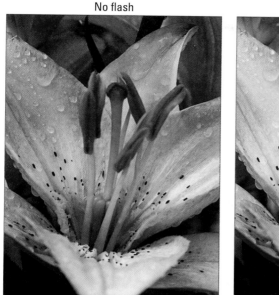 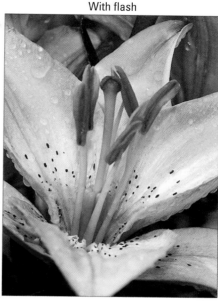

Figure 7-32: For this flower photo, adding flash resulted in better illumination and a slight warming effect.

✔ **Colors may need tweaking when you mix light sources.** When you combine multiple light sources, such as flash with daylight, colors may appear warmer or cooler than neutral. In Figure 7-32, colors became warmer with the addition of flash. For outdoor portraits, the warming effect is usually flattering, and I usually like the result with nature shots as well. If you prefer a neutral color rendition, see the Chapter 8 section related to the white balance control to find out how to address this issue. You can adjust white balance only in P, S, A, and M exposure modes.

✔ **In P and A modes, shutter speeds may drop low enough to require a tripod to steady the camera.** Remember, in these two modes, the camera controls shutter speed. And by default, the camera can drop the shutter speed as low as 1/60 second to ensure a good exposure when you use flash. A slower shutter speed raises the risk of blurring caused by camera shake or any movement of the subject, as explained in the introduction to shutter speed at the beginning of this chapter. Use a tripod if you're unsure whether you can handhold the camera at 1/60 second, and warn your subject to stay still as well.

✔ **You can lower the slow limit of the shutter speed used for the P and A modes.** Again, the camera restricts itself to using a shutter speed no slower than 1/60 second when you use flash in the P and A modes. If you need a longer exposure, you can waive that limit through the Flash Shutter Speed option; shown in Figure 7-33, you can set the minimum shutter speed as slow as 30 seconds. The option appears in the Bracketing/Flash section of the Custom Setting menu.

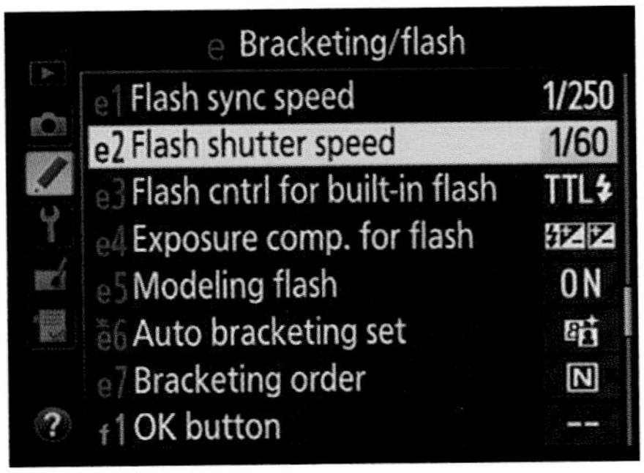

e Bracketing/flash	
e1 Flash sync speed	1/250
e2 Flash shutter speed	1/60
e3 Flash cntrl for built-in flash	TTL⚡
e4 Exposure comp. for flash	⚡±
e5 Modeling flash	ON
e6 Auto bracketing set	⚡⚡
e7 Bracketing order	N
f1 OK button	--

Figure 7-33: You can set the minimum shutter speed the camera can select when you use flash in the P and A exposure modes.

This setting applies only to the normal, Front-Curtain Sync Flash mode as well as to the Red-Eye Reduction mode and Rear-Sync mode, both discussed in upcoming sections. The camera completely ignores your limit if you choose Slow-Sync flash, Slow-Sync with Red Eye, or Slow Rear-Curtain Sync, also discussed later.

Red-Eye Reduction flash

Red-Eye is caused when flash light bounces off a subject's retinas and is reflected back to the camera lens. Red-eye is a human phenomenon, though; with animals, the reflected light usually glows yellow, white, or green.

Man or beast, this issue isn't nearly the problem with the type of pop-up flash found on your camera as it is on non-SLR cameras. Your camera's flash is positioned in such a way that the flash light usually doesn't hit a subject's eyes straight on, which lessens the chances of red-eye. However, red-eye may still be an issue when you use a lens with a long focal length (a telephoto lens) or you shoot subjects from a distance.

 If you notice red-eye, try the Red-Eye Reduction mode, represented by the icon shown in the margin here. In this mode, the AF-assist lamp on the front of the camera lights up briefly before the flash fires. The subject's pupils constrict in response to the light, allowing less flash light to enter the eye and cause that glowing red reflection. Be sure to warn your subjects to wait for the flash, or they may step out of the frame or stop posing after they see the light from the AF-assist lamp.

For an even better solution, try the flash-free portrait tips covered in Chapter 9. If you do a lot of portrait work that requires flash, consider investing in an external flash unit that offers a rotating head. You then can aim the flash toward the ceiling and "bounce" the light off the ceiling instead of aiming it directly at your subject. That technique produces softer lighting and also virtually eliminates the possibility of red-eye.

If all else fails, check out Chapter 10, which shows you how to use the built-in red-eye removal tool on your camera's Retouch menu.

Slow-Sync and Rear-Curtain Sync flash

In Front-Curtain Sync (normal flash) and Red-Eye Reduction Flash modes, the flash and shutter are synchronized so that the flash fires at the exact moment the shutter opens; technical types refer to this flash arrangement as *Front-Curtain Sync.*

Your camera also offers some special sync modes, which work as follows:

✔ **Slow-Sync Flash:** This mode, available in the P and A exposure modes and used by default in some Scene modes, also uses Front-Curtain Sync but allows a shutter speed slower than the 1/60 second minimum that is in force by default when you use normal Front-Curtain Sync flash and Red-Eye Reduction flash. Remember that in these two exposure modes, you can't directly control shutter speed, so the camera automatically lowers the shutter speed for you.

The benefit of this longer exposure is that the camera has time to absorb more ambient light, which in turn has two effects: Background areas that are beyond the reach of the flash appear brighter, and less flash power is needed, resulting in softer lighting.

The downside of the slow shutter speed is, well, the slow shutter speed. As I discuss earlier in this chapter, the longer the exposure time, the more you have to worry about blur caused by movement of your subject or your camera. A tripod is essential to a good outcome, as are subjects that can hold very, very still. I find that the best practical use for this mode is shooting nighttime still-life subjects, such as the one in Figure 7-34. If you have an adult portrait subject, using Slow-Sync can also produce good results; Chapter 9 has an example.

Some photographers, though, turn the downside of Slow-Sync flash to an upside, using it to blur their subjects, thereby emphasizing motion.

Whatever your creative goals, if you want to use flash with a slow shutter in the S or M exposure mode, just choose the normal Flash mode (Front-Curtain Sync) and then select the shutter speed you want to use. The flash will fire at the beginning of the exposure. Or as an alternative choice, choose Rear-Curtain Sync, explained next.

Normal flash

Slow-sync flash

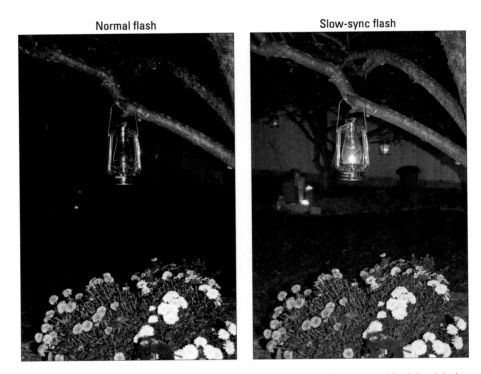

Figure 7-34: Slow-Sync flash produces softer, more even lighting than normal flash in nighttime pictures.

✔ **Rear-Curtain Sync:** In this mode, available in P, S, A, and M exposure modes, the flash fires at the very end of the exposure, just before the shutter's second curtain draws across the frame to prevent any more light from hitting the image sensor.

The classic use of this mode is to combine the flash with a slow shutter speed to create trailing-light effects like the one shown in Figure 7-35. With Rear-Curtain Sync, the light trails extend behind the moving object (my hand, and the match, in this case), which makes visual sense. If instead you use Slow-Sync flash (or Front-Curtain Sync with a slow shutter), the light trails appear in front of the moving object.

When you shoot in the P and A exposure modes, the camera actually combines Slow-Sync flash with Rear-Curtain Sync when you select this Flash mode. Shutter speeds automatically drop below normal because the camera assumes that when you use Rear-Curtain flash, you're after the longer exposure time needed to produce the "trailing ghost" effect. In the M and S modes, you dial in that slow shutter speed yourself.

✔ **Slow-Sync with Red-Eye Reduction:** In P and A exposure modes, you can also combine a Slow-Sync flash with the Red-Eye Reduction feature. Given the potential for blur that comes with a slow shutter, plus the potential for subjects to mistake the prelight from the AF-assist lamp for the real flash and walk out of the frame before the image is actually recorded, I vote this Flash mode as the most difficult to pull off.

All these modes are somewhat tricky to use successfully. Have fun playing around, but at the same time, don't feel too badly if you don't have time right now to master these modes plus all the other exposure options presented to you in this chapter. In the meantime, do a web search for Slow-Sync and Rear-Sync image examples if you want to get a better idea of the effects that other photographers create with these Flash modes.

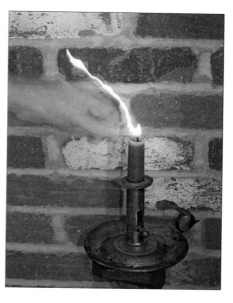

Figure 7-35: I used Rear-Curtain flash and a shutter speed of about 1.5 seconds to create this candle-lighting image.

Adjusting flash output

Your camera calculates the necessary flash output depending on your exposure metering mode:

✔ **In matrix and center-weighted modes,** flash power is adjusted to expose the picture using a balance of ambient light and flash light. Nikon uses the term *i-TTL Balanced Fill Flash* for this technology. The *i* stands for *intelligent;* again, the *TTL* means that the camera calculates exposure by reading the light that's coming through-the-lens. The *balanced fill* part refers to the fact that the flash is used to fill in shadow areas, while brighter areas are exposed by the available light, resulting (usually) in a pleasing balance of the two light sources.

✔ **In spot-metering mode,** the camera assumes that you're primarily interested in a single area of the frame, so it calculates flash power on the same single area it uses to calculate overall exposure, without much regard for the background. This mode is *Standard i-TTL Flash.* (See the earlier discussion of metering modes to find out how the specific metering spot, which is based on a single autofocus point, is chosen.)

Regardless of your metering mode, if you want a little more or less flash light than the camera thinks is appropriate, you can adjust the flash output by using Flash Compensation. Available only when you set the exposure mode to P, S, A, or M, this feature works just like Exposure Compensation, discussed earlier in the chapter, except that it enables you to tweak flash power instead of the overall exposure. As with Exposure Compensation, the Flash Compensation settings are stated in terms of EV numbers. A setting of 0.0 indicates no flash adjustment; you can increase the flash power to EV +1.0 or decrease it to EV –3.0.

As an example of the benefit of this feature, look at the carousel images in Figure 7-36. The first image shows you a flash-free shot. Clearly, I needed a flash to compensate for the fact that the horses were shadowed by the roof of the carousel. But at normal flash power, as shown in the image, the flash was too strong, creating glare in some spots on the horse's neck and blowing out the highlights in the white mane. By dialing the flash power down to EV –1.0, I got a softer flash that straddled the line perfectly between no flash and too much flash.

| No flash | Flash EV 0.0 | Flash EV –1.0 |

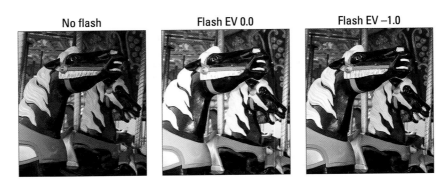

Figure 7-36: When normal flash output is too strong, dial in a lower Flash Compensation setting.

As for boosting the flash output, well, you may find it necessary on some occasions, but don't expect the built-in flash to work miracles even at a Flash Compensation of +1.0. Any built-in flash has a limited range, and you simply can't expect the flash light to reach faraway objects. In other words, don't even try taking flash pictures of a darkened recital hall from your seat in the balcony — all you'll wind up doing is annoying everyone.

With that preface in mind, here are the two controls you need to know to take advantage of this feature:

✔ **Setting the Flash Compensation amount:** Press the Flash button while rotating the Sub-command dial to adjust the setting. (Rotating the Main command dial adjusts the Flash mode.) As long as you hold the Flash button, the Flash Compensation setting appears in the Control panel and Information display. (See Figure 7-37.) In the viewfinder, the current setting takes the place of the usual shots-remaining value, and a plus or minus sign also appears to indicate whether you're dialing in a positive or negative value.

After you release the Flash button, you see the Flash Compensation amount in the Information display, but the viewfinder and Control panel show just the Flash Compensation icon. You can press the Flash button at any time to reveal the value in those two displays.

✔ **Disabling flash adjustment during Exposure Compensation:** By default, if you use flash when Exposure Compensation is in force, the flash power is affected by your Exposure Compensation setting. But as I cover in the earlier section "Applying Exposure Compensation," you can tell the camera to leave the flash out of the equation when you apply Exposure Compensation. To do so, track down the Exposure Compensation for Flash Option on the Custom Setting menu and choose Background Only as the setting. You then can use Flash Compensation to vary the flash output as you see fit.

Any flash-power adjustment you make remains in force until you reset the control. So be sure to check the setting before you next use your flash. Set the value to 0.0 to disable Flash Compensation.

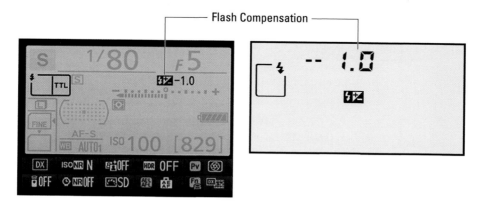

Figure 7-37: Rotate the Sub-command dial while pressing the Flash button to adjust flash power.

Locking flash exposure on your subject

With FV Lock (or Flash Value Lock), you can lock flash power similar to the way you can use the AE-L/AF-L button to lock autoexposure. (Note that not all external flash units support this function; the camera manual and your flash manual provide a list of supported flash features.)

This option can come in handy when you want to compose your photo so that your subject is located at the edge of the frame, for example. You frame the scene initially so the subject is at the center of the frame, lock the flash power, and then reframe. If you didn't lock the flash value, the camera would calculate flash power on your final framing, which could be inappropriate for your subject. You also can use FV Lock to maintain a consistent flash power for a series of shots.

This feature is one of the few advanced flash options that works in Auto mode and in the Scene and Effects modes that permit flash — but only if the camera sees the need for flash in the first place. In Food Scene mode, you must pop up the flash to use flash.

 However, regardless of your exposure mode, you can't use FV Lock until you first assign the function to the Fn button, which is set up by default to give you access to the Image Area setting (DX or 1.3x crop) or to the Depth of Field Preview button, which normally lets you see how your f-stop will affect depth of field. Visit the Controls section of the Custom Setting menu, choose Assign Fn button or Assign Preview button, and select FV Lock as the setting. (Chapter 11 explains more about adjusting button functions.)

After assigning a button to the FV Lock feature, follow these steps to use it:

1. **Frame the shot so that your subject is in the center of the viewfinder.**

2. **Press and hold the shutter button halfway to engage the exposure meter and, if autofocusing is used, set focus.**

3. **Press and release the button that you assigned to FV Lock.**

   The flash fires a little preflash to determine the correct flash power. When flash power is locked, you see a little flash symbol with the letter L at the left end of the viewfinder, next to the metering mode icon. The same symbol appears in the Information display (look under the exposure meter).

4. **Recompose the picture if desired and then take the shot.**

To release the FV Lock, just press the assigned button again.

Exploring a few additional flash options

For most people, the flash options covered to this point in the chapter are the most useful on a regular basis, but your camera does offer a few other flash options that you may appreciate on occasion, so the next several sections provide a quick look-see. Again, keep in mind that I'm touching on the highlights — be sure to dive into the camera manual or your flash manual, if you use an external flash unit, for all the nitty-gritty.

Enabling high-speed flash (Auto FP)

To properly expose flash pictures, the camera has to synchronize the timing of the flash output with the opening and closing of the shutter. On the D7100, this synchronization normally dictates a maximum shutter speed of 1/250 second when you use the built-in flash.

Through a Nikon feature called Auto FP flash, you can bump the maximum sync speed up to 1/320 second for the built-in flash, however. Furthermore, if you attach some specific Nikon flash units, you can access the full range of shutter speeds.

When Auto FP flash is used, the flash fires a little differently. Instead of a single pop of light, it emits a continuous, rapid-fire burst for the entire time that the shutter is open. Although that sounds like a good thing, it actually forces a reduction of the flash power, thereby shortening the distance over which subjects remain illuminated. The faster your shutter speed, the greater the impact on the flash power. So at very high speeds, your subject needs to be pretty close to the camera to be properly exposed by the flash.

Because of this limitation, high-speed flash is mostly useful for shooting portraits or other close-up subjects. In fact, it's very useful when you're shooting portraits outside in the daytime because it permits you to use a wider aperture to blur the background. At a shutter speed of 1/250 second, a very wide aperture would normally overexpose the picture even at ISO 100. With high-speed flash, you can increase the shutter speed enough to compensate for the large aperture.

To access the high-speed flash option, open the Bracketing/Flash section of the Custom Setting menu and select the Flash Sync Speed option, as shown in Figure 7-38. You can choose from the following settings:

- ✔ **1/320 s (Auto FP):** At this setting, you can use the built-in flash with shutter speeds up to 1/320 second. For select Nikon flash units (including models SB-910, SB-900, SB-800, SB-700, SB-600, and SB-R200), you can use any shutter speed.

- ✔ **1/250 s (Auto FP):** For compatible external flash units, the high-speed flash behavior kicks in at shutter speeds over 1/250 second. With the built-in flash, the flash sync speed is set to 1/250 second. In P and A exposure modes, the high-speed flash sync is activated if the camera needs to use a shutter speed faster than 1/250 second. (Note that the camera may sometimes use a shutter speed faster than 1/250 second in those modes even if the shutter speed readout is 1/250.)

✓ **1/250 s to 1/60 s:** The other settings on the menu (see the right image in Figure 7-37) establish a fixed maximum sync speed. By default, it's set to 1/250 second, and high-speed flash operation is disabled.

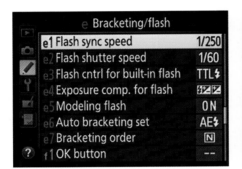
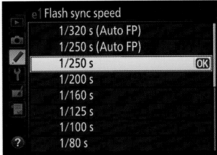

Figure 7-38: Through this option, you can enable high-speed flash, permitting a faster maximum shutter speed for flash photos.

Enabling manual, repeating, or commander-mode flash

The Bracketing/Flash submenu of the Custom Setting menu also offers a setting called Flash Cntrl (Control) for Built-In Flash, as shown in Figure 7-39. Normally, your flash operates in the TTL mode, in which the camera automatically determines the right flash output for you.

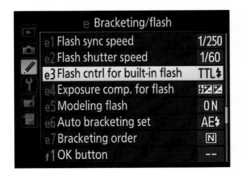
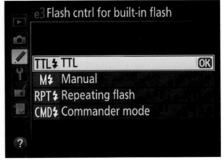

Figure 7-39: You also can change the behavior of the built-in flash through this menu option.

However, if you're an advanced flash user, you may want to a few other options available when you shoot in the P, S, A, or M exposure modes:

- **Manual:** You can select a specific flash power, with settings ranging from full power to 1/128 power. (If you're hip to rating flash power by Guide Numbers, the manual spells out the ratings for the built-in flash.)

- **Repeating Flash:** The flash fires repeatedly as long as the shutter is open. The resulting picture looks as though it was shot with a strobe light — a special-effects function. You can modify certain aspects of the flash output, including how often the flash fires per second.

- **Commander Mode:** Enables the built-in flash to act as a *master flash,* which just means that you can use it to trigger off-camera, remote-control flash units. (When the remote units "see" the light from the master flash, they fire.) You can set the power of the remote flashes through the Commander Mode options and specify whether you want the built-in flash to simply trigger other flashes or add its light to the scene.

To use this feature, your remote flash heads must support the Nikon Creative Lighting System, or CLS. Visit Nikon online to get a better idea of how the system works. It's pretty cool, and it can provide great added lighting flexibility without requiring you to spend tons of money or rely on bulky, traditional lighting equipment.

Firing a modeling flash

Found on the right front side of the camera, just under the AF-assist lamp, the Depth-of-Field Preview button has two functions by default. First, pressing the button enables you to preview the depth of field that your current f-stop setting will produce. (Chapter 8 explains in detail.) When you use flash, pressing the button also causes the flash to emit a modeling flash when you shoot in the P, S, A, or M exposure modes.

When the modeling flash feature is turned on, the flash emits a repeating, strobelike series of flash light while you press the button. The idea is to enable you to preview how the light will fall on your subject. However, living subjects aren't likely to appreciate the feature — it's a bit blinding to have the flash going off repeatedly in your face. And obviously, using the feature drains the camera battery or the battery of an external flash.

To disable the modeling flash, hunt down the Modeling Flash option, found on the Bracketing/Flash submenu of the Custom Setting menu, and set the option to Off. Changing the function of the Depth-of-Field Preview button from the default setting, which I show you how to do in Chapter 11, also disables the modeling flash.

Bracketing Exposures

Many photographers use exposure bracketing to ensure that at least one shot of a subject is properly exposed. *Bracketing* simply means to shoot the same subject multiple times, slightly varying the exposure settings for each image.

In the P, S, A, and M exposure modes, your camera offers automatic bracketing. When you enable this feature, your only job is to press the shutter button to record the shots; the camera adjusts exposure settings between each image. The D7100, however, takes things one step further than most cameras that offer automatic bracketing, enabling you to bracket not just exposure, but also flash power, Active D-Lighting, and white balance.

The next section explains how to bracket exposure and flash. Following that, you can find details about bracketing Active D-Lighting. Chapter 8 walks you through the process of bracketing white balance.

Bracketing exposure and flash

After setting the mode dial to P, S, A, or M, follow these steps to bracket exposure only, flash only, or both together. (Don't be put off by the length of these steps; although describing the features takes quite a few words, actually using them isn't all that complicated.)

1. **Specify what you want to bracket through the Auto Bracketing Set option, located in the Bracketing/Flash section of the Custom Setting menu.**

   Shown in Figure 7-40, this option determines what aspect of your picture you want to vary between shots. For exposure and flash bracketing, you have three choices:

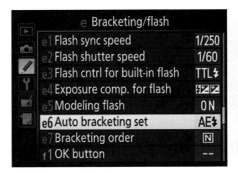 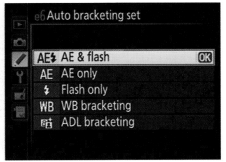

Figure 7-40: Use this option to select the setting you want the camera to adjust between shots.

- *AE & Flash:* Brackets exposure settings and flash power.

- *AE Only:* Brackets exposure settings only.

In P mode, the camera may vary shutter speed, aperture, or both between shots to produce the different exposures. In S mode, it adjusts aperture only; in A and M modes, it changes shutter speed only. In all modes, ISO may be adjusted if you enable ISO Sensitivity Auto Control, as I outline earlier in this chapter.

- *Flash Only:* Brackets flash power only.

2. **Choose the order in which you want the bracketed shots recorded.**

   Make the call via the Bracketing Order option, found with the other bracketing options on the Custom Setting menu. As shown in Figure 7-41, you have two options:

   - *MTR>Under>Over:* This setting is the default. For a three-shot exposure bracketing series, your first shot is captured at your original settings. (MTR stands for *metered* and designates the initial settings suggested by the camera's exposure meter.) The second image is captured at settings that produce a darker image, and the third, at settings that produce a brighter image.

     This sequence can vary depending on how many frames you include in your bracketed series; if you're a detail nut, you can find out the specific order used in every scenario in the camera manual.

   - *Under>MTR>Over:* The darkest image is captured first, then the metered image, and then the brightest image.

 3. **Select the number of frames in each series by pressing the BKT button while rotating the Main command dial.**

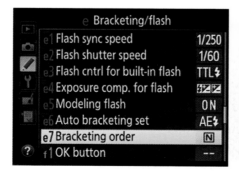 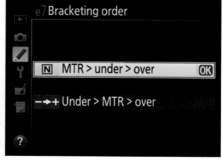

Figure 7-41: You can choose the order in which you want the bracketed shots to be captured.

As soon as you press the button, you see the current bracketing settings in the Control panel and Information display, as shown in Figure 7-42. You also see an exposure meter with some symbols related to bracketing; more on how to interpret the bracketing information a little later.

With the BKT button pressed, rotate the Main command dial to cycle to through the available settings. Here's what you can accomplish at each of the frame-count settings:

- *+3F:* One image at the selected exposure settings and two brighter frames.
- *–3F:* One image at the selected exposure settings and two darker frames.
- *+2F:* One image at the selected exposure settings and one brighter frame.
- *–2F:* One image at the selected exposure settings and one darker frame.
- *3F:* One image at the selected exposure settings, one darker image, and one brighter image.
- *5F:* One image at the selected exposure settings, two darker frames, and two brighter frames.

4. **Set the level of exposure adjustment between frames by pressing the BKT button while rotating the Sub-command dial.**

You can choose values ranging from 1/3 stop (0.3, in the display) to two stops (2.0).

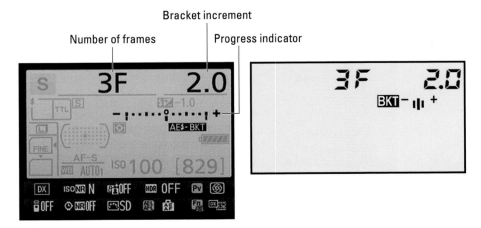

Figure 7-42: Rotate the Main command dial while pressing BKT button to adjust the number of bracketed frames; press the button and rotate the Sub-command dial to adjust the bracketing increment.

Now for the promised decoder guide to the bracketing information displayed with the meter: In the Information display, the meter serves as a bracketing progress indicator and appears as shown on the left in Figure 7-42 when you enable the three-frame bracketing option (3F). The markings near the meter indicate the following:

- The symbol below the meter tells you what you're bracketing — AE+Flash, in the figure.

- The notches under the meter show you how many frames are enabled and the amount of adjustment between frames. For example, in the figure, the notch at the zero point represents the neutral shot — the one that will be recorded with no adjustment. The notches to the left and right show that the other two shots will be recorded at settings that produce a two-stop increase and a two-stop decrease in exposure.

The Control panel shows a miniaturized version of the progress indicator; for a three-shot series, you see a three vertical lines, with a plus and minus at each end, as shown on the right in the figure. Frankly, the indicator is so miniature that I can't make it out even with my strongest reading glasses on, but that's the price of living past your twenties, I guess.

5. **Release the BKT button to return to shooting mode.**

   The bracketing frame and increment settings disappear from the Control panel and Information display; the bracketing indicators remain.

6. **Take your first shot.**

   After you take the picture, the indicator representing the shot you just took disappears from under the meter in the Information display. For example, if you're bracketing three frames, the notch at the 0 position disappears after your first shot. Likewise, the middle bar of the indicator in the Control panel goes away.

7. **Take the remaining shots in the series.**

   When the series is done, the indicator scale returns to its original appearance, and you can begin shooting the next bracketed series.

8. **To disable bracketing, press the BKT button and rotate the Main command dial until the number of frames returns to 0.**

Bracketing Active D-Lighting

Active D-Lighting, introduced earlier in this chapter, adjusts exposure in a way that brightens shadows without blowing out highlights. In the P, S, A, or M exposure modes, you can set up a bracketed series that applies different levels of the adjustment to each shot.

The process varies only slightly from the steps in the preceding section, so instead of repeating it all here, I'll just hit the highlights:

1. **Set the Auto Bracketing Set option to ADL Bracketing, as shown in Figure 7-43.**

   Look in the Bracketing/Flash section of the Custom Setting menu.

   The Bracketing Order option discussed in Step 2 in the preceding section doesn't matter for Active D-Lighting bracketing; the camera always uses the default setting.

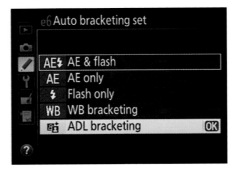

Figure 7-43: You can capture a series of up to three shots, each with a different amount of Active D-Lighting applied.

2. **Press the BKT button while rotating the Main command dial to set up the bracketed series.**

   When you press the BKT button, the Information display and Control panel display the data shown in Figure 7-44. Notice that instead of the bracket increment that appears for exposure and flash bracketing, you see just the frame count, the symbol ADL (to let you know that Active D-Lighting bracketing is enabled), and a progress indicator. With Active D-Lighting bracketing, you don't set the frame count and level of shot-to-shot adjustment as you do for exposure and flash bracketing. Instead, the number of frames you select determines what Active D-Lighting setting is used for each frame.

   Here are your options:

   - *2 Frames:* Records one image with Active D-Lighting turned off and another at the value currently selected for Active D-Lighting. (You set that value via the Shooting menu or the Information panel control strip; see the earlier section "Expanding tonal range with Active D-Lighting" for help.) If Active D-Lighting happens to be set to Off, the second shot is recorded using the Auto setting.

   - *3 Frames:* Records one shot with Active D-Lighting off, one at the Normal setting, and one at the High setting.

   In the Information display, the labels next to the progress indicator tell you which settings are used for the different frame counts. For example, in Figure 7-44, the labels display the settings associated with recording three frames: Off, N (Normal), and H (High). The Control panel shows — er, wait, I have to go find a stronger pair of glasses — two bars and a triangle for three frames, and two bars for two frames.

3. Release the BKT button and take your shots.

As with exposure and flash bracketing, each little bar under the meter represents one frame in the series. After you capture a shot, the bar representing that frame disappears. When you've captured all shots in the series, the meter indicators return to their starting position.

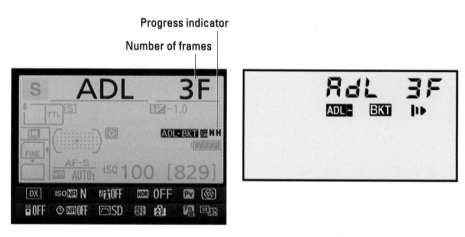

Figure 7-44: With Active D-Lighting, a single value controls both the frame count and the level of Active D-Lighting adjustment.

8

Manipulating Focus and Color

In This Chapter

▷ Controlling the camera's autofocusing performance

▷ Understanding depth of field

▷ Exploring white balance and its effect on color

▷ Investigating other color options

*T*o many people, the word *focus* has just one interpretation when applied to a photograph: Either the subject is in focus or it's blurry. But an artful photographer knows that there's more to focus than simply getting a sharp image of a subject. You also need to consider *depth of field,* or the distance over which objects appear sharply focused.

This chapter explains all the ways to control depth of field and also explains how to use your camera's advanced focusing options. Additionally, this chapter dives into the topic of color, explaining such features as white balance, which compensates for the varying color casts created by different light sources.

Note: Autofocusing features covered here relate to viewfinder photography; Chapter 4 focuses (yuk yuk) on Live View and movie autofocusing, which involves a different techniques.

Mastering the Autofocusing System

The first step in putting the autofocus system to work is to set the Focus-mode selector on the front of the camera to AF, as shown in Figure 8-1. With the 18–105mm kit lens, also set the switch on the lens to the A position, as shown in the figure.

For autofocusing, you then need to specify two settings:

Lens focus-mode switch

AF-mode button

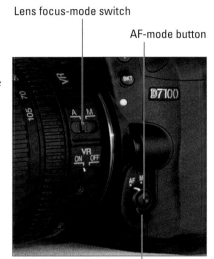

Focus-mode selector

Figure 8-1: These switches control whether the camera uses autofocusing or manual focusing.

- ✓ **Autofocus mode:** Determines whether the camera locks focus when you press the shutter button halfway, or it continually adjusts focus up to the time you take the picture.

- ✓ **AF-area mode:** Determines which of the camera's 51 autofocusing points are used to establish focus.

The next few sections explain both options in detail. For now, familiarize yourself with how you check and adjust these settings:

- ✓ **Checking the current settings:** Symbols representing the current Autofocus mode and AF-area mode appear in the Information display and Control panel, in the areas labeled in Figure 8-2. Upcoming sections help you decode the symbols you see here.

- ✓ **Changing the settings:** The key to adjusting the settings is the AF-mode button, labeled in Figure 8-1:
    - • *To change the Autofocus mode:* Press the button while rotating the Main command dial.
    - • *To change the AF-area mode:* Press the button while rotating the Sub-command dial.

While the button is pressed, all data disappears from the Information screen and Control panel except readouts representing the Autofocus mode setting and the AF-area mode, as shown in Figure 8-3.

AF-area mode

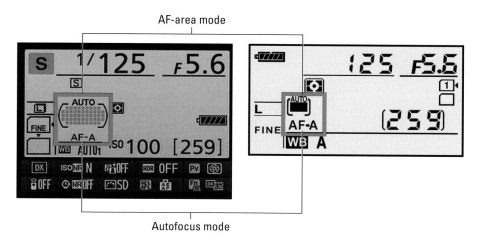

Autofocus mode

Figure 8-2: You can see the current Autofocus mode and AF-area mode settings here.

AF-area mode

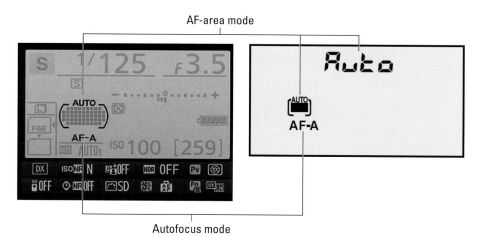

Autofocus mode

Figure 8-3: Press the AF-mode button to access the settings; then use the command dials to adjust them.

The viewfinder display also changes, with the Autofocus mode and AF-area mode settings appearing in the areas labeled in Figure 8-4. The viewfinder also shows the autofocus brackets, which indicate the area of the frame that contain the camera's autofocus points, and rectangles representing the active points. One quirk here, though: In the default AF-area mode, Auto Area, all 51 autofocus points are active. But the viewfinder display shows points only around the perimeter of the autofocus brackets, as shown in the figure, so that you can still get a good view of your subject. All 51 points are active just the same; the rest are spaced evenly throughout the area enclosed by the autofocus brackets.

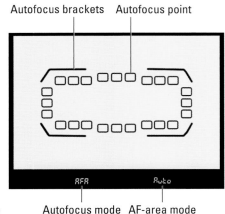

Figure 8-4: The viewfinder also shows the current settings while you press the AF-mode button.

Okay, with the how-to's out of the way, read on for details that will help you understand which Autofocus mode and AF-area mode options work best for different types of subjects.

Choosing an Autofocus mode

When you use autofocusing, you press the shutter button halfway to kick-start the autofocusing system. Whether the camera locks focus at that point or continually adjusts focus until you press the button the rest of the way depends on the Autofocus mode. You can choose from three options, which work as follows:

- **AF-S (single-servo autofocus):** With this option, designed for shooting stationary subjects, the camera locks focus when you depress the shutter button halfway. (Think *S* for *still, stationary.*)

- **AF-C (continuous-servo autofocus):** In this mode, designed for moving subjects, the camera focuses continuously for the entire time you hold the shutter button halfway down. (Think *C* for *continuous motion.*)

- **AF-A (auto-servo autofocus):** This mode is the default setting. The camera analyzes the scene, and if it detects motion, automatically selects continuous-servo mode (AF-C). If the camera instead believes you're shooting a stationary object, it selects single-servo mode (AF-S).

  This mode is easiest to use, but it can get confused sometimes. For example, if your subject is motionless but something is moving in the background, the camera may mistakenly switch to continuous autofocus. By the same token, if the subject is moving only slightly, the camera may not make the switch to continuous autofocusing. So my advice is to choose either AF-S or AF-C instead.

Shutter speed and blurry photos

A poorly focused photo isn't always related to the issues discussed in this chapter. Any movement of the camera or subject can also cause blur. Both of these problems are related to shutter speed, an exposure control that I cover in Chapter 7. To eliminate camera shake, use a tripod. Be sure to also visit Chapter 9, which provides additional tips for capturing moving objects without blur.

To change the Autofocus setting, press the AF-mode button (refer to Figure 8-1) while rotating the Main command dial. Refer to Figures 8-3 and 8-4 for help locating the setting in the displays.

One other critical thing to know about this setting: By default, the camera refuses to take a picture in AF-S mode if it can't achieve focus. With AF-C mode, the opposite occurs. The camera assumes that because this mode is designed for shooting action, you want to capture the shot at the instant you fully depress the shutter button, regardless of whether it had time to set focus.

You can change this behavior through the AF Priority Selection options found in the Autofocus section of the Custom Setting menu and shown in Figure 8-5. The AF-C Priority Selection option affects how things work in AF-C mode; the AF-S Priority Selection option, the AF-S mode. For both options, you can choose from two settings:

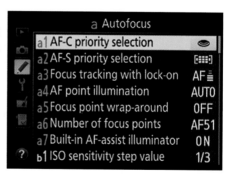

Figure 8-5: You can tell the camera whether to go ahead and take the picture even if focus hasn't been achieved.

 ✔ **Release:** You can take the picture regardless of whether focus is achieved.

 ✔ **Focus:** You can't take the picture until focus is achieved.

To decide which option is right for you, you have to consider whether you'd rather have any shot, even if it's out of focus, or capture only those that are in focus. I prefer the latter, so I set both options to Focus. Why waste battery power, memory card space, and inevitable time deleting out-of-focus pictures, after all? Yes, if you're shooting rapid action, you may miss a few shots waiting for the focus to occur — but if they're going to be lousy shots, who cares? Sports shooters who fire off hundreds of shots while covering an event, though, may want to unlock the shutter release for AF-C mode. Again, you may wind up with lots of wasted shots, but you increase the odds that you'll capture that split-second "highlight reel" moment.

Choosing an AF-area mode: One focus point or many?

The AF-area mode setting determines which autofocusing points the camera considers when choosing its focusing target. To adjust the setting, press the AF-mode button while rotating the Sub-command dial. (Refer to Figure 8-1 for a look at the button.)

When the button is pressed, all data except the current AF-area mode setting and the Autofocus mode setting disappear from the Information screen and Control panel, as shown in Figure 8-3. The viewfinder also shows you which autofocus points are active, and the current AF-area mode setting appears at the right end of the display, as shown in Figure 8-4.

The Control panel displays the icons you see in the margins in the upcoming list to represent the current AF-Area mode. The Information display also contains an AF-Area mode icon, and this one provides more details about the setting: Active autofocus points are represented by gray squares; inactive points appear as small plus signs; and the selected point is a black square. Too much to remember? Then take the easy way out and just look through the viewfinder while pressing the AF-mode button to see which points are active. The viewfinder also displays a text readout telling you the active AF-area mode (refer to Figure 8-4): A for Auto Area, S for Single Point, d9 for 9-point Dynamic Area, and so on.

Here's how each of the AF-area mode settings works:

✔ **Single Point:** This mode is designed to help you quickly and easily lock focus on a still subject. You select a single focus point, and the camera bases focus on that point only. See the next section for details on selecting an autofocus point.

✔ **Dynamic Area:** This option is designed for focusing on a moving subject. You select an initial focus point, but if your subject moves out of that point before you snap the picture, the camera looks to surrounding points for focusing information.

To use Dynamic Area autofocusing, you must set the Autofocus mode to AF-C or AF-A. Assuming that condition is met, you can choose from three Dynamic Area settings:

- *9-point Dynamic Area:* The camera takes focusing cues from your selected point plus the eight surrounding points. This setting is ideal when you have a moment or two to compose your shot and your subject is moving in a predictable way, making it easy to reframe as needed to keep the subject within the 9-point area.

  This setting also provides the fastest Dynamic Area autofocusing because the camera has to analyze the fewest autofocusing points.

- *21-point Dynamic Area:* Focusing is based on the selected point plus the 20 surrounding points. This setting enables your subject to move a little farther afield from your selected focus point and still remain in the target zone, so it works better than 9-point mode when you can't quite predict the path your subject is going to take.

- *51-point Dynamic Area:* The camera makes use of the full complement of autofocus points. This mode is designed for subjects that are moving so rapidly that it's hard to keep them within the framing area of the 21-point or 9-point setting — a flock of birds, for example. The drawback to this setting is focusing time: With all 51 points on deck, the camera has to work a little harder to find a focus target.

✔ **3D Tracking:** This one is a variation of 51-point Dynamic Area autofocusing. As in that mode, you start by selecting a single focus point and then press the shutter button halfway to set focus. The goal of the 3D Tracking mode is to maintain focus on your subject if you recompose the shot after you press the shutter button halfway to lock focus.

The problem with 3D Tracking is that the way the camera detects your subject is by analyzing the colors of the object under your selected focus point. So, if not much difference exists between the subject and other objects in the frame, the camera can get fooled. And if your subject moves out of the frame, you must release the shutter button and reset focus by pressing it halfway again.

If you want to try 3D Tracking autofocus, set the Autofocus mode to AF-C or AF-A; you can't access this AF-area mode when the Autofocus mode is set to AF-S.

✔ **Auto Area:** At this setting, the camera automatically chooses which of the 51 focus points to use. Focus priority is typically assigned to the object closest to the camera. Remember that in this mode, only the points around the perimeter of the autofocus brackets light up in the viewfinder when you press the AF-mode button (refer to Figure 8-4), but all 51 points are active nonetheless.

Although Auto Area mode requires the least input from you, it's also typically the slowest option because of the technology it uses to set focus. First, the camera analyzes all 51 focus points. Then it consults an internal database to try to match the information reported by those points to a huge collection of reference photographs. From that analysis, it makes an educated guess about which focus points are most appropriate for your scene. Although it's still amazingly fast considering what's happening in the camera's brain, it's slower than the other AF-area options.

Choosing the right autofocus combo

You'll get the best autofocus results if you pair your chosen Autofocus mode with the most appropriate AF-area mode because the two settings work in tandem. Here are the combinations that I suggest for the maximum autofocus control:

✔ **For still subjects:** Opt for AF-S and Single Point. You select a specific focus point, and the camera locks focus on that point when you press the shutter button halfway. Focus remains locked on your subject even if you reframe the shot after you press the button halfway. (It helps to remember the *s* factor: For *s*till subjects, *S*ingle Point and AF-*S*.)

✔ **For moving subjects:** Choose AF-C and 51-point Dynamic Area. You still begin by selecting a focus point, but the camera adjusts focus as needed if your subject moves within the frame after you press the shutter button halfway to establish focus. (Think *motion, dynamic, continuous.*) Remember to reframe as needed to keep your subject within the boundaries of the autofocus points, though. And if you want speedier autofocusing, consider switching to 21-point or 9-point Dynamic Area mode — just remember that you need to keep your subject within that smaller portion of the frame for the focus adjustment to work properly.

Upcoming sections in this chapter spell out the steps for setting focus with these autofocus pairings. First, though, I need to take a detour to explain how you select a specific focus point when you use Single Point, Dynamic Area, or 3D Tracking mode.

Selecting (and locking) an autofocus point

When you use any AF-area mode except Auto Area, you see a single autofocus point in the viewfinder. That point is the *selected autofocus point* — the one the camera will use to set focus in the Single Point mode and to choose the starting focusing distance in the Dynamic Area and 3D Tracking modes. By default, the center point is selected, as shown in Figure 8-6.

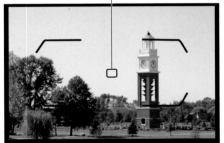

Selected autofocus point

Figure 8-6: By default, the center focus point is selected.

To choose a different focus point, set the Focus Selector Lock switch to the position shown in Figure 8-7. Then press the Multi Selector right, left, up, or down to cycle through the available focus points, which are all located within the area surrounded by the autofocus brackets. I moved the focus point over the clock tower, for example, in the second image in Figure 8-7. (If nothing happens when you press the Multi Selector, press the shutter button halfway to activate the metering system. Then release the button and try again.)

Unlocked position

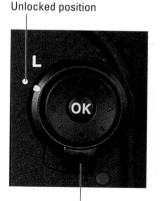
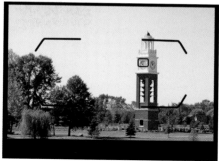

Focus Selector Lock switch

Figure 8-7: When the Focus Selector Lock switch is set to this position, you can press the Multi Selector to select a different focus point.

A couple of additional tips:

✓ **You can reduce the number of focus points available for selection from 51 to 11.** Why would you do this? Because it enables you to choose a focus point more quickly — you don't have to keep pressing the Multi Selector zillions of times to get to the one you want to use. Make the change via the Number of Focus Points option, found on the Autofocus section of the Custom Setting menu and shown on the left in Figure 8-8. The right half of the figure shows you which autofocus points are available at the reduced setting.

Note that when the camera establishes focus, it still uses the full complement of normal focus points in the Dynamic Area and 3D Tracking modes. This setting just limits the points you can choose for your initial focus point.

✓ **You can quickly select the center focus point by pressing OK.** This assumes that you haven't changed the function of that button, an option you can explore in Chapter 11.

✓ **If you want to use a certain focus point for a while, you can "lock in" that point by moving the Focus Selector Lock switch to the L position.** This feature ensures that an errant press of the Multi Selector doesn't accidentally change your selected point.

✓ **The selected focus point is also used to meter exposure when you use spot metering.** See Chapter 7 for details about metering.

✓ **Focus-point wraparound is disabled by default.** That simply means that when you're cycling through the available focus points, you hit a "wall" when you reach the top, bottom, left, or right focus point in the group. So if the leftmost point is selected, for example, pressing left again gets you nowhere. But if you turn on the Focus Point Wrap-Around option, found with the other autofocus options on the Custom Setting menu, you instead jump to the rightmost point.

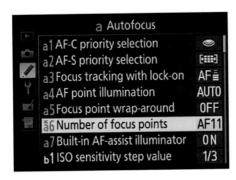 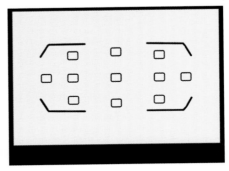

Figure 8-8: You can limit the number of available focus points to the 11 shown here.

Autofocusing with still subjects: AF-S + Single Point

For stationary subjects, the fastest, most precise autofocus option is to pair the AF-S (single-servo) Autofocus mode with the Single Point AF-area mode. To select these settings, press and hold the AF-mode button (refer to Figure 8-1). Then rotate the Main command dial to change the Autofocus mode; rotate the Sub-command dial to change the AF-area mode.

Next, follow these steps to establish focus and take the picture:

1. **Looking through the viewfinder, use the Multi Selector to position the focus point over your subject.**

   If the focus point doesn't respond, press the shutter button halfway and release it to jog the camera awake. Then try again. Also be sure that the Focus Selector Lock switch is set to the position shown in Figure 8-7.

2. **Press the shutter button halfway to set focus.**

   The camera displays a focus light in the viewfinder, as shown in Figure 8-9.

Focus indicator light

Selected focus point

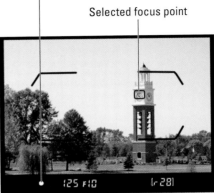

Figure 8-9: The focus light tells you that focus has been achieved.

Focus remains locked as long as you keep the shutter button pressed halfway. In any exposure mode but M, the initial exposure settings are also chosen at the moment you press the shutter button halfway, but they're adjusted as needed up to the time you take the shot.

3. **Press the shutter button the rest of the way to take the shot.**

By default, the camera doesn't let you take the picture when focus isn't set. To modify that behavior, change the AF-S Priority Selection option on the Custom Setting menu from Focus to Release.

Now for a few nuances of this autofocusing process:

✔ **A triangle symbol in the viewfinder indicates incorrect focusing.** I cover this issue in the part of Chapter 3 that shows you how to take a picture in the Auto and Auto Flash Off exposure modes, but what the heck, the illustrations are small, so Figure 8-10 shows you what the triangles look like again so you don't have to tromp back to Chapter 3. A right-pointing arrow means that focus is set in front of the object under the focus point; a left-pointing arrow means that focus is set behind the object. Typically, you see one or both of the triangles while the camera is hunting for the correct focusing distance. If the triangles don't go away, the subject is confusing the autofocus system, and your best bet is to switch to manual focusing in that situation. You also may simply be too close to your subject, so try backing away a little to see whether that helps.

✔ **You can position your subject outside a focus point if needed.** Just compose the scene initially so that your subject is under a point, press the shutter button halfway to lock focus, and then reframe. However, note that if you're using autoexposure, you may want to lock focus and exposure together by pressing the AE-L/AF-L button, as covered in Chapter 7. Otherwise, exposure is adjusted to match your new framing, which may not work well for your subject. In fact, the Chapter 7 technique for locking exposure is designed to work when teamed up with the AF-S/Single Point autofocus settings.

✔ **Which focus points you can select depends on the setting of the Number of Focus Points option on the Custom Setting menu.** By default, you can choose from all 51 points, but if you change the menu setting to 11, you're limited to the points shown in Figure 8-8. See the preceding section for details on this topic.

Focus in front of subject   Focus behind subject

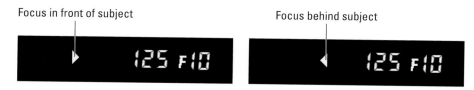

Figure 8-10: The triangles indicate that focus isn't accurately set on the object under the selected focus point.

✔ **For an audio cue that focus is set in AF-S mode, enable the Beep option on the Custom Setting menu.** You can find the option in the Shooting/Display section of the menu. If you enable the option, you also hear the beep during self-timer shooting and in a number of other scenarios.

Focusing on moving subjects: AF-C + Dynamic Area

To autofocus on a moving target, select AF-C for the Autofocus mode and choose one of the three Dynamic Area options for the AF-area mode. The earlier section "Choosing an AF-area mode: One focus point or many?" provides some information to help you decide whether to use the 9-, 21-, or 51-point Dynamic Area setting.

The focusing process is the same as just outlined, with a couple of exceptions:

✔ **When you press the shutter button halfway, the camera sets the initial focusing distance based on your selected autofocus point.** If your subject moves from that point, the camera checks surrounding points for focus information.

✔ **Focus is adjusted until you take the picture.** You see the focus indicator light in the viewfinder, but it may flash on and off as focus is adjusted.

✔ **Try to keep the subject under the selected focus point to increase the odds of good focus.** As long as the subject falls within one of the other focus points (9, 21, or 51, depending on which Dynamic Area mode you select), focus should be adjusted accordingly, however. Note that you don't see the focus point actually move in the viewfinder, but the focus tweak happens just the same. (You can hear the focus motor doing its thing if you listen closely.)

✔ **By default, the camera lets you take the picture regardless of whether focus has been achieved.** To change this behavior, head for the AF-C Priority Selection option on the Custom Setting menu and change the option from Release to Focus. At that setting, the camera won't release the shutter until focus is achieved.

Getting comfortable with continuous autofocusing takes some time, so practice before you need to photograph an important event. After you get the hang of the AF-C/Dynamic Area system, though, I think you'll really like it. When you're up to speed on the basics, explore these related options:

✔ **Using autofocus lock:** Should you want to stop the focus adjustment so that focus remains set at a specific distance, press and hold the AE-L/AF-L button. Remember, though, that the default setup for this button locks both focus and exposure. If you use this option a lot, you may want to decouple the two functions by using the button customization options covered in Chapter 11. You can use the AE-L/AF-L button to lock exposure only, for example, and then set the Fn or Depth-of-Field preview button to lock focus.

✔ **Preventing focusing miscues with tracking lock-on:** So you're shooting your friend's volleyball game, practicing your action-autofocusing skills. You set the initial focus, and the camera is doing its part by adjusting focus to accommodate her pre-serve moves. Then all of a sudden, some clueless interloper walks in front of the camera. Okay, it *was* the referee, who probably did have a right to be there, but *still.*

The good news is that as long as the ref gets out of the way before the action happens, you're probably okay. A feature called *focus tracking with lock-on,* designed for just this scenario, tells the camera to ignore objects that appear temporarily in the scene after you begin focusing. Instead of resetting focus on the newcomer, the camera continues focusing on the original subject.

You can vary the length of time the camera waits before starting to refocus through the Focus Tracking with Lock-On option, found on the Custom Setting menu and shown in Figure 8-11. Normal (3 seconds) is the default setting. You can choose a longer or shorter delay or turn off the lock-on altogether. If you turn off the lock-on, the camera starts refocusing on any object that appears in the frame between you and your original subject.

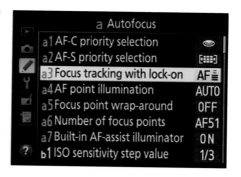

Figure 8-11: This option controls how the autofocus system deals with objects that come between the lens and the subject after you initiate focusing.

Exploring a few last autofocus tweaks

All these autofocus options making your brain hurt? Hang in there — just a few more to go, and they're no-brainers. Well, easy-brainers, at least. They're found in the Autofocus section of the Custom Setting menu and work as follows:

✔ **AF Point Illumination:** It happens so fast that you might not notice it unless you pay close attention, but when you press the shutter button halfway, the selected focus point in the viewfinder flashes red and then goes back to black. At the default setting for this option (Auto), the red highlights are displayed only when the background is dark, which would make the black focus points difficult to see. You can choose the On setting to force the highlights no matter whether the background is dark. Or you can choose Off to disable the highlights altogether.

✔ **Built-in AF-Assist Illuminator:** In dim lighting, the camera may emit a beam of light from the AF-assist light, the little lamp just below the Control panel, on the front of the camera, when you press the shutter button halfway to set focus. If the light is distracting to your subject or others in the room, you can disable it by setting this menu option to Off. You may need to focus manually, though, because without the light to help it find its target, the autofocus system may have trouble.

Additionally, the Setup menu offers an AF Fine Tune option, which is provided to enable you to create custom focusing adjustments for specific lenses. This feature is one for the experts, though; Nikon doesn't recommend that you use the fine-tuning tool unless it's unavoidable. If you consistently have focusing trouble with a lens, I recommend that you start by having your local camera tech inspect the lens to be sure it doesn't need repair. If everything checks out and you want to try the fine-tuning feature, the D7100 camera manual provides instructions.

And now for the very last (I promise) autofocus customization options: Through settings on the Controls section of the Custom Setting menu, you can set the Function (Fn) button, AE-L/AF-L button, and Depth-of-Field Preview button to lock focus or lock focus and exposure together. And you can set the OK button to highlight the active autofocus point instead of selecting the center point. But what say we leave this whole button customization discussion for Chapter 11, okay?

Focusing Manually

Some subjects confuse even the most sophisticated autofocusing systems, causing the camera's autofocus motor to spend a long time hunting for its focus point. Animals behind fences, reflective objects, water, and low-contrast subjects are just some of the autofocus troublemakers. Autofocus systems also struggle in dim lighting, although that difficulty is often offset on the D7100 by the AF-assist lamp, which shoots out a beam of light to help the camera find its focusing target.

When you encounter situations that cause an autofocus hang-up, you can try adjusting the autofocus options discussed earlier in this chapter. Often, it's simply easier to focus manually. For best results, follow these manual-focusing steps:

1. **If your lens has a manual/auto focusing switch, set that switch to the manual position.**

   On the 18–105mm kit lens, set the switch to M.

2. **Set the Focus-mode selector switch (front left side of the camera) to the M position.**

   Refer to Figure 8-1 if you need help locating the switch.

If you're using an AF-S lens (the kit lens is included in this category), you actually can skip this step. However, if you're not sure whether your lens is an AF-S type, set the switch to the M position to be safe. Otherwise, damage to the lens and camera can occur.

3. **Select a focus point.**

   Use the same technique as when selecting a point during autofocusing: Looking through the viewfinder, press the Multi Selector right, left, up, or down until the point you want to use flashes red. Again, you may need to press the shutter button halfway and release it to wake up the display first. And make sure that the Focus Selector Lock switch is set to the position shown in Figure 8-7.

During autofocusing, the selected focus point tells the camera what part of the frame to use when establishing focus. And technically speaking, you don't *have* to choose a focus point for manual focusing — the camera will set the focus according to the position that you set by turning the focusing ring. However, choosing a focus point is still a good idea, for two reasons: First, even though you're focusing manually, the camera provides some feedback to let you know whether the focus is correct, and that feedback is based on your selected focus point. Second, if you use spot metering, an exposure option covered in Chapter 7, exposure is based on the selected focus point.

4. **Frame the shot so that your subject is under your selected focus point.**

5. **Turn the lens focusing ring to focus.**

When the focus is set on the object under your focus point, the focus lamp in the lower-left corner of the viewfinder lights, just as it does during autofocusing. If you see a triangle in that part of the display instead, focus is set in front of or behind the object in the focus point. (Refer to Figure 8-10.)

6. **Press the shutter button halfway to initiate exposure metering.**

   Adjust exposure as needed; see Chapter 7 for help.

7. **Press the shutter button the rest of the way to take the shot.**

Manipulating Depth of Field

Getting familiar with the concept of *depth of field* is one of the biggest steps you can take to becoming a better photographer. I introduce you to depth of field in Chapters 3 and 7, but here's a quick recap:

   ✔ *Depth of field* refers to the distance over which objects in a photograph appear acceptably sharp.

✔ With a shallow, or small, depth of field, distant objects appear more softly focused than the main subject (assuming that you set focus on the main subject, of course).

✔ With a large depth of field, the zone of sharp focus extends to include objects at a distance from your subject.

Which arrangement works best depends entirely on your creative vision and your subject. In portraits, for example, a classic technique is to use a short depth of field, as I did for the photo in Figure 8-12. This approach increases emphasis on the subject while diminishing the impact of the background. But for the photo shown in Figure 8-13, I wanted to emphasize that the foreground figures were in St. Peter's Square, so I used a large depth of field, which kept the background buildings sharply focused and gave them equal weight in the scene.

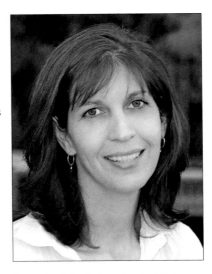

Figure 8-12: A shallow depth of field blurs the background and draws added attention to the subject.

So how do you manipulate depth of field? You have three points of control:

✔ **Aperture setting (f-stop):** The aperture is one of three main exposure settings, all explained fully in Chapter 7. Depth of field increases as you stop down the aperture (by choosing a higher f-stop number). For shallow depth of field, open the aperture (by choosing a lower f-stop number). Figure 8-14 offers an example; in the f/22 version, focus is sharp all the way through the frame; in the f/13 version, focus softens as the distance from the center lure increases. I snapped both images using the same focal length and camera-to-subject distance, setting focus on the front of the center lure.

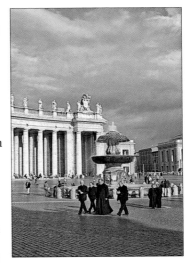

Figure 8-13: A large depth of field keeps both foreground and background subjects in focus.

Aperture, f/22; Focal length, 92mm

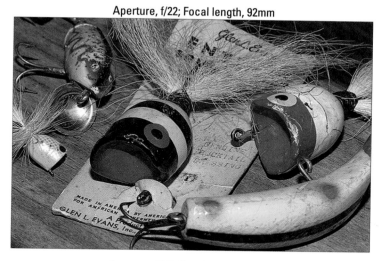

Aperture, f/13; Focal length, 92mm

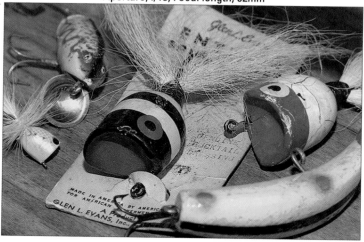

Figure 8-14: A lower f-stop number (wider aperture) decreases depth of field.

✔ **Lens focal length:** In lay terms, _focal length_ determines what the lens "sees." As you increase focal length, measured in millimeters, the angle of view narrows, objects appear larger in the frame, and — the important point for this discussion — depth of field decreases. Additionally, the spatial relationship of objects changes as you adjust focal length. As an example, Figure 8-15 compares the same scene shot at a focal length of 127mm and 183mm. I used the same aperture, f/5.6, for both examples.

Aperture, f/5.6; Focal length, 127mm

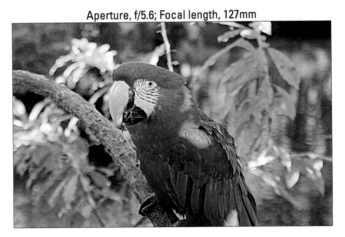

Aperture, f/5.6; Focal length, 183mm

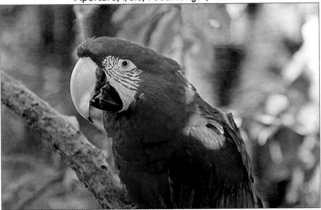

Figure 8-15: Zooming to a longer focal length also reduces depth of field.

Whether you have any focal length flexibility depends on your lens: If you have a zoom lens, you can adjust the focal length by zooming in or out. If you don't have a zoom lens, the focal length is fixed, so scratch this means of manipulating depth of field.

For more details about focal length and your camera, flip to Chapter 1 and explore the section related to choosing lenses.

✔ **Camera-to-subject distance:** As you move the lens closer to your subject, depth of field decreases. This assumes that you don't zoom in or out to reframe the picture, thereby changing the focal length. If you do, depth of field is affected by both the camera position and focal length.

Together, these three factors determine the maximum and minimum depth of field that you can achieve, as follows:

- **To produce the shallowest depth of field:** Open the aperture as wide as possible (the lowest f-stop number), zoom in to the maximum focal length of your lens, and get as close as possible to your subject.

- **To produce maximum depth of field:** Stop down the aperture to the highest possible f-stop number, zoom out to the shortest focal length (widest angle) your lens offers, and move farther from your subject.

A couple of final tips related to depth of field:

- **Aperture-priority autoexposure mode (A) enables you to easily control depth of field while enjoying exposure assistance from the camera.** In this mode, you rotate the Sub-command dial to set the f-stop, and the camera selects the appropriate shutter speed to produce a good exposure. The range of available aperture settings depends on your lens.

- **For greater background blurring, move the subject farther from the background.** The extent to which background focus shifts as you adjust depth of field also is affected by the distance between the subject and the background.

- **Press the Depth-of-Field Preview button to get an idea of how your f-stop will affect depth of field.** When you look through your viewfinder and press the shutter button halfway, you can get only a partial indication of the depth of field that your current camera settings will produce. You can see the effect of focal length and the camera-to-subject distance, but not how your selected f-stop will affect depth of field because the camera doesn't close down the aperture to your selected setting until you take the picture.

  By using the Depth-of-Field Preview button, however, you can preview how the f-stop will affect the image. Almost hidden away on the front of your camera, the button is highlighted in Figure 8-16. When you press the button, the camera temporarily sets the aperture to your selected f-stop so that you can preview depth of field. At small apertures (high f-stop settings), the viewfinder display may become quite dark, but this doesn't indicate a problem with exposure — it's just a function of how the preview works.

Depth-of-Field Preview button

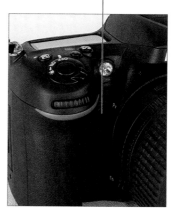

Figure 8-16: Press this button to get a preview of the effect of aperture on depth of field.

By default, the camera also emits a modeling flash when you preview depth of field and have flash enabled. If you want to experiment with this feature, visit the flash discussion in Chapter 7 for details. Turn the feature off via the Modeling Flash option on the Custom Setting menu. And if you don't use the Depth-of-Field Preview button often, see Chapter 11 to find out how to assign the button a different role in life.

Controlling Color

Compared with understanding some aspects of digital photography — resolution, aperture and shutter speed, depth of field, and so on — making sense of your camera's color options is easy-breezy. First, color problems aren't all that common, and when they are, they're usually simple to fix with a quick shift of your camera's white balance control. And getting a grip on color requires learning only a couple of new terms, an unusual state of affairs for an endeavor that often seems more like high-tech science than art.

The rest of this chapter explains the aforementioned white balance control, plus a couple of menu options that enable you to fine-tune the way your camera renders colors.

Correcting colors with white balance

Every light source emits a particular color cast. Science-y types measure the color of light, officially known as *color temperature,* on the Kelvin scale, which is named after its creator. You can see the Kelvin scale in Figure 8-17.

When photographers talk about "warm light" and "cool light," though, they aren't referring to the position on the Kelvin scale — or at least not in the way we usually think of temperatures, with a higher number meaning hotter. Instead, the terms describe the visual appearance of the light. Warm light, produced by candles and incandescent lights, falls in the red-yellow spectrum you see at the bottom of the Kelvin scale in Figure 8-17; cool light, in the blue-green spectrum, appears at the top of the Kelvin scale.

At any rate, most people don't notice these fluctuating colors of light because our eyes automatically compensate for them. Similarly, a

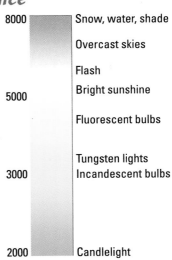

Figure 8-17: Each light source emits a specific color.

digital camera compensates for different colors of light through *white balancing*. Simply put, white balancing neutralizes light so that whites are always white, which in turn ensures that other colors are rendered accurately. If the camera senses warm light, it shifts colors slightly to the cool side of the color spectrum; in cool light, the camera shifts colors in the opposite direction.

By default, the camera uses automatic white balancing — the AWB setting (for Auto White Balance) — which tackles this process remarkably well in most situations. But if your scene is lit by two or more light sources that cast different colors, the white balance sensor can get confused, producing an unwanted color cast.

For example, when shooting the figurine shown in Figure 8-18, I lit the scene with photo lights that use tungsten bulbs, which produce light with a color temperature similar to regular household incandescent bulbs. Some strong daylight was filtering in through nearby windows, though, and in Auto White Balance mode, the camera reacted to that daylight — which has a cool color cast — and applied too much warming, giving my original image (left) a yellow tint. No problem: I just switched the White Balance mode from Auto to the Incandescent setting. The right image in Figure 8-18 shows the corrected colors.

The next section explains how to make a simple white balance correction; following that, you can explore some advanced white balance options.

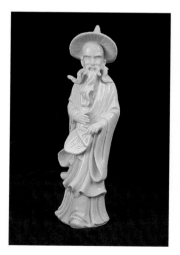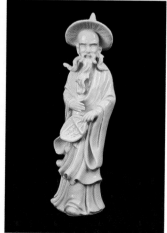

Figure 8-18: For this photo, multiple light sources resulted in a yellow color cast in Auto White Balance mode (left); switching to the Incandescent setting solved the problem (right).

Changing the White Balance setting

You can adjust the White Balance setting only in the P, S, A, and M exposure modes. If you have a color issue and want to use the other exposure modes, you're out of luck. See Chapter 7 to find out how to step up from the fully automatic exposure modes to one of these advanced exposure modes.

The current White Balance setting appears in the Control panel and Information display, as shown in Figure 8-19. The figures show the symbols that represent the Auto setting; other settings are represented by the icons you see in Table 8-1.

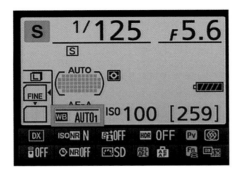
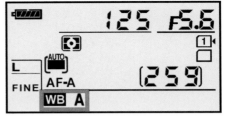

Figure 8-19: These icons represent the current White Balance setting.

Table 8-1	Manual White Balance Settings
Symbol	**Light Source**
	Incandescent
	Fluorescent
	Direct sunlight
	Flash
	Cloudy
	Shade
K	Choose color temperature
PRE	Custom preset

WB The quickest way to change the setting is to press and hold the WB button as you rotate the Main command dial, but you also can get the job done via the Shooting menu, as shown in Figure 8-20. After highlighting the setting you want to use, press OK.

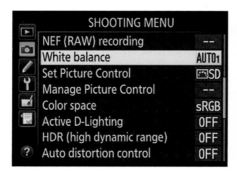 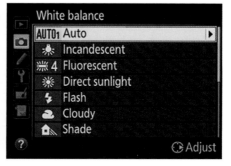

Figure 8-20: The White Balance option on the Shooting menu gives you access to some fine-tuning options.

If you go the menu route, you can access options that modify the White Balance setting, as follows:

✓ **Selecting from two Auto settings:** I know what you're thinking: "For heaven's sake, even the Auto setting is complicated?" Yeah, but just a little: You can choose from two Auto White Balance settings. At the default setting, Normal, things happen as you'd expect: The camera analyzes the color temperature of the light and adjusts colors to render the scene accurately. If you use the other setting, Keep Warm Lighting Colors, the warm hues produced by incandescent lighting are left intact. I prefer the default, but if you want to choose the other setting, open the Shooting menu, choose White Balance, and then choose Auto and press the Multi Selector right. You see the screen shown in Figure 8-21; make your choice and press OK.

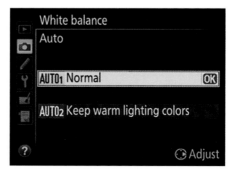

Figure 8-21: The Auto 2 setting preserves some of the warm hues that incandescent lighting lends to a scene.

You can tell which Auto setting is selected by looking at the Shooting menu and Information display; a little 1 appears next to the word *Auto* when the Normal option is active, as shown in the left screens in Figures 8-19 and 8-20. A 2 appears when the other setting is in force.

✔ **Specifying a color temperature through the K White Balance setting:** If you know the exact color temperature of your light source — perhaps you're using some special studio bulbs, for example — you can tell the camera to balance colors for that precise temperature. (Well, technically, you have to choose from a preset list of temperatures, but you should be able to get close to the temperature you have in mind.) First, select the K White Balance setting. (*K* for *Kelvin,* get it?) Then, while pressing the WB button, rotate the Sub-command dial to set the color temperature, which appears at the top of the Control panel and Information display.

You also can set the temperature through the White Balance option on the Shooting menu. Select Choose Color Temp as your White Balance setting and then press the Multi Selector right to display a list of the available temperature options. Highlight your choice and press OK.

✔ **Specifying a fluorescent bulb type:** For the Fluorescent setting, you can select a specific type of bulb. To do so, you must go through the Shooting menu. Select Fluorescent as the White Balance setting and then press the Multi Selector right to display the list of bulbs, as shown in Figure 8-22. Select the option that most closely matches your bulbs and then press OK.

After you select a fluorescent bulb type, that option is always used when you use the WB button to select the Fluorescent White Balance setting. Again, you can change the bulb type only through the Shooting menu.

✔ **Creating a custom White Balance preset:** The PRE (Preset Manual) option enables you to create and store a precise, customized White Balance setting, as explained in the upcoming "Creating custom White Balance presets" section. This setting is the fastest way to achieve accurate colors when your scene is lit by multiple light sources that have differing color temperatures.

✔ **Fine-tuning a White Balance setting:** You can tweak the way colors are rendered at any setting via the Shooting menu as well; the next section shows you how.

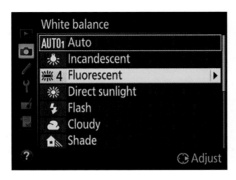
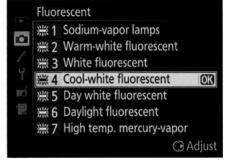

Figure 8-22: You can select a specific type of fluorescent bulb.

Your selected White Balance setting remains in force for the P, S, A, and M exposure modes until you change it. So you may want to get in the habit of resetting the option to the Auto setting after you finish shooting whatever subject it was that caused you to switch to manual White Balance mode.

Fine-tuning White Balance settings

To fine-tune any White Balance option but PRE (Preset Manual), take the following steps. (For the PRE option, you first need to create your preset, which I tell you how to do in the next two sections; see the "Editing presets" section later on to find out how to fine-tune a preset.)

1. **Set the Mode dial to P, S, A, or M.**

   You can modify white balance in these exposure modes only.

2. **Display the Shooting menu, highlight White Balance, and press OK.**

3. **Highlight the White Balance setting you want to adjust, and press the Multi Selector right.**

   You're taken to a screen where you can do your fine-tuning, as shown in Figure 8-23.

   If you select Auto, Fluorescent, or K (Choose Color Temp.), you first go to a screen where you select the Auto setting you want to use, the specific type of bulb, or Kelvin color temperature, as covered in the preceding section. After you take that step, press the Multi Selector right to get to the fine-tuning screen.

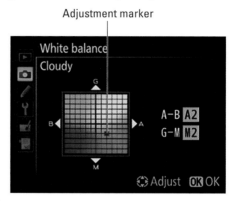

Figure 8-23: You can fine-tune the White Balance settings via the Shooting menu.

4. **Fine-tune the setting by using the Multi Selector to move the adjustment marker in the color grid.**

   The grid is set up around two color pairs: Green and Magenta, represented by G and M; and Blue and Amber, represented by B and A. By pressing the Multi Selector, you can move the adjustment marker around the grid. (The adjustment marker is labeled in Figure 8-23.)

   As you move the marker, the A–B and G–M boxes on the right side of the screen show you the current amount of color shift. A value of 0 indicates the default amount of color compensation applied by the selected White Balance setting. In Figure 8-23, for example, I moved the marker two levels toward amber and two levels toward magenta to specify that I wanted colors to be a tad warmer.

If you're familiar with traditional colored lens filters, you may know that the density of a filter, which determines the degree of color correction it provides, is measured in *mireds* (pronounced *my-redds*). The white balance grid is designed around this system: Moving the marker one level is the equivalent of adding a filter with a density of five mireds.

5. Press OK to complete the adjustment.

After you adjust a White Balance setting, an asterisk appears next to that setting in the White Balance menu and next to the WB symbol in the Information display and Control panel.

For all White Balance settings but K (Choose Color Temp.) and PRE (Preset Manual), you can apply a white balance shift along the blue-to-amber axis without going through the Shooting menu. Instead, press and hold the WB button and then rotate the Sub-command dial. You see the amount of adjustment in the Control panel and Information display. An *a* value indicates a shift toward the amber direction; a *b* value, toward blue. For example, the value A2 indicates a shift two steps toward amber (A). Set the value to 0 to remove the adjustment.

Creating custom White Balance presets

If none of the standard White Balance settings do the trick and you don't want to fool with fine-tuning them, take advantage of the PRE (Preset Manual) feature. This option enables you to do two things:

- ✔ Base white balance on a direct measurement of the actual lighting conditions.
- ✔ Match white balance to an existing photo.

You can create up to six custom White Balance presets, which are assigned the names d-1 through d-6. The next two sections provide you with the step-by-step instructions; following that, you can find out how to fine-tune, protect, and otherwise edit presets.

Setting white balance with direct measurement

To use this technique, you need a piece of card stock that's either neutral gray or absolute white — not eggshell white, sand white, or any other close-but-not-perfect white. (You can buy reference cards made just for this purpose in many camera stores for less than $20.)

Position the reference card so that it receives the same lighting you'll use for your photo. Then take these steps:

1. **Set the exposure mode to P, S, A, or M.**

   As with all white balance features, you can take advantage of this one only in those exposure modes.

2. **Open the Shooting menu, choose White Balance, and highlight PRE (Preset Manual), as shown on the left in Figure 8-24.**

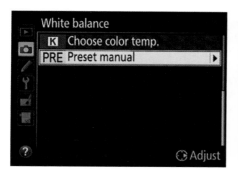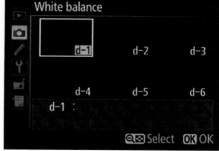

Figure 8-24: You can store as many as six custom White Balance presets.

3. **Press the Multi Selector right to display the screen shown on the right in Figure 8-24.**

4. **Highlight the preset number (d-1 through d-6) you want to assign to the custom White Balance setting.**

   Preset d-1 is selected by default the first time you go through this process, as shown in Figure 8-24. If you select an existing preset, it will be overwritten by your new preset.

5. **Press OK, press the shutter button halfway, and release it to return to shooting mode.**

6. **Frame your shot so that the reference card completely fills the viewfinder.**

7. **Check exposure and adjust settings if needed.**

   This process won't work if your settings produce an underexposed or overexposed shot of your reference card.

WB

8. Press the WB button.

You see the letters PRE in the white balance area of the Control panel as well as in the Information display. You also see the number of the preset you chose in Step 4.

9. Keep pressing the WB button until the letters PRE begin flashing in the Control panel and viewfinder.

10. Release the WB button and take a picture of the reference card before the PRE warning stops flashing.

You have about 6 seconds to snap the picture.

If the camera is successful at recording the white balance data, the letters _Gd_ flash in the viewfinder. In the Control panel, the word _Good_ flashes. If you instead see the message _No Gd,_ adjust your lighting or exposure settings and then try again. Remember, the reference card shot must be properly exposed for the camera to create the preset successfully.

To use a stored preset as your White Balance setting, take either of these approaches:

WB

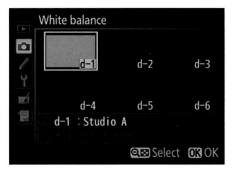

Figure 8-25: Highlight the thumbnail representing the preset you want to use.

✔ **WB button + command dials:** First, select PRE as the White Balance setting by pressing the WB button as you rotate the Main command dial. Keep holding the button and rotate the Sub-command dial to cycle through the available presets (d-1 through d-6). The number of the selected preset appears in the Control panel and Information display while the button is pressed.

✔ **Shooting menu:** Repeat Steps 1–5 of the preceding list to select your custom preset from the menu. In Step 4, you see a thumbnail representing your preset, as shown in Figure 8-25. The thumbnail will be white (or gray) if you based the preset on a reference card, as shown in the figure.

After creating a preset, you can use the feature I explain in the upcoming section "Editing presets" to add a text identifier to help you remember what lighting conditions you used to create the preset, as I did before capturing the screen you see in Figure 8-25.

One final tip: In Live View mode, you can base your preset on any neutral gray or white object in the frame — you don't have to fill the frame with a reference card. Follow Steps 1–5, skip Step 6, and then continue on through Step 9 to display a small white-balance target (a yellow rectangle) in the frame. Position that frame over your neutral object and then press OK to establish the preset.

Matching white balance to an existing photo

Suppose that you're the marketing manager for a small business, and one of your jobs is to shoot portraits of the company bigwigs for the annual report. You build a small studio just for that purpose, complete with a couple of photography lights and a nice, conservative, beige backdrop.

Of course, the bigwigs can't all come to get their pictures taken in the same month, let alone on the same day. Still, you have to make sure that the colors in that beige backdrop remain consistent for each shot, no matter how much time passes between photo sessions. This scenario is one possible use for an advanced white balance feature that enables you to base white balance on an existing photo.

Basing white balance on an existing photo works well only in strictly controlled lighting situations, where the color temperature of your lights is consistent from day to day. Otherwise, the White Balance setting that produces color accuracy when you shoot Big Boss Number One may add an ugly color cast to the one you snap of Big Boss Number Two.

To give this option a try, follow these steps:

1. **Copy the picture that you want to use as the reference photo to a camera memory card, if it isn't already stored there.**

   You can copy the picture to the card using a card reader and whatever method you usually use to transfer files from one drive to another. The main folder on the card is DCIM; open that folder and store the picture in the camera's image folder, named 100D7100 by default.

   You can put the card containing the photo in either memory card slot.

2. **Set the exposure mode to P, S, A, or M; then open the Shooting menu, highlight White Balance, and press OK.**

3. **Select PRE (Preset Manual) and press the Multi Selector right.**

   You see the screen shown earlier in Figure 8-25. (If you haven't yet created any presets, the d-1 thumbnail appears black instead of gray.)

4. **Use the Multi Selector to highlight the number of the preset you want to create (d-1 through d-6).**

If you already created a preset, choosing its number will overwrite that first preset with your new one.

5. **Press the ISO button.**

You see the menu shown in Figure 8-26.

6. **Highlight Select Image and press the Multi Selector right.**

You see thumbnails of your photos.

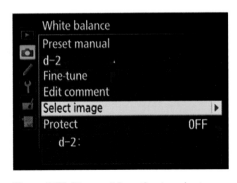

Figure 8-26: Choose this option to select an image to use as the basis for a White Balance preset.

7. **Use the Multi Selector to move the yellow highlight box over the picture you want to use as your white balance photo.**

8. **Press OK.**

You return to the screen showing your White Balance preset thumbnails. The thumbnail for the photo you selected in Step 7 appears as the thumbnail for the preset slot you chose in Step 4.

9. **Press OK to return to the Shooting menu.**

The White Balance setting you just created is now selected. See the end of the preceding section to find out how to select a different preset.

Editing presets

After creating a preset, you can't delete it — the only way to get rid of it is to overwrite it by creating a new preset with the same number (d-1 through d-6). However, you can edit a preset in a couple ways.

To access these features, choose White Balance from the Shooting menu. Then select PRE (Preset Manual), press the Multi Selector right, and highlight the number of the preset you want to edit. Finally, press the ISO button to display the screen shown on the left in Figure 8-27.

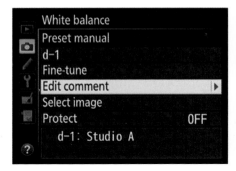 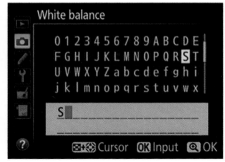

Figure 8-27: Add a text label to a preset to remind you which lighting conditions you used when creating it.

Here's what you can accomplish with each menu option:

- **Preset number (d-1, in the figure):** To edit a different preset, highlight this first option and press the Multi Selector right or left to cycle through the six presets.

- **Fine-tune:** Press the Multi Selector right to access the same fine-tuning screen that's available for other White Balance settings. See "Fine-tuning White Balance settings," earlier in this chapter, for help.

- **Edit comment:** This is a great option: It enables you to add a brief text label to the preset so that you can easily remember what lighting conditions the White Balance setting is designed to address. For example, you might add the label "Studio A" to one preset and "Studio B" to another to help you remember which is which. The label then appears with the preset thumbnail.

  After highlighting Edit Comment, press the Multi Selector right to display the text-entry screen shown on the right in Figure 8-27. Use these techniques to create your text comment:

  - *To enter a character:* On the "keyboard" in the top half of the screen, use the Multi Selector to highlight the letter you want to enter. Then press OK.

  - *To move the cursor in the text entry area:* Hold down the ISO button while pressing the Multi Selector right or left. Release the ISO button to return to the keyboard.

  - *To delete a character:* First use the preceding technique to highlight the offending character in the text-entry box. Then release the ISO button and press the Delete button to erase the character.

ISO

When you finish entering your label, press the Qual button to finalize things and store the comment with your preset.

✓ **Select Image:** This option enables you to base a preset on an existing photo; see the preceding section for how-to's.

✓ **Protect:** Set this option to On to lock a preset so that you can't accidentally overwrite it when you create a new one. If you enable this feature, however, you can't alter the preset comment or fine-tune the setting.

To exit the edit screen and return to shooting, press the shutter button halfway and release it, or press Menu to return to the menu screens.

Bracketing white balance

Chapter 7 introduces you to your camera's automatic bracketing feature, which enables you to easily record the same image at several different exposure settings. In addition to being able to bracket autoexposure, flash, and Active D-Lighting settings, you can use the feature to bracket white balance.

Note a couple of things about this feature:

✓ **You must set the Mode dial to P, S, A, or M.** You can't take advantage of auto bracketing in the other exposure modes.

✓ **You can bracket JPEG shots only.** You can't use white balance bracketing if you set the camera's Image Quality setting to either Raw (NEF) or any of the RAW+JPEG options. And frankly, there isn't any need to do so because you can precisely tune colors of Raw files when you process them in your Raw converter. Chapter 6 has details on Raw processing.

✓ **You take just one picture to record each bracketed series.** Each time you press the shutter button, the camera records a single image and then makes the bracketed copies, each at a different White Balance setting. One frame is always captured with no white balance adjustment.

✓ **You can apply white balance bracketing only along the blue-to-amber axis of the fine-tuning color grid.** You can't shift colors along the green-to-magenta axis, as you can when tweaking a specific White Balance setting. (For a reminder of this feature, see the earlier section "Fine-tuning White Balance settings.")

✓ **You can shift colors a maximum of three steps between frames.** For those familiar with traditional lens filters, each step on the axis is equivalent to a filter density of five mireds.

I used white balance bracketing to record the three candle photos in Figure 8-28. For the blue and amber versions, I set the bracketing to shift colors the maximum three steps from neutral. In this photo, I find the shift most noticeable in the color of the backdrop.

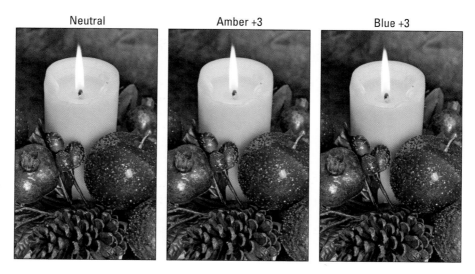

Figure 8-28: I used white balance bracketing to record three variations on the subject.

To apply white balance bracketing, you first need to take these steps:

1. **Set the Mode dial to P, S, A, or M.**

2. **Set the Image Quality setting to one of the JPEG options (Fine, Normal, or Basic).**

   Chapter 2 explains these options. To adjust the setting quickly, press the Qual button while rotating the Main command dial.

3. **Display the Custom Setting menu, select the Bracketing/Flash submenu, and press OK.**

4. **Select Auto Bracketing Set, as shown on the left in Figure 8-29, and press OK.**

   You see the screen shown on the right in the figure.

5. **Select WB Bracketing and press OK.**

   The bracketing feature is now set up to adjust white balance between your bracketed shots.

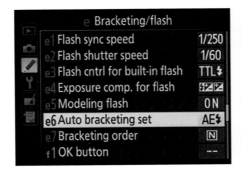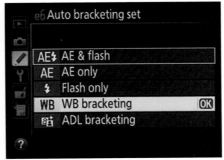

Figure 8-29: Set the Auto Bracketing Set option to WB Bracketing.

From here on, bracketing works pretty much as detailed in the steps at the end of Chapter 7. Rather than repeating everything here, I'll save some page space and provide just a quick summary of how to establish the bracketing settings.

✔ **To set the number of frames and direction of the bracketing adjustment:** Press and hold the BKT button (right-front side of the camera) while rotating the Main command dial. For white balance bracketing, the options are as follows:

- *b3F:* Records three frames: one with no adjustment and two shifted toward blue.

- *a3F:* Records three frames: one neutral and two shifted toward amber.

- *b2F:* Records two frames: one without any adjustment and one shifted toward blue.

- *a2F:* Again, you get two frames, but the second is shifted toward amber.

- *3F:* This setting records three frames: one neutral, one pushed toward amber, and one shifted toward blue.

- *5F:* Produces one neutral shot, two shifted toward amber and two shifted toward blue.

- *0F:* Select this setting to turn off bracketing.

✔ **To set the amount of white-balance adjustment:** Press the BKT button and rotate the Sub-command dial. Again, you can set the bracketing amount to 1, 2, or 3.

While the BKT button is pressed, you can view both settings in the Control panel and Information display. When you release the button, you see the same BKT symbol and progress indicator that appears when you bracket exposure settings. (Again, check out Chapter 7 for details.)

After establishing the bracketing parameters, just shoot your bracketed frames. Remember: Press the shutter button just once, and the camera records the entire bracketed series. Bracketing remains in force until you disable it (by setting the frame number to 0F).

Choosing a Color Space: sRGB versus Adobe RGB

By default, your camera captures images using the *sRGB color mode,* which refers to an industry-standard spectrum of colors. (The *s* is for *standard,* and the RGB is for *red-green-blue,* which are the primary colors in the digital color world.) The sRGB color mode was created to help ensure color consistency as an image moves from camera (or scanner) to monitor and printer; the idea was to create a spectrum of colors that all devices can reproduce.

However, the sRGB color spectrum leaves out some colors that *can* be reproduced in print and onscreen, at least by some devices. So as an alternative, your camera also enables you to shoot in the Adobe RGB color mode, which includes a larger spectrum (or *gamut*) of colors. Figure 8-30 offers an illustration of the two spectrums.

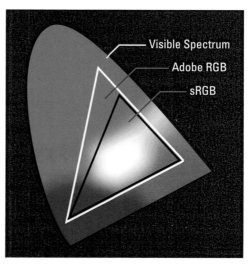

Some colors in the Adobe RGB spectrum can't be reproduced in print. (The printer just substitutes the closest printable color, if necessary.) Still, I usually shoot in Adobe RGB mode because I see no reason to limit myself to a smaller spectrum from the get-go.

However, just because I use Adobe RGB doesn't mean that it's right for you. First, if you plan to print and share your photos without making any adjustments in your

Figure 8-30: Adobe RGB includes some colors not found in the sRGB spectrum.

photo editor, you're better off sticking with sRGB because most printers and web browsers are designed around that color space. Second, know that to retain all your original Adobe RGB colors when you work with your photos, your editing software must support that color space — not all programs do. You also must be willing to study the whole topic of digital color a little bit because you need to use some specific settings to avoid really mucking up the color works.

If you want to go with Adobe RGB instead of sRGB, you can make the change via the Color Space option on the Shooting menu, as shown in Figure 8-31.

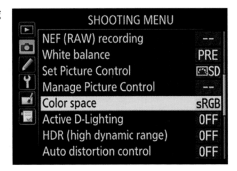

SHOOTING MENU	
NEF (RAW) recording	--
White balance	PRE
Set Picture Control	SD
Manage Picture Control	--
Color space	sRGB
Active D-Lighting	OFF
HDR (high dynamic range)	OFF
Auto distortion control	OFF

Figure 8-31: Stick with sRGB unless you understand color management and have software that supports the Adobe RGB color space.

You can tell whether you captured an image in the Adobe RGB format by looking at its filename: Adobe RGB images start with an underscore, as in _DSC0627.jpg. For pictures captured in the sRGB color space, the underscore appears in the middle of the filename, as in DSC_0627.jpg.

Taking a Quick Look at Picture Controls

The Picture Control setting gives you one more way to modify color intensity as well as to adjust image contrast and sharpening. *Sharpening,* in case you're new to the term, refers to a software process that adjusts contrast in a way that creates the illusion of slightly sharper focus. I emphasize, "slightly sharper focus." Sharpening produces a subtle tweak, not a fix for poor focus.

Two things to note before you explore Picture Controls:

✔ **Picture Controls affect only those photos that you shoot in the JPEG format.** If you select Raw (NEF) as the format, the Picture Control setting affects only the picture preview you see during playback and when you view the picture thumbnail in your photo software. (See Chapter 2 for help understanding the JPEG and Raw formats.)

✔ You can specify a Picture Control only in the P, S, A, and M exposure modes. In all other modes, the camera selects the Picture Control for you.

You can choose from the six Picture Control settings:

✔ **Standard (SD):** The default setting, this option captures the image normally — that is, using the characteristics that Nikon offers as suitable for the majority of subjects.

✔ **Neutral (NL):** At this setting, the camera doesn't enhance color, contrast, and sharpening as much as in the other modes. The setting is designed for people who want to precisely manipulate these picture characteristics in a photo editor. By not overworking colors, sharpening, and so on when producing your original file, the camera delivers an original that gives you more latitude in the digital darkroom.

✔ **Vivid (VI):** In this mode, the camera amps up color saturation, contrast, and sharpening.

✔ **Monochrome (MC):** This setting produces black-and-white photos. Only in the digital world, they're called *grayscale images* because a true black-and-white image contains only black and white, with no shades of gray.

I'm not keen on creating grayscale images this way. I prefer to shoot in full color and then do my own grayscale conversion in my photo editor. That technique just gives you more control over the look of your black-and-white photos. Assuming that you work with a decent photo editor, you can control what original tones are emphasized in your grayscale version, for example. Additionally, keep in mind that you can always convert a color image to grayscale, but you can't go the other direction. You can create a black-and-white copy of your color image right in the camera, in fact; Chapter 10 shows you how.

✔ **Portrait (PT):** This mode tweaks colors and sharpening in a way that is designed to produce nice skin texture and pleasing skin tones. (If you shoot in the Portrait or Night Portrait Scene modes, the camera selects this Picture Control for you.)

✔ **Landscape (LS):** This mode emphasizes blues and greens. As you might expect, it's the mode used by the Landscape Scene mode.

The extent to which the Picture Control setting affects your image depends on the subject as well as the exposure settings you choose and the lighting conditions, but Figure 8-32 gives you a general idea of what to expect. As you can see, the differences between the Picture Controls are pretty subtle, with the exception of the Monochrome setting.

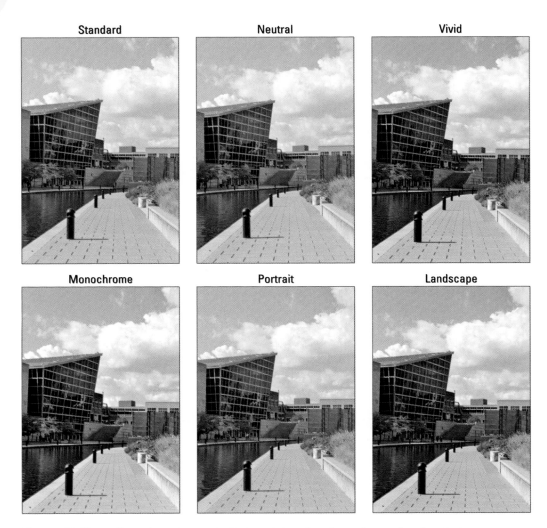

Figure 8-32: Picture Controls apply preset adjustments to color, sharpening, and contrast to images you shoot in the JPEG file format.

You can view the current setting in the Information display: It's represented by the two-letter code highlighted in Figure 8-33. (See the preceding list for the code-decoder.)

To adjust the setting, follow either of these paths:

- ✔ **Shooting menu:** Select Set Picture Control and press OK to display the list of options, as illustrated in Figure 8-34. Highlight your choice and press OK.

- ✔ **Information display control strip:** Here's an even faster option: Press the *i* button to go activate the control strip, highlight the Picture Control setting, and press OK to display the Picture Control menu screen (the right screen in Figure 8-34).

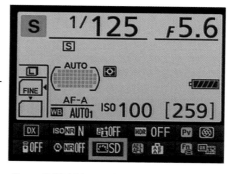

Figure 8-33: This two-letter code represents the current Picture Control setting.

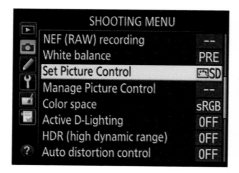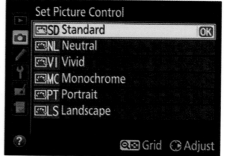

Figure 8-34: You can adjust the setting via the Shooting menu.

At least while you're new to the camera, I recommend that you stick with the default Picture Control setting, for two reasons. First, you have way more important camera settings to worry about — aperture, shutter speed, autofocus, and all the rest. Why add one more setting to your list, especially when the impact of changing it is minimal?

Second, if you really want to mess with the characteristics that the Picture Control options affect, you're much better off shooting in the Raw (NEF) format and then making those adjustments on a picture-by-picture basis in your Raw converter. In Nikon ViewNX 2, you can even assign any of the existing Picture Controls to your Raw files and then compare how each one affects the image. The camera does tag your Raw file with whatever Picture Control is active when you take the shot, but the image adjustments are in no way set in stone, or even in sand — you can tweak your photo at will.

However, in the interest of full disclosure, I should alert you to a feature that may make Picture Controls a little more useful to some people: You can modify any Picture Control to more closely render a scene the way you envision it. So, for example, if you like the bold colors of Landscape mode but don't think the effect goes far enough, you can adjust the setting to amp up colors even more.

To reserve page space in this book for functions that experience tells me will be the most useful to the most readers, I opted not to provide full details about customizing Picture Controls. The following steps provide a quick overview of the process so that if you encounter the menu screens that contain the related options, you'll have some idea of what you're seeing:

1. **Set the Mode dial to P, S, A, or M.**

   You can select and modify Picture Controls only in these exposure modes.

2. **Access the Set Picture Control option via the Information display control strip (press the *i* button to activate the strip) or the Shooting menu. Then press OK.**

   Either way, you see the screen shown on the left in Figure 8-35.

3. **Highlight the Picture Control you want to modify.**

   For example, I highlighted the Vivid setting on the left screen in Figure 8-35.

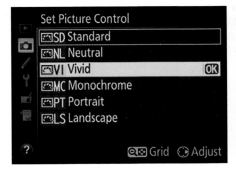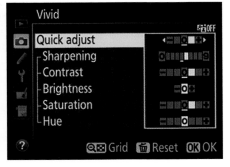

Figure 8-35: After selecting a Picture Control, press right to display options for adjusting its effect on your pictures.

4. **Press the Multi Selector right.**

You see the screen shown on the right in Figure 8-35, containing slid-
ers that you use to modify the Picture Control. Which options you can
adjust depend on your selected Picture Control.

5. **Highlight a picture characteristic and then press the Multi Selector
right or left to adjust the setting.**

A few tips:

- Some Picture Controls offer a Quick Adjust setting, which enables
you to easily increase or decrease the overall effect of the Picture
Control. A positive value produces a more exaggerated effect; set
the slider to 0 to return to the default setting.

- The large vertical line in the slider bar indicates the current setting
for the option.

- After you adjust a setting, you see a little line under the slider bar
to represent the default setting.

- Reset all the options to their defaults by pressing the Delete
button.

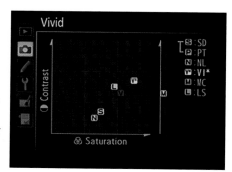

Figure 8-36: Press the Zoom In button to
display a grid that ranks each Picture Control
according to its level of saturation and
contrast.

- To display a grid that lets
you see how your selected
Picture Control compares
with the others in terms of
color saturation and con-
trast, as shown in Figure
8-36, press and hold the ISO
button. (I vote this screen
most likely to confound new
camera users who stumble
across it.) Note that the
Standard and Portrait settings are identical in terms
of contrast and saturation,
so the P for Portrait doesn't
appear in the grid unless
you selected that Picture
Control initially.

If you changed any settings before getting to the screen, you see
an asterisk next to the setting, as in the figure. You also see two
grid markers for the Picture Control you're adjusting: the highlighted one represents the current, adjusted setting, and the
dimmed gray one shows you where the default settings put
the Picture Control on the grid.

You can't change any settings via the grid — it's for informational purposes only. However, if you display the grid from the first Set Picture Control menu (the left screen in Figure 8-35), you can press the Multi Selector up or down to select a different Picture Control. You then can press right to access the Picture Control adjustment screen.

6. **Press OK to save your changes and exit the adjustment screen.**

As when you fine-tune a White Balance setting, an asterisk appears next to the edited Picture Control in the menu and Information screen to remind you that you have adjusted it.

Again, these steps are intended just as a starting point for those who are interested in playing with Picture Controls. Complete details on each of the Picture Control adjustment options are found in the camera manual.

Putting It All Together

*E*arlier chapters of this book break down every picture-taking feature on your camera, describing in detail how the various controls affect exposure, picture quality, focus, color, and the like. This chapter pulls together all that information to help you set up your camera for specific types of photography.

Keep in mind, though, that there are no hard-and-fast rules as to the "right way" to shoot a portrait, a landscape, or whatever. So feel free to wander off on your own, tweaking this exposure setting or adjusting that focus control, to discover your own creative vision. Experimentation is part of the fun of photography, after all — and thanks to your camera monitor and the Delete button, it's an easy, completely free proposition.

Recapping Basic Picture Settings

Your subject, creative goals, and lighting conditions determine which settings you should use for some picture-taking options, such as aperture and shutter speed. I offer my take on those options throughout this chapter. But for many basic options, I recommend the same settings for almost every shooting scenario. Table 9-1 shows you those recommendations and also lists the chapter where you can find details about each setting.

One key point: Instructions in this chapter assume that you set the exposure mode to P, S, A, or M, as indicated in the table. These modes, detailed in Chapter 7, are the only ones that give you access to the entire cadre of camera features. In most cases, I recommend using S (shutter-priority autoexposure) when controlling motion blur is important, and A (aperture-priority autoexposure) when controlling depth of field is important. These two modes let you concentrate on one side of the exposure equation and let the camera handle the other. Of course, if you're comfortable making both the aperture and shutter speed decisions, you may prefer to work in M (manual) exposure mode instead. P (programmed autoexposure) is my last choice because it makes choosing a specific aperture or shutter speed more cumbersome.

Additionally, this chapter discusses choices for viewfinder photography; Chapter 4 guides you through the options available for Live View photography and movie recording. (For Live View photography, however, most settings work the same as discussed here, with the exception of the autofocus options.)

Table 9-1	All-Purpose Picture-Taking Settings	
Option	*Recommended Setting*	*Chapter*
Exposure mode	P, S, A, or M	7
Image Quality	JPEG Fine or Raw (NEF)	2
Image Size	Large or medium	2
Image Area	DX	2
White Balance	Auto$_1$	8
ISO Sensitivity	100	7
Autofocus mode	For still subjects, AF-S; moving subjects, AF-C	8
AF-area mode	Still subjects, Single Point; moving subjects, 9-, 21-, or 51-point Dynamic Area	8
Release mode	Action photos: Continuous Low or High; all others: Single Frame	2
Metering	Matrix	7
Active D-Lighting	Off	7

Shooting Still Portraits

By *still portrait,* I mean that your subject isn't moving. For subjects who aren't keen on sitting still, skip to the next section and use the techniques given for action photography instead. Assuming that you do have a subject willing to pose, the classic portraiture approach is to keep the subject sharply focused while throwing the background into soft focus. This artistic choice emphasizes the subject and helps diminish the impact of any distracting background objects. The following steps show you how to achieve this look:

1. **Set the Mode dial to A (aperture-priority autoexposure) and select a low f-stop value.**

   A low f-stop setting opens the aperture, which not only allows more light to enter the camera but also shortens *depth of field,* or the distance over which focus appears sharp. So dialing in a low f-stop value is the first step in softening your portrait background. However, for a group portrait, don't go too low, or the depth of field may not be enough to keep everyone in the sharp-focus zone. Take test shots and inspect your results at different f-stops to find the right setting.

   I recommend using aperture-priority mode when depth of field is a concern, because you can control the f-stop while relying on the camera to select the shutter speed. Just rotate the command dial to select your f-stop. (You need to pay attention to shutter speed as well, however, to make sure that it's not so slow that movement of the subject or camera will blur the image.)

   You can monitor the current f-stop and shutter speed in the Information display, Control panel, and viewfinder, as shown in Figure 9-1.

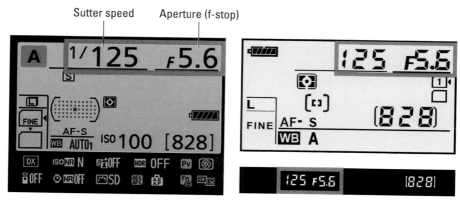

Figure 9-1: You can monitor aperture (f-stop) and shutter speed settings in the displays.

2. **To further soften the background, zoom in, get closer, and put more distance between the subject and background.**

   Zooming in to a longer focal length reduces depth of field, as does moving physically closer to your subject. And the greater the distance between the subject and background, the more the background blurs. (A good rule is to place the subject at least an arm's length away from the background.)

   A lens with a focal length of 85–120mm is ideal for a classic head-and-shoulders portrait. You should avoid using a short focal length (a wide-angle lens) for portraits. They can cause features to appear distorted — sort of like how people look when you view them through a security peephole in a door.

3. **Check composition.**

   Two quick pointers on this topic:

   - *Consider the background.* Scan the frame looking for background objects that may distract the eye from the subject. If necessary, reposition the subject against a more flattering backdrop.

   - *Frame the subject loosely to allow for later cropping to a variety of frame sizes.* Your camera produces images that have an aspect ratio of 3:2. That means that your portrait perfectly fits a 4 x 6" print size but will require cropping to print at any other proportions, such as 5 x 7 or 8 x 10. Leaving some extra background margin around your subject gives you the flexibility of cropping to those frame sizes.

4. **For indoor portraits, shoot flash-free if possible.**

   Shooting by available light rather than flash produces softer illumination and avoids the problem of red-eye. To get enough light to go flash-free, turn on room lights or, during daylight, pose your subject next to a sunny window, as I did in Figure 9-2.

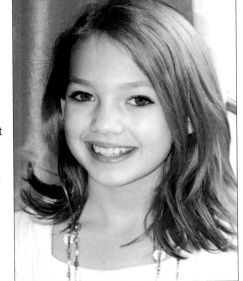

   In the A exposure mode, simply keeping the built-in flash unit closed disables the flash. If flash is unavoidable, see my list of flash tips at the end of these steps to get better results.

Figure 9-2: For more pleasing indoor portraits, shoot by available light instead of using flash.

**5. For outdoor por-
traits, use a flash if
possible.**

Even in daylight, a
flash adds a ben-
eficial pop of light
to subjects' faces,
as illustrated in
Figure 9-3. A flash
is especially impor-
tant when the back-
ground is brighter
than the subjects, as
in this example.

In the A exposure
mode, press the
Flash button on the
side of the camera to
raise the built-in
flash. For daytime
portraits, set the
Flash mode to Fill
Flash. (That's the
regular, basic Flash
mode.) For nighttime
images, try Red-Eye
Reduction or Slow-
Sync flash; again, see
the flash tips at the
end of these steps to
use either mode
most effectively.

No flash

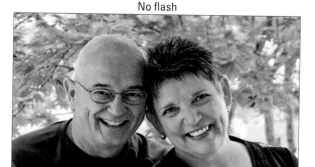

Fill flash

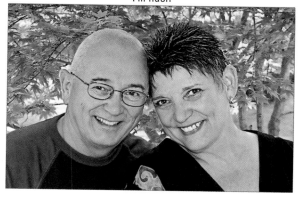

Figure 9-3: To properly illuminate the face in outdoor
portraits, use flash.

By default, the top shutter speed for flash photography is 1/250 second,
so in bright light, you may need to stop down the aperture to avoid overexposing the photo, as I did for the second image in Figure 9-3. Doing so,
of course, brings the background into sharper focus, so if that creates an
issue, move the subject into a shaded area instead.

**6. Press and hold the shutter button halfway to initiate exposure meter-
ing and autofocusing.**

If focusing manually, rotate the focusing ring to set focus.

7. Press the shutter button the rest of the way to capture the image.

When flash is unavoidable, try these tricks to produce better results:

✔ **Indoors, turn on as many room lights as possible.** With more ambient light, you need less flash power to expose the picture. Adding light also causes the pupils to constrict, further reducing the chances of red-eye. As an added benefit, the smaller pupil allows more of the subject's iris to be visible in the portrait, so you see more eye color.

✔ **Pay attention to white balance when you combine flash with other light sources.** If you set the White Balance setting to Auto$_1$, as I recommend in Table 9-1, enabling flash tells the camera to warm colors to compensate for the cool light of a flash. If your subject is also lit by another light source, whether it's the sun or indoor room lighting, the result may be colors that are slightly warmer or cooler (more blue) than neutral. A warming effect typically looks nice in portraits, giving the skin a subtle glow. If you aren't happy with the result, see Chapter 8 to find out how to fine-tune white balance.

✔ **Try using a Flash mode that enables Red-Eye Reduction or Slow-Sync flash.** If you choose the first option, warn your subject to expect both a preliminary light from the AF-assist lamp, which constricts pupils, and the flash. And remember that Slow-Sync flash modes use a slower-than-normal shutter speed, which produces softer lighting and brighter backgrounds than normal flash. (Chapter 7 explains the various Flash modes.)

Take a look at Figure 9-4 for an example of how using Slow-Sync flash can improve an indoor portrait. When I used regular flash, the shutter speed was 1/60 second. At that speed, the camera has little time to soak up any ambient light. As a result, the scene is lit primarily by the flash. That caused two problems: The strong flash created some glare on the subject's skin, and the window panes and frame are much more prominent because of the contrast between them and the darker bushes outside the window. Although it was daylight when I took the picture, the skies were overcast, so at 1/60 second, the exterior appears dark.

In the Slow-Sync flash example, shot at 1/4 second, the exposure time was long enough to permit the ambient light to brighten the exteriors to the point that the window frame almost blends into the background. And because much less flash power was needed to expose the subject, the lighting is much more flattering. In this case, the bright background also helps to set the subject apart because of her dark hair and shirt. If the subject had been a pale blonde, this setup wouldn't have worked as well. Note, too, the subtle color shift between the normal flash and slow-sync example — again, that's a result of using the Auto$_1$ White Balance setting when the subject is lit by multiple light sources. In this case, colors became warmer.

Regular fill flash, 1/60 second   Slow-sync flash, 1/4 second

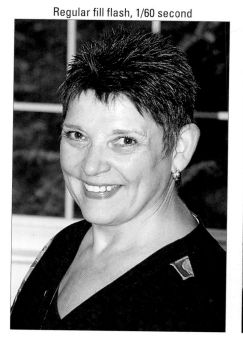 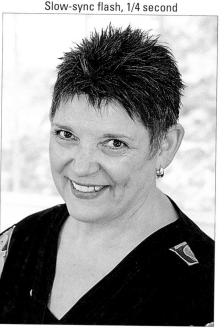

Figure 9-4: Slow-Sync flash produces softer, more even lighting and brighter backgrounds.

Don't forget that using a slower-than-normal shutter speed means an increased risk of blur due to camera shake, so use a tripod. Remind your subjects to stay absolutely still, too, because they'll appear blurry if they move during the exposure. I was fortunate to have both a tripod and a cooperative subject for my examples, but I probably wouldn't opt for slow-sync for portraits of young children or pets.

✓ **For professional results, use an external flash with a rotating flash head.** Aim the flash head upward so that the flash light bounces off the ceiling and falls softly down onto the subject. External flashes can be pricey, but the results make the purchase worthwhile if you shoot lots of portraits. Compare the two portraits in Figure 9-5 for an illustration. In the first example, using the built-in flash resulted in strong shadowing behind the subject and harsh, concentrated light. To produce the better result on the right, I used a Nikon Speedlight external flash and bounced the light off the ceiling. I also moved the subject a few feet farther in front of the background to create more background blur.

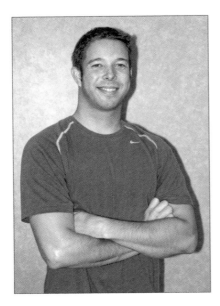 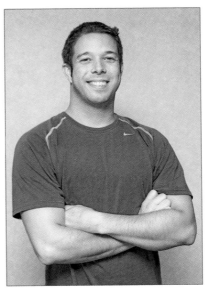

Figure 9-5: To eliminate harsh lighting and strong shadows (left), use bounce flash and move the subject farther from the background (right).

Make sure that the ceiling or other surface you use to bounce the light is white; otherwise, the flash light will pick up the color of the surface and influence the color of your subject.

✒ **Invest in a flash diffuser to further soften the light.** Whether you use the built-in flash or an external flash, attaching a diffuser is also a good idea. A *diffuser* is simply a piece of translucent plastic or fabric that you place over the flash to soften and spread the light — much like how sheer curtains diffuse window light. Diffusers come in lots of different designs, including small, fold-flat models that fit over the built-in flash.

Capturing Action

Using a fast shutter speed is the key to capturing a blur-free shot of any moving subject, whether it's a flower in the breeze, a spinning Ferris wheel, or, as in the case of Figure 9-6, a racing cyclist.

Along with the basic capture settings outlined earlier in Table 9-1, try the techniques in the following steps to photograph a subject in motion:

1. **Set the Mode dial to S (shutter-priority autoexposure).**

   In this mode, you control the shutter speed, and the camera takes care of choosing an aperture setting that will produce a good exposure.

2. **Rotate the command dial to select the shutter speed.**

   Refer to Figure 9-1 to locate shutter speed in the camera displays. After you select the shutter speed, the camera selects an aperture (f-stop) to match.

   What shutter speed should you choose? Well, it depends on the speed at which your subject is moving, so you need to experiment. But generally speaking,

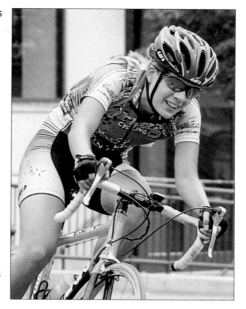

Figure 9-6: Use a high shutter speed to freeze motion.

1/320 second should be plenty for all but the fastest subjects (race cars, boats, and so on). For very slow subjects, you can even go as low as 1/250 or 1/125 second. My subject in Figure 9-6 was zipping along at a pretty fast pace, so I set the shutter speed to 1/500 second. Remember, though, that when you increase shutter speed in S exposure mode, the camera opens the aperture to maintain the same exposure. At low f-stop numbers, depth of field becomes shorter, so you have to be more careful to keep your subject within the sharp-focus zone as you compose and focus the shot.

You also can take an entirely different approach to capturing action: Instead of choosing a fast shutter speed, select a speed slow enough to blur the moving objects, which can create a heightened sense of motion and, in scenes that feature very colorful subjects, cool abstract images. I took this approach when shooting the carnival ride featured in Figure 9-7, for example. For the left image, I set the shutter speed to 1/30 second; for the right version, I slowed things down to 1/5 second. In both cases, I used a tripod, but because nearly everything in the frame was moving, the entirety of both photos is blurry — the 1/5 second version is simply more blurry because of the slower shutter.

1/30 second

1/5 second

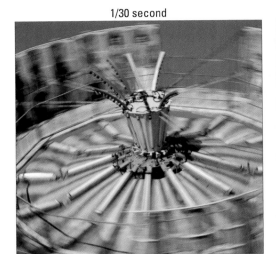 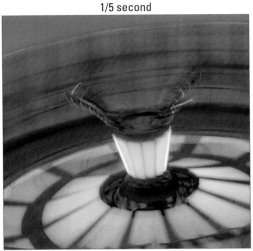

Figure 9-7: Using a shutter speed slow enough to blur moving objects can be a fun creative choice, too.

3. **In dim lighting, raise the ISO setting if necessary to allow a fast shutter speed.**

   Unless you're shooting in bright daylight, you may not be able to use a fast shutter speed at a low ISO, even if the camera opens the aperture as far as possible. If auto ISO override is in force, ISO may go up automatically when you increase the shutter speed — Chapter 7 has details on that feature. Raising the ISO does increase the possibility of noise, so you have to decide whether a noisy shot is better than a blurry shot.

   Why not add flash to brighten the scene? Well, adding flash is tricky for action shots, unfortunately. First, the flash needs time to recycle between shots, which slows your capture rate. Second, the built-in flash has limited range, so don't waste your time if your subject isn't close by. And third, remember that the fastest shutter speed you can use with flash is 1/250 second by default, which may not be high enough to capture a quickly moving subject without blur.

4. **For rapid-fire shooting, set the Release mode to Continuous Low or Continuous High.**

   In both modes, the camera shoots a continuous burst of images as long as you hold down the shutter button. At the camera's default settings,

Continuous Low captures up to 3 frames per second (fps), and Continuous High bumps the frame rate up to about 6 fps. Here again, though, you need to go flash-free; otherwise, you get one shot per press of the shutter button, just as in Single Frame release mode.

5. **Select speed-oriented focusing options.**

For fastest shooting, try manual focusing: It eliminates the time the camera needs to lock focus when you use autofocusing. If you use auto-focus, select these two autofocus settings for best performance:

- Set the AF-area mode to one of the Dynamic Area settings. Chapter 8 has information to help you decide whether the 9-point, 21-point, or 51-point Dynamic Area setting is best for your subject.

- Set the Autofocus mode to AF-C (continuous-servo autofocus).

At these settings, the camera sets focus initially on your selected focus point but then looks to the surrounding points for focusing information if your subject moves away from the selected one. Focus is adjusted continuously until you take the shot.

6. **Compose the subject to allow for movement across the frame.**

Frame your shot a little wider than you normally might so that you lessen the risk that your subject will move out of the frame before you record the image. You can always crop to a tighter composition later. (I used this approach for my cyclist image — the original shot includes a lot of background that I later cropped away.)

Using these techniques should give you a better chance of capturing any fast-moving subject, but action-shooting strategies also are helpful for shooting candid portraits of kids and pets. Even if they aren't currently running, leaping, or otherwise cavorting, snapping a shot before they do move is often tough. So if an interaction catches your eye, set your camera into action mode and fire off a series of shots as fast as you can.

Capturing Scenic Vistas

Providing specific capture settings for landscape photography is tricky because there's no single best approach to capturing a beautiful stretch of countryside, a city skyline, or other vast subject. Most people, for example, prefer using a wide-angle lens to incorporate a large area of the landscape into the scene, but if you're far away from your subject, you may like the results you get from a telephoto or medium-range lens. When shooting the scene in Figure 9-8, for example, I had to position myself across the street from the buildings, so I captured the shot using a focal length of 82mm. And consider depth of field: One person's idea of a super cityscape might be to keep all buildings sharply focused, but another photographer might prefer to shoot the same scene so that a foreground building is sharply focused while the others are less so, thus drawing the eye to that first building.

That said, I can offer tips to help you photograph a landscape the way *you* see it:

- **Shoot in aperture-priority autoexposure mode (A) so that you can control depth of field.** If you want extreme depth of field so that both near and distant objects are sharply focused, as in Figure 9-8, select a high f-stop value. I used an aperture of f/18 for this shot. For short depth of field, use a low value.

- **Remember that the shorter your lens focal length, the greater the depth of field.** With the 18–105mm kit lens, for example, zoom out to the 18mm position for the largest depth of field (and widest angle of view).

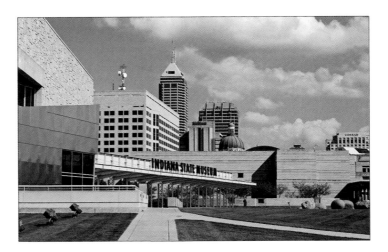

Figure 9-8: Use a high f-stop value to keep foreground and background sharply focused.

- **If the exposure requires a slow shutter speed, use a tripod to avoid blurring.** The downside to a high f-stop is that you may need a slower shutter speed to produce a good exposure. If the shutter speed drops below what you can comfortably handhold, use a tripod to avoid picture-blurring camera shake.

- **For dramatic waterfall shots, consider using a slow shutter to create that "misty" look.** The slow shutter blurs the water, giving it a soft, romantic appearance, as shown in Figure 9-9. Again, use a tripod to ensure that the rest of the scene doesn't also blur due to camera shake. The shutter speed for the image in Figure 9-9 was 1/5 second.

In very bright light, you may overexpose the image at a very slow shutter, even if you stop the aperture all the way down and select the camera's lowest ISO setting. As a solution, consider investing in a *neutral density filter* for your lens. This type of filter works something like sunglasses for your camera: It simply reduces the amount of light that passes through the lens, without affecting image colors, so that you can use a slower shutter than would otherwise be possible.

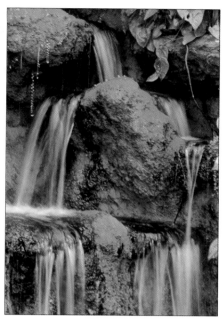

Figure 9-9: For misty waterfalls, use a slow shutter speed and a tripod.

- **At sunrise or sunset, base exposure on the sky.** The foreground will be dark, but you can usually brighten it in a photo editor if needed. If you base exposure on the foreground, on the other hand, the sky will become so bright that all the color will be washed out — a problem you usually can't fix after the fact. You can also invest in a *graduated neutral-density filter,* which is clear on one side and dark on the other. You orient the filter so that the dark half falls over the sky and the clear side over the dimly lit portion of the scene. This setup enables you to better expose the foreground without blowing out the sky colors.

Also experiment with the Active D-Lighting and HDR features that I cover in Chapter 7; both are designed to create images that contain a greater range of brightness values than is normally possible.

- **For cool nighttime city pics, experiment with slow shutter speeds.** Assuming that cars or other vehicles with their lights on are moving through the scene, the result is neon trails of light like those you see in the foreground of the image in Figure 9-10. Shutter speed for this image was about 10 seconds.

Instead of changing the shutter speed manually between each shot, try *Bulb* mode. Available only in M (manual) exposure mode, this option records an image for as long as you hold down the shutter button. So just take a series of images, holding down the button for different lengths of time for each shot. In Bulb mode, you also can exceed the standard maximum exposure time of 30 seconds.

✔ **For the best lighting, shoot during the *magic hours*.** That's the term photographers use for early morning and late afternoon, when the light cast by the sun is soft and warm, giving everything that beautiful, gently warmed look.

Can't wait for the perfect light? Tweak your camera's White Balance setting, using the instructions laid out in Chapter 8, to simulate the color of magic-hour light.

✔ **In tricky light, bracket exposures.** *Bracketing* simply means to take the same picture at several different exposure settings to increase the odds that at least one of them will capture the scene the way you envision. Bracketing is especially a good idea in difficult lighting situations, such as sunrise and sunset. Chapter 7 shows you how to make bracketing easier by using automatic exposure bracketing.

✔ **When shooting fireworks, use manual exposure, manual focus, and a tripod.** Fireworks require a long exposure, and trying to handhold your camera simply isn't going to work. If using a zoom lens, zoom out to the shortest focal length (widest angle). Switch to manual focusing and set focus at the farthest focus point possible on your lens. Set the exposure mode to manual, choose a relatively high f-stop setting — say, f/16 or so — and start at a shutter speed of 1 to 5 seconds. From there, it's simply a matter of experimenting with different shutter speeds. Also play with the timing of the shutter release, starting some exposures at the moment the fireworks are shot up, some at the moment they burst open, and so on. For the example featured in Figure 9-11, I used a shutter speed of about 5 seconds and began the exposure as the rocket was going up.

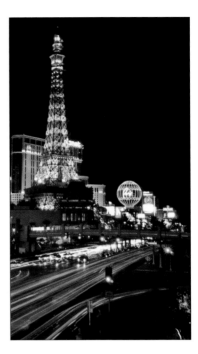

Figure 9-10: Using a slow shutter speed creates neon light trails in nighttime city street scenes.

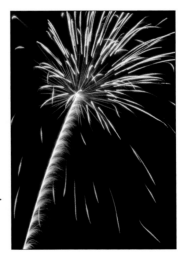

Figure 9-11: Use a slow shutter speed to capture fireworks.

Again, for an easy way to vary exposure time between shots, try using the Bulb shutter speed. This technique enables you to experiment with shutter speed more easily because you don't have to use the Main command dial to adjust the setting between each shot. Remember that this option is available only in the M (manual) exposure mode; it's the setting one step below the slowest shutter speed (30 seconds).

Capturing Dynamic Close-Ups

For great close-up shots, try these techniques:

✔ **Check your lens manual to find out its minimum close-focusing distance.** How "up close and personal" you can get to your subject depends on your lens.

✔ **Take control over depth of field by setting the camera mode to A (aperture-priority autoexposure) mode.** Whether you want a shallow, medium, or extreme depth of field depends on the point of your photo. In classic nature photography, for example, the artistic tradition is a very shallow depth of field, as shown in Figure 9-12, and requires an open aperture (low f-stop value). If you want the viewer to be able to clearly see all details throughout the frame — for example, you're shooting a product shot for a sales catalog — you need to go the other direction, stopping down the aperture as far as possible.

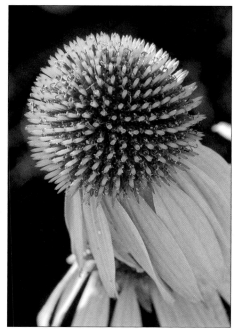

Figure 9-12: Shallow depth of field is a classic technique for close-up floral images.

✔ **Remember that zooming in and getting close to your subject both decrease depth of field.** So back to that product shot: If you need depth of field beyond what you can achieve with the aperture setting, you may need to back away, zoom out, or both. (You can always crop your image to show just the parts of the subject that you want to feature.)

✔ **When shooting flowers and other nature scenes outdoors, pay attention to shutter speed, too.** Even a slight breeze may cause your subject to move, causing blur at slow shutter speeds.

✔ **Use flash for better outdoor lighting.** Just as with portraits, a tiny bit of flash typically improves close-ups when the sun is your primary light source. Again, though, keep in mind that the maximum shutter speed possible when you use the built-in flash is 1/250 second. So in very bright light, you may need to use a high f-stop setting to avoid overexposing the picture. You can also adjust the flash output via the Flash Compensation control. Chapter 7 offers details.

✔ **When shooting indoors, try not to use flash as your primary light source.** Because you're shooting at close range, the light from your flash may be too harsh even at a low Flash Compensation setting. If flash is inevitable, turn on as many room lights as possible to reduce the flash power that's needed — even a shop light from a hardware store can do in a pinch as a lighting source. (Remember that if you have multiple light sources, though, you may need to tweak the White Balance setting.)

✔ **To really get close to your subject, invest in a macro lens or a set of diopters.** A true macro lens, which enables you to get really, really close to your subjects, is an expensive proposition; expect to pay many hundreds of dollars. If you enjoy capturing the tiny details in life, though, it's worth the investment.

Nikon has a great guide to its macro lenses — officially titled "Micro-Nikkor Lenses" — at its www.nikonusa.com website, if you're ready to start shopping.

For a less expensive way to go, you can spend about $40 for a set of *diopters,* which are sort of like reading glasses that you screw onto your existing lens. Diopters come in several strengths — +1, +2, +4, and so on — with a higher number indicating a greater magnifying power. I took this approach to capture the extreme close-up in Figure 9-13, attaching a +2 diopter to my lens. The downfall of using diopters, sadly, is that they typically produce images that are very soft around the edges, a problem that doesn't occur with a good macro lens.

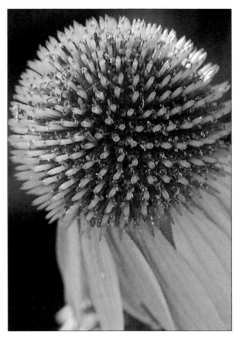

Figure 9-13: To extend your lens's close-focus capability, you can add magnifying diopters.

Part IV
The Part of Tens

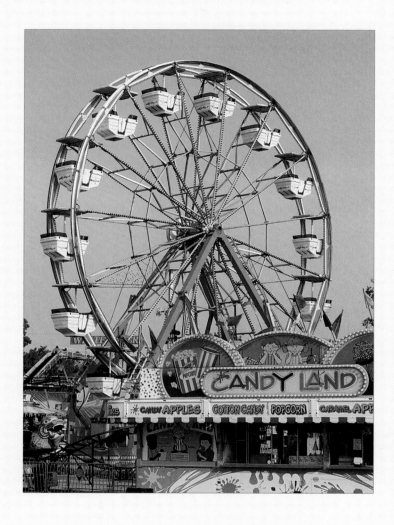

Enjoy an additional Part of Tens article about ten cool digital photography websites at
www.dummies.com/extras/nikon.

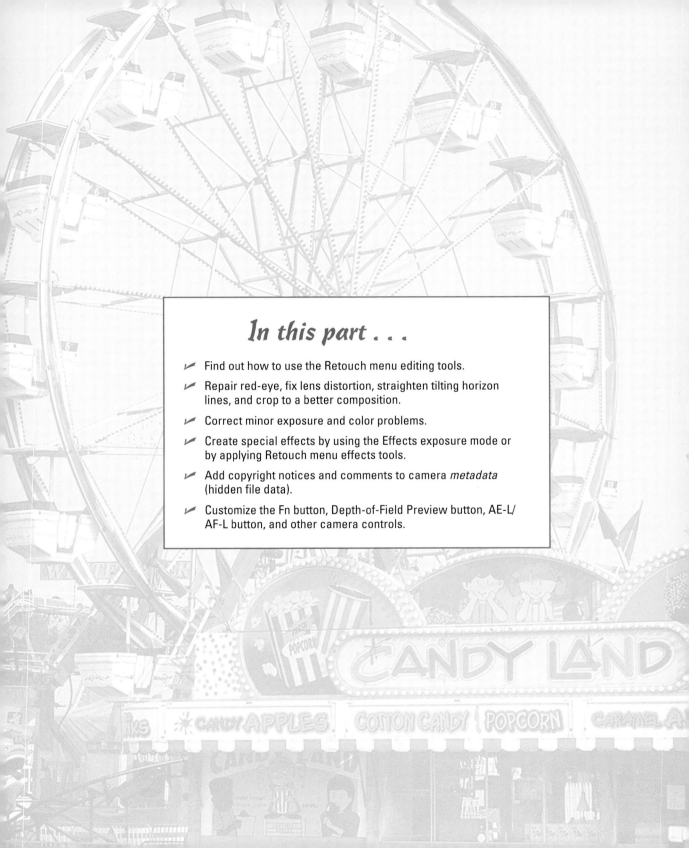

In this part . . .

- ✍ Find out how to use the Retouch menu editing tools.

- ✍ Repair red-eye, fix lens distortion, straighten tilting horizon lines, and crop to a better composition.

- ✍ Correct minor exposure and color problems.

- ✍ Create special effects by using the Effects exposure mode or by applying Retouch menu effects tools.

- ✍ Add copyright notices and comments to camera *metadata* (hidden file data).

- ✍ Customize the Fn button, Depth-of-Field Preview button, AE-L/ AF-L button, and other camera controls.

Ten Fun (And Practical) Ways to Manipulate Your Photos

In This Chapter

▶ Applying Retouch menu filters

▶ Removing red-eye

▶ Correcting crooked horizon lines, lens distortion, and perspective

▶ Cropping away excess background

▶ Tweaking exposure, contrast, and color

▶ Creating a black-and-white version of a photo

▶ Having fun with special effects

*E*very photographer produces a clunker now and then. When it happens to you, don't be too quick to press the Delete button, because many common problems are surprisingly easy to fix. In fact, you often can repair your photos right in the camera, thanks to tools found on the Retouch menu.

This chapter starts with the basics of navigating the Retouch menu and then provides specifics for using its photo-repair tools. Then I show you how to create special effects by using other Retouch menu options and by shooting in Effects mode.

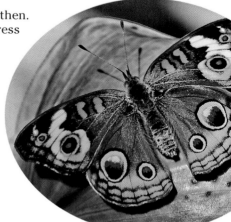

Applying the Retouch Menu Filters

You can get to most Retouch menu features in two ways:

✔ **Display the menu, select the tool you want to use, and press OK.**
You're presented with thumbnails of your photos; use the Multi Selector to move the yellow highlight box over the photo you want to adjust and press OK. You then see options related to the selected tool.

The only menu item you can't access this way is Side-By-Side Comparison, explained shortly.

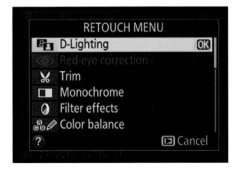

Figure 10-1: In single-frame playback view, press the *i* button to access the Retouch menu.

✔ **Switch the camera to playback mode, display your photo in single-frame view, and press the *i* button.** The Retouch menu appears superimposed over your photo, as shown in Figure 10-1. Select the tool you want to use and press OK to display options related to that tool. I prefer the second method so that's how I approach things in this chapter, but it's entirely a personal choice.

However, you can't use the *i* button method to access the Image Overlay menu item. That feature, which combines two Raw (NEF) photos to create a third, blended image, is only available when you display the Retouch menu by pressing the Menu button.

A few other facts to note:

✔ **Your originals remain intact.** When you apply a Retouch menu tool, the camera creates a copy of your original photo and makes the changes to the copy. An icon that looks like the one that represents the Retouch menu (a box with a little paintbrush) appears with the image during playback to let you know that you're looking at an edited photo.

✔ **All menu options work with either JPEG or Raw (NEF) originals except Image Overlay and NEF (Raw) Processing.** Those two tools work only with Raw files.

✔ **Retouched copies for all alterations except Image Overlay are saved in the JPEG file format.** The retouched copy uses the same JPEG quality setting as the original (Fine, Normal, or Basic). Retouched copies of Raw originals are saved in the JPEG Fine format. For the Image Overlay option, the retouched image is stored using the current Image Quality and Image Size settings.

✔ **You can apply each correction to a picture only once.** The exception, again, is Image Overlay. If you save the composite in the Raw format, you can combine the composite with a third Raw image. In fact, you can keep combining photos until your memory card is full, if the urge hits you.

✔ **The camera automatically assigns the next available file number to the retouched image.** Make note of the filename of the retouched version so that you can easily track it down later.

✔ **You can compare the original and the retouched version through the Side-by-Side Comparison menu option.** To use this feature, start by displaying either the original or the retouched version in full-frame playback. Then press the *i* button, select Side-by-Side Comparison, as shown on the left in Figure 10-2, and press OK. You see the original image on one side and the retouched version on the other, as shown in the second screen in the figure. At the top of the screen, a label indicates the Retouch tool that you applied to the photo.

These tricks work in Side-by-Side Comparison display:

- If you applied more than one Retouch tool to the picture, press the Multi Selector right and left to display thumbnails that show how each tool affected the picture.

- If you create multiple retouched versions of the same original — for example, you create a monochrome version, save that, and then crop the original image and save that — use a different technique to compare the versions. First, press the Multi Selector right or left to surround the after image with the yellow highlight box. Now press the Multi Selector up and down to scroll through the retouched versions.

QUAL

- To temporarily view the original or retouched image at full-frame size, use the Multi Selector to highlight its thumbnail and then press the Qual button. Release the button to return to Side-by-Side Comparison view.

To exit Side-by-Side Comparison view, press the Playback button. The retouched photo appears on the screen.

TIP

If you want to view the original image in full-screen playback instead of the retouched version, use the Multi Selector to highlight the original while the Side-by-Side Comparison screen is active. Then press OK instead of the Playback button.

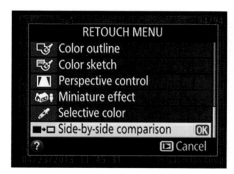
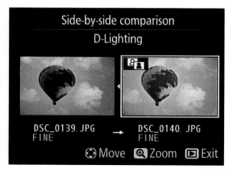

Figure 10-2: Use Side-by-Side Comparison to see whether you prefer the retouched version to the original.

Removing Red-Eye

For portraits marred by red-eye, give the Red-Eye Correction filter a whirl. After you select the tool, as shown on the left in Figure 10-3, press OK. If the camera can't find any red-eye, it displays a message telling you so. But if it detects red-eye, it applies the removal filter and displays the results on the screen, as shown on the right in the figure.

 QUAL After the filter does its thing, press the Qual button to magnify the display so that you can check the camera's work. To scroll the display, press the Multi Selector up, down, right, or left.

To go forward with the correction, press OK twice. The first OK returns the display to normal magnification; the second creates the retouched copy. To instead cancel the repair, press OK to return to normal magnification and then press the Playback button.

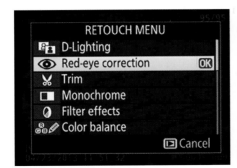 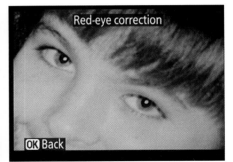

Figure 10-3: An automated red-eye remover is built right into your camera.

Straightening Tilting Horizon Lines

I have a knack for shooting with the camera slightly misaligned with respect to the horizon, which means that photos like the one on the left in Figure 10-4 often wind up crooked — in this case, everything tilts down toward the right corner of the frame. Luckily for me, the D7100 offers a Straighten tool that can rotate tilting horizons back to the proper angle, as shown in the right image in the figure.

 To achieve this rotation magic, the camera must crop your image and then enlarge the remaining area — that's why the after photo in Figure 10-4 contains slightly less subject matter than the original. (The same cropping occurs if you make this kind of change in a photo editor.) The camera updates the display as you rotate the photo so that you can get an idea of how much of the original scene may be lost.

Here's how to put the tool to work:

1. **Display the photo in single-frame playback mode and then press the *i* button to get to the Retouch menu.**

2. **Highlight Straighten, as shown on the left in Figure 10-5, and press OK.**

   You see a screen similar to the one on the right in the figure, with a grid superimposed on your photo to serve as an alignment aid.

3. **To rotate the picture clockwise, press the Multi Selector right.**

   Each press spins the picture by about 0.25 degrees. You can achieve a maximum rotation of five degrees. The yellow pointer on the little scale under the photo shows you the current amount of rotation.

4. **To rotate the picture counterclockwise, press the Multi Selector left.**

5. **When things are no longer off-kilter, press OK to create your retouched copy.**

Original

Straightened

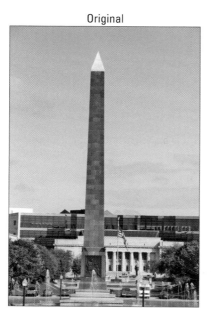 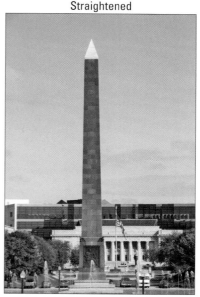

Figure 10-4: You can rotate crooked photos back to a level orientation with the Straighten tool.

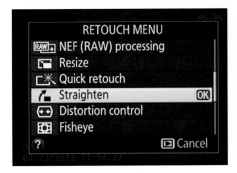
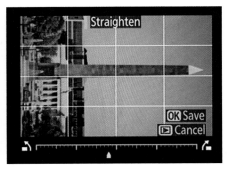

Figure 10-5: Press the Multi Selector right or left to rotate the image in increments of 0.25 degrees.

Removing (Or Creating) Lens Distortion

Certain lenses can produce a type of distortion that causes straight lines to appear curved. Wide-angle lenses, for example, often create *barrel distortion,* in which objects at the center of a picture appear to be magnified and pushed forward — as if you wrapped the photo around the outside of a barrel. The effect is perhaps easiest to spot in a rectangular subject like the oil painting in Figure 10-6. Notice that in the original image, on the left, the edges of the painting appear to bow slightly outward. *Pincushion distortion* affects the photo in the opposite way, making center objects appear smaller and farther away.

If you notice either type of distortion, try enabling the Auto Distortion Control option on the Shooting menu. This feature attempts to correct distortion as you take the picture. (Chapter 1 has details.) Or you may prefer to wait until after reviewing your photos and then use the Distortion Control tool on the Retouch menu to try to fix things. I applied the filter to create the second version of the subject in Figure 10-6, for example. Less helpful, in my opinion, is a related filter, the Fisheye filter, that actually creates distortion in an attempt to replicate the look of a photo taken with a fisheye lens.

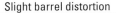

Slight barrel distortion   After Distortion Correction filter

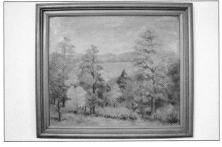
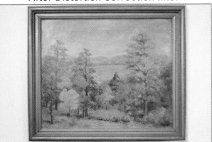

Figure 10-6: Barrel distortion makes straight lines appear to bow outward.

With either filter, you lose part of your original image area as a result of the distortion correction, just as you do when you apply the Straighten tool. So if you're shooting a photo that you think may benefit from these filters, frame your subject a little loosely.

With that warning out of the way, here's what you need to know to apply the filters:

- **Distortion Control:** After selecting the filter, as shown on the left in Figure 10-7, press the Multi Selector right to see the screen shown on the right. An Auto option is available for some lenses, as long as you didn't apply the Auto Distortion Control feature when taking the picture. As its name implies, the Auto option attempts to automatically apply the right degree of correction. If the Auto option is dimmed or you prefer to do the correction on your own, choose Manual, as shown on the right in the figure and press OK. You then see the screen featured in Figure 10-8. The scale under the image represents the degree and direction of shift that you're applying. Press the Multi Selector right to reduce barrel distortion; press left to reduce pincushioning. Press OK to make your corrected copy of the photo.

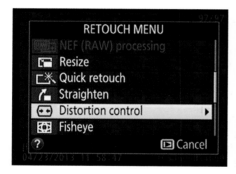
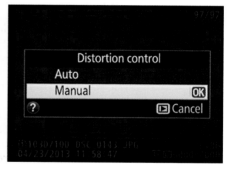

Figure 10-7: Use the Distortion Control filter to reduce barrel or pincushion distortion.

- **Fisheye:** After you select the filter and press OK, you see a screen similar to the one in Figure 10-8, but this time, you see the word Fisheye at the top of the screen. The scale at the bottom of the image indicates the strength of the distortion effect. Press the Multi Selector right or left to adjust the amount. Then press OK to create the fisheye copy.

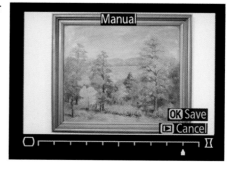

Figure 10-8: Press the Multi Selector right or left to adjust the amount and type of correction.

Correcting Perspective

When you photograph a tall building and tilt the camera up to get it all in the frame, a *convergence* or *keystoning* effect occurs. This effect causes vertical structures to tilt toward the center of the frame. Buildings sometimes even appear to be falling away from you, as shown in the left image in Figure 10-9. (If the lens is tilting down, verticals instead lean outward, and the building appears to be falling toward you.) Through the Retouch menu's Perspective Control feature, you can right those tilting verticals, as shown in the after photo on the right in Figure 10-9.

Note, though, that just as with the Straighten, Distortion Correction, and Fisheye tools, you lose some area around the perimeter of your photo when you apply the Perspective Control tool. So again, when you're shooting this type of subject, frame loosely — that way, you ensure that you don't sacrifice an important part of the scene due to the correction.

To try out the feature, follow these steps:

1. **Display your photo in single-image view and press the *i* button to bring the Retouch menu to life.**

2. **Select Perspective Control, as shown on the left in Figure 10-10, and press OK.**

   You see a grid and a horizontal and vertical scale, as shown on the right in the figure.

3. **Press the Multi Selector left and right to move the out-of-whack object horizontally.**

4. **Press the Multi Selector up and down to rotate the object toward or away from you.**

Original | After perspective correction

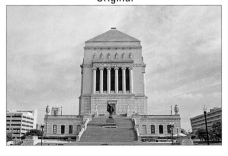 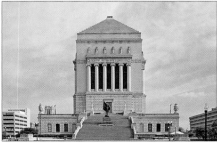

Figure 10-9: The original photo exhibited convergence (left); applying the Perspective Control filter corrected the problem (right).

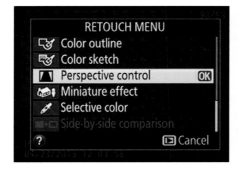
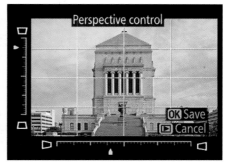

Figure 10-10: Press the Multi Selector to adjust the correction type and amount.

5. When you're happy with the results, press OK.

Depending on the scene, you may not be able to get all structures fully corrected, so just pay attention to the most prominent ones. For severe distortion problems, you may be able to get better results in your photo editor; in some programs, you can pull and push each side of the image independently of the others, which enables you to more freely shift perspective than is possible with the type of tool provided in the camera.

Cropping (Trimming) Your Photo

To *crop* a photo means to trim away some of its perimeter. Cropping away excess background can often improve an image, as illustrated by Figures 10-11 and 10-12. When shooting this scene, I couldn't get close enough to the ducks to fill the frame with them, so I simply cropped it after the fact to achieve the desired composition.

With the Trim function on the Retouch menu, you can crop a photo right in the camera. Note a few things about this feature:

- **Crop aspect ratio:** You can crop to one of five aspect ratios: 3:2, 4:3, 5:4, 1:1, and 16:9.

- **Crop size:** For each aspect ratio, you can choose from a variety of crop sizes, which depend on the size of your original. The sizes are stated in pixel terms, such as 3600 x 2880. If you're cropping in advance of printing the image, remember to aim for at least 200 pixels per linear inch of the print — 800 x 1200 pixels for a 4 x 6 print, for example.

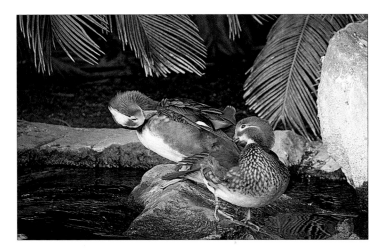

Figure 10-11: The original contains too much extraneous background.

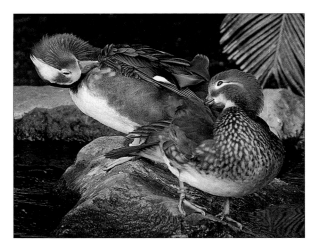

Figure 10-12: Cropping creates a better composition and eliminates background clutter.

After you crop, you can't apply any other fixes from the Retouch menu, so make cropping the last of your retouching steps.

Keeping those caveats in mind, trim your image as follows:

1. **Display your photo in single-image view and press the *i* button to launch the Retouch menu.**

2. **Select Trim and press OK.**

   You see the screen shown in Figure 10-13. The yellow highlight box indicates the cropping frame.

3. **Rotate the command dial to change the crop aspect ratio.**

   The selected aspect ratio appears in the upper-right corner of the screen.

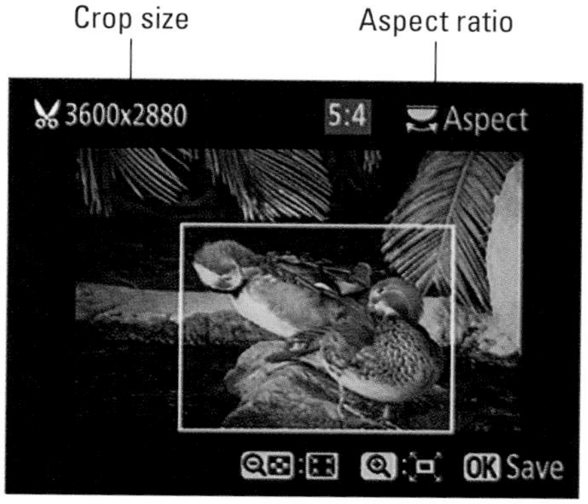

4. **Adjust the cropping frame size and placement as needed.**

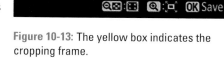

Crop size   Aspect ratio

Figure 10-13: The yellow box indicates the cropping frame.

   The current crop size appears in the upper-left corner of the screen. You can adjust the size and placement of the cropping frame like so:

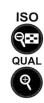

   - *Reduce the size of the cropping frame.* Press and release the ISO button. Each press of the button further reduces the crop size.

   - *Enlarge the cropping frame.* Press the Qual button to expand the crop boundary.

   - *Reposition the cropping frame.* Press the Multi Selector up, down, right, and left to shift the frame position.

5. **Press OK to create your cropped copy.**

   When you view the cropped image in Playback mode, a scissors symbol appears next to the image size to tell you that you're looking at a trimmed photo.

Manipulating Exposure and Color

Chapters 7 and 8 discuss the bazillion exposure and color controls on the D7100. But even pros at using those controls sometimes produce images that are just a little off. For major problems, using a photo-editing program to make corrections is usually the answer, but for images that need just a little exposure or color tweak, try these Retouch menu tools:

- **D-Lighting:** Chapter 7 explains Active D-Lighting, a feature that brightens too-dark shadows in a way that leaves highlight details intact. You can apply a similar adjustment after you take a picture by choosing the D-Lighting filter. I used the filter on the photo in Figure 10-14, where strong backlighting left the balloon underexposed in the original image.

Original image

D-Lighting, High

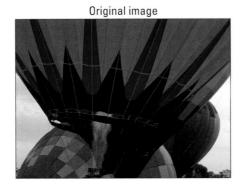
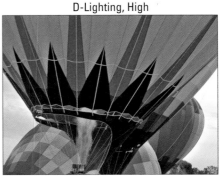

Figure 10-14: An underexposed photo (left) gets help from the D-Lighting filter (right).

QUAL

When you choose the D-Lighting filter, you see before-and-after views of the image, as shown in Figure 10-15. Press the Multi Selector up or down to set the strength of the adjustment to Low, Normal, or High. I used High for the balloon image. To get a closer view of the adjusted photo, press and hold the Qual button. Release the button to return to the two-thumbnail display.

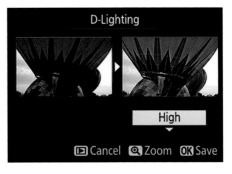

Figure 10-15: Press the Multi Selector up or down to vary the strength of the correction.

You can't apply D-Lighting to a picture taken using the Monochrome Picture Control, introduced in Chapter 8. Nor does D-Lighting work on any pictures to which you've applied the Quick Retouch filter, covered next, or the Monochrome filter, detailed a little later in this chapter.

✔ **Quick Retouch:** This filter increases contrast and color saturation and, if your subject is backlit, also applies a D-Lighting adjustment to restore some shadow detail that otherwise might be lost. In other words, Quick Retouch is sort of like D-Lighting on steroids.

As with D-Lighting, you can choose from three levels of Quick Retouch correction. And the same restrictions apply: You can't apply the filter to monochrome images or on pictures that you adjusted via D-Lighting.

✔ **Filter Effects:** Shown in Figure 10-16, the Filter Effects option offers filters that are designed to mimic the results produced by traditional lens filters. The first five are color-manipulation filters. The other two, Cross Screen and Soft (not shown in the figure), are special-effects filters; you can read about both later in this chapter.

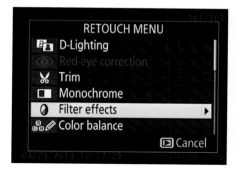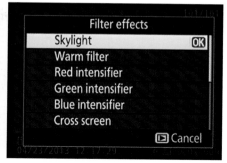

Figure 10-16: You can choose from filter effects that mimic traditional lens filters.

The color filters work like so:

- *Skylight filter:* This filter reduces the amount of blue in an image. The result is a very subtle warming effect.

- *Warm filter:* This one produces a warming effect that's just a bit stronger than the Skylight filter.

- *Color intensifiers:* You can boost the intensity of reds, greens, or blues individually by applying these filters. When you choose these filters, you can press the Multi Selector up or down to control the strength of the adjustment.

As an example, Figure 10-17 shows you an original image and three adjusted versions. As you can see, the Skylight and Warm filters are both very subtle; in this image, the effects are most noticeable in the sky. The fourth example shows a variation created by using the Color Balance filter, explained next, and shifting colors toward the cool (bluish) side of the color spectrum.

✔ **Color Balance:** Offering more flexibility than the Filter Effects options, this tool enables you to shift colors toward any part of the color spectrum. After you select the filter from the Retouch menu, as shown on the left in Figure 10-18, press OK to display a screen similar to the one shown on the right. The important control is the color grid in the lower-left corner. You shift image colors by using the Multi Selector to move the tiny black square (labeled *Color shift marker* in the figure) around the grid. In the figure, I positioned the marker to strengthen blue tones, for example.

The histograms on the right side of the display show you the resulting impact on overall image brightness as well as on the individual red, green, and blue brightness values — a bit of information that's helpful if you're experienced in the science of reading histograms. Chapter 5 gives you an introduction.

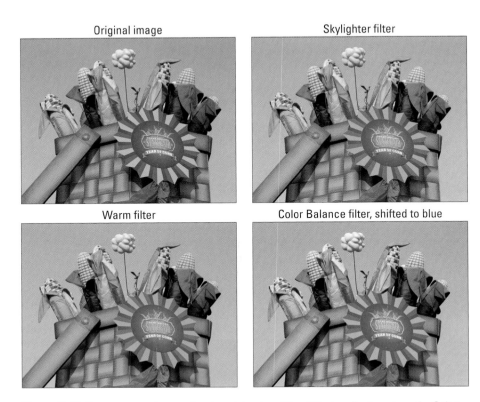

Figure 10-17: Here you see the results of applying two Filter Effects adjustments and a Color Balance shift.

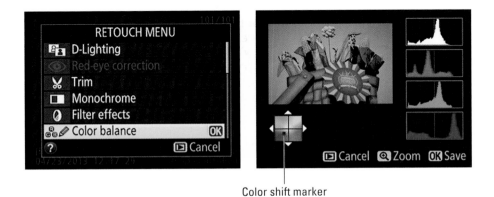

Figure 10-18: Press the Multi Selector to move the color shift marker and adjust color balance.

Use these tricks to inspect your image more closely:

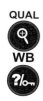
QUAL

WB

ISO

- Press the Qual In button to magnify the image and display the usual picture-in-picture zoom navigation thumbnail.

- When the display is magnified, press the WB button to toggle between that thumbnail and the color-balance control box. When the thumbnail is active, pressing the Multi Selector scrolls the display; when the control box is active, pressing the Multi Selector adjusts color balance.

- Use the ISO button to reduce the magnification.

Creating Monochrome Images

With the Monochrome Picture Control feature covered in Chapter 8, you can shoot black-and-white photos. As an alternative, you can create a black-and-white copy of an existing color photo by applying the Monochrome option on the Retouch menu. You can also create sepia and *cyanotype* (blue and white) images via the Monochrome option. Figure 10-19 shows you examples.

I prefer to convert my color photos to monochrome images in my photo editor; going that route offers more control, not to mention it's easier to preview your results on a large computer monitor than on the camera monitor. Still, I know that not everyone's as much of a photo-editing geek as I am, and there's certainly no harm in trying the in-camera filter. Just note that you can't apply some Retouch menu options to your photo after you do the conversion; the D-Lighting, Quick Retouch, and Soft filters are among those that don't work on a monochrome copy. (Obviously, filters related to color adjustment also are no longer available.)

That said, going from color to monochrome is easy: Just select Monochrome from the Retouch menu, press OK, select the type of monochrome image you want to create (black and white, sepia, or cyanotype), and press OK again. For the Sepia and Cyanotype options, you then see a screen that asks you to set the intensity of the tint; press the Multi Selector up and down to do so and then give OK one final tap.

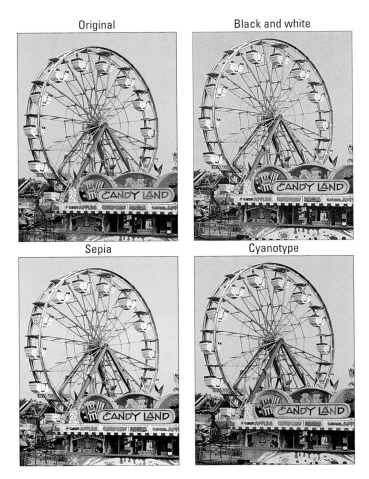

Figure 10-19: You can create three monochrome effects through the Monochrome tool on the Retouch menu.

Playing with Special Effects

If you want to alter reality beyond what you can achieve with the tools mentioned so far, the Retouch menu offers a number of special-effects filters. And through the Effects exposure mode, you can add certain effects at the moment you capture the image — you don't have to shoot the picture and then tweak it through the Retouch menu. The Effects exposure mode also enables you to record movies by using special effects.

The next section describes the remaining Retouch menu effects; following that, I show you how to take advantage of the Effects exposure mode.

Retouch menu special-effects filters

For some easy special-effects fun, experiment with these Retouch menu filters:

✒ **Cross Screen:** The Cross Screen filter adds a starburst effect to the brightest part of your image, as shown in Figure 10-20. To try it, select Filter Effects from the Retouch menu and then scroll down to the Cross Screen option.

Original   Cross Screen filter applied

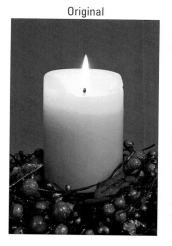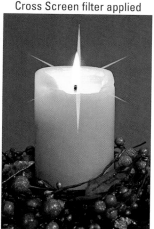

Figure 10-20: The Cross Screen filter adds a starburst effect to the brightest parts of the photo.

When you choose the filter, you see a screen showing a preview along with a column of options along the right side of the screen. The options enable you to adjust the number of points on the star, the intensity of the effect, the length of the star's rays, and the angle of the effect. Just use the Multi Selector to highlight an option (the label at the top of the screen tells you the name of the current option) and then press right to display the available settings. Highlight your choice and press OK. To update the preview after changing a filter setting, highlight Confirm and press OK. When you're happy with the effect, choose Save and press OK.

It's important to frame your original image with a little extra margin around the object that will get the starburst, as I did in my example. Otherwise, there isn't room in the picture for the effect.

✓ **Soft:** Also found on the Filter Effects menu, the Soft filter blurs your photo to give it a dreamy, watercolor-like look. You can choose from three levels of blur: Low, Normal, and High.

✓ **Color Outline:** Select this tool to create a black-and-white line drawing based on a photo, as illustrated in Figure 10-21. This is a fun project to do with kids — you can, in essence, create a custom coloring-book page that they can then fill in with watercolors, crayons, or markers.

✓ **Color Sketch:** This filter also creates a sketch of your photo, but this time with a result similar to a drawing done in colored pencils. I used the filter on the architectural image shown in Figure 10-22, for example. When you select the effect, you can play with two options: Vividness, which affects the boldness of the colors; and Outlines, which determines the thickness of outlines. Highlight an option, press the Multi Selector right or left to adjust the setting, and then press OK.

✓ **Miniature Effect:** Have you ever seen an architect's small-scale models of planned developments? The ones complete with tiny trees and even people? The Miniature Effect attempts to create a photographic equivalent by applying a strong blur to all but one portion of an image, as shown in Figure 10-23. The left photo is the original; the right shows the result of applying the filter. For this example, I set the focus point on the part of the street occupied by the cars.

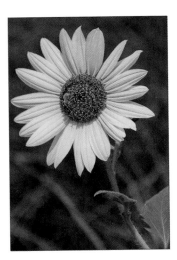 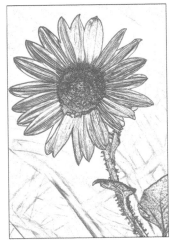

Figure 10-21: Use Color Outline to create a black-and-white line drawing out of a photo.

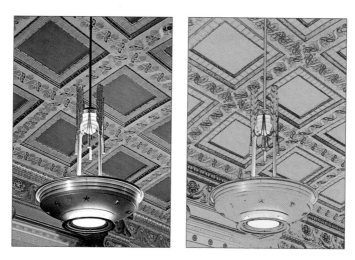

Figure 10-22: Color Sketch produces this type of effect.

Original   Miniature Effect filter

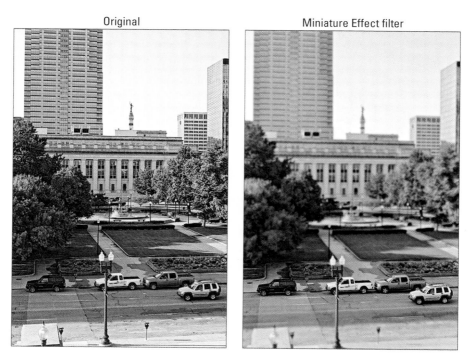

Figure 10-23: The Miniature Effect throws all but a small portion of a scene into very soft focus.

The Miniature Effect works best if you shoot your subject from a high angle — otherwise, you don't get the miniaturization result. To try it, display your photo in playback mode, press the *i* button, and then choose Miniature Effect from the Retouch menu, as shown on the left in Figure 10-24. Press OK to display a preview like the one shown on the right. Then experiment with the effect as follows:

ISO
QUAL

- Use the Multi Selector to position the yellow box over the area you want to keep in sharp focus.

- To rotate the box 90 degrees, press the ISO button.

- To preview the effect, press the Qual In button.

- When you get a result you like, press OK to save a copy of the original with the effect applied.

✔ **Selective Color:** This effect enables you to *desaturate* (remove color from) parts of a photo while leaving specific colors intact. For example, in Figure 10-25, I desaturated everything but the yellows and peaches in the rose. The result lends additional drama to your subject because the eye goes first to the areas of color.

When you choose the filter from the Retouch menu, you see a screen similar to the one on the left in Figure 10-26. Here, you can select up to three colors to retain and specify how much a color can vary from the selected one and still be retained. Make your wishes known as follows:

AE-L
AF-L

- *Select the first color to be retained.* Using the Multi Selector, move the yellow highlight box over the color. Then press the AE-L/AF-L button to tag that color, which appears in the left color swatch at the top of the screen, as shown on the left in Figure 10-26.

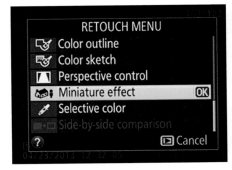
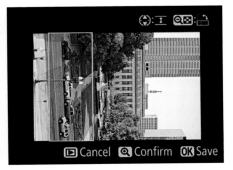

Figure 10-24: Use the Multi Selector to position the yellow rectangle over the area you want to keep in sharp focus.

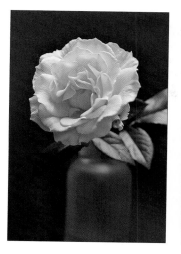
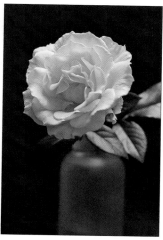

Figure 10-25: I used the Selective Color filter to desaturate everything but the rose petals.

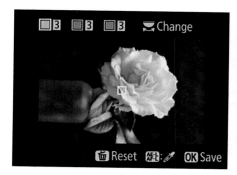
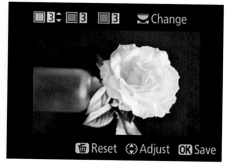

Figure 10-26: To select a color you want to keep, move the yellow box over it and press the AE-L/AF-L button.

- *Set the range of the selected color.* Rotate the Main command dial to display a preview of the desaturated image and highlight the number box to the right of the color swatch, as shown on the right in the figure. Then press the Multi Selector up or down to choose a value from 1 to 7. The higher the number, the more a pixel can vary in color from the selected hue and still be retained. At a low value, only pixels that are very similar to the one you selected are retained. The display updates to show you the impact of the setting.

- *Choose one or two additional colors.* Rotate the Main command dial to highlight the second color swatch box. Then repeat the selection process: Move the yellow highlight box over the color and press the AE-L/AF-L button to select that color. Rotate the Main command dial to display the preview and activate the range value box; press the Multi Selector up and down to set the range. To choose a third color, lather, rinse, and repeat.

- *Fine-tune your settings.* You can keep rotating the Main command dial to cycle through the color swatch boxes and range values, adjusting each as necessary.

- *Reset a color swatch box.* To empty a selected swatch box, press the Delete button. You can then move the yellow highlight box over a new color and press the AE-L/AF-L button to select it.

  To reset all the swatch boxes, hold down the Delete button until you see a message asking whether you want to get rid of all selected colors. Highlight Yes and press OK.

- *Save a copy of the image with the effect applied.* Press OK.

Shooting in Effects mode

When you set the Mode dial to Effects, as shown in Figure 10-27, you can apply special effects on the fly: That is, the effect is added as the camera writes the picture to the memory card.

For still photos, I prefer to capture my originals sans effect and then go through the Retouch menu to alter them. That way, I wind up with one normal image and one with the effect applied, just in case I decide I prefer the unaltered photo to the effects version. Shooting in the Effects mode also brings up another problem: To create the effects, the camera puts most picture-taking controls, such as White Balance and Metering mode, off limits.

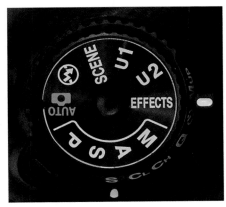

Figure 10-27: Effects mode lets you apply special effects to movies and still photos.

However, Effects mode does offer some artistic filters not available through the Retouch menu. In addition, it enables you to add effects to movies, which isn't possible through the Retouch menu. So even though I suspect that you won't find use for the Effects mode very often, I'd be remiss if I didn't spend a little time discussing it.

You use the same technique to select an effect in Live View mode for still photography. But for movies, you must select the effect you want to use before switching the Live View switch to the movie-camera icon. That is, start out in Live View still photography mode, choose your effect, and then switch to movie mode. After you're in movie mode, you can't choose a different effect. (See Chapter 4 for details on Live View.)

Although the screen displays a thumbnail to indicate the result of each effect, as shown on the right in Figure 10-28, you don't have to rely on that artwork: Instead, set the camera to Live View mode. The monitor then shows a live preview of each effect as you select it. To shift to Live View mode, set the Live View switch to the still photo or movie position — depending on what you want to shoot — and then press the LV button. (See Chapter 4 for complete details on Live View.)

Either way, you can choose from the following effects:

> **Night Vision:** Use this setting in low-light situations to produce a grainy, black-and-white image that resembles what you see with night-vision goggles. Figure 10-29 has an example. To achieve the grainy effect, the camera uses a high ISO Sensitivity setting — that high ISO produces noise, which results in the grainy look. How high the ISO climbs and, thus, how much noise becomes visible, depends on the ambient light.
>
> A few critical points about using Night Vision mode:
>
> - *Flash is disabled.* The whole idea is to create a picture taken in little light, after all.
>
> - *Use a tripod to avoid blur.* A slow shutter speed is needed to capture the image in dark conditions, and you must be careful to avoid camera movement during the exposure. If your subject is moving, however, it could appear blurry even if the camera is on a tripod.
>
> - *The image is always recorded in the JPEG format.* You can't record a Night Vision photo in the Raw (NEF) format.

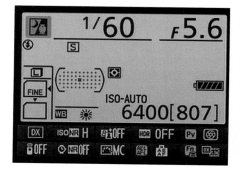
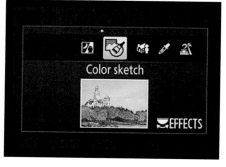

Figure 10-28: Rotate the Command dial to cycle through the available effects.

✔ **Color Sketch:** This produces the same effect as the Color Sketch filter on the Retouch menu. (Refer to Figure 10-22.) And, if you engage Live View when the effect is selected, you can adjust the same options available through the Retouch menu: Vividness and Color Outlines. First, press OK to display the options; then press the Multi Selector up or down to highlight the option you want to change, and press right or left to adjust the value for that option. Press OK again to hide the options and return to shooting. The camera remembers your settings and uses them any time you select the Color Sketch effect until you change them again.

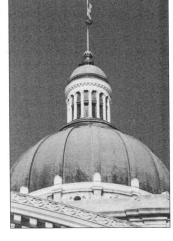

Figure 10-29: The Night Vision effect creates an exceptionally noisy black-and-white image.

Three points worth knowing:

- *It's best to compose the image by using the viewfinder and then switch to Live View.* When the effect is selected, the Live View display updates very slowly, making it a pain to play with composition using the monitor.

- *Using the effect puts some limitations on movie recording.* Movies recorded using this effect play back as a series of still images rather than a standard movie. In addition, autofocusing during recording is disabled.

- *For still photos, you can shoot only in the JPEG format.* As with the Night Vision mode, you can't create a Raw (NEF) file with this effect.

✔ **Miniature Effect:** This one is also a double of the one on the Retouch menu; Figure 10-23 shows an example of the result.

You must set the camera to Live View mode in order to position the box that specifies the part of the scene that will remain in sharp focus. After switching to Live View, first set focus on the area that you want to remain sharp. If you're using autofocusing, next press OK to display horizontal markings that indicate the width of the sharp-focus region. (The marks appear right away if you're focusing manually.) Press the Multi Selector up and down to adjust the width of the in-focus region; press right or left to change the orientation of the box. When you achieve the look you want, press OK again.

A few other limitations also apply: Flash is disabled, as is the AF-assist lamp. If you use the Continuous Release mode, the frames per second rate is reduced. For movies, sound recording is disabled, autofocus is disabled during recording, and movies play back at high speed. (The high-speed playback means that a movie that contains about 45 minutes of footage is compressed into a 3-minute clip, for example.) Finally, you're limited to creating a JPEG file for still photography. (If you're thinking that this Effects mode is a tad complex, I'm right there with ya.)

✔ **Selective Color:** Use this effect to create an image in which all but one to three colors are desaturated, just as when you use the Selective Color option on the Retouch menu. Figure 10-25 has an example.

To choose the colors you want to retain and specify the range of similar colors that are included, you must use Live View. You see the normal three-color swatch boxes and their accompanying value boxes at the top of the screen, but the process of choosing the colors and setting the range is a little different than when you go through the Retouch menu. Use these tactics instead:

- *Access the color options:* Press OK. A little yellow selection box appears on the screen.

- *Choose a color to retain:* Frame the image so that the selection box is over the color you want to preserve. Then press the Multi Selector up.

- *Set the color range:* After setting the color, press the Multi Selector up or down to adjust the color range value. A higher value retains a broader spectrum of similar shades than the one you chose.

- *Choose additional color to retain:* Rotate the Main command dial to select the second color swatch box and repeat the process of choosing a color and setting its range value.

- *Deselect a color:* Change your mind about retaining one of your chosen colors? Rotate the Main command dial to highlight its color swatch and then press the Delete button. Or hold down the button for a few seconds to delete all your selected colors.

After setting your color preferences, press OK to lock in your decisions and hide the options. The camera will use those settings any time you choose the Selective Color effect until you specify new settings.

Note that just as with the preceding Effects settings, you're limited to using JPEG as the file type when you use the Selective Color mode. Flash is disabled.

✔ **Silhouette:** Choosing this setting ensures that backlit subjects will be captured as dark silhouettes against a bright background, as shown in Figure 10-30. To help ensure that the subject is dark, flash is disabled. If you want your subject instead

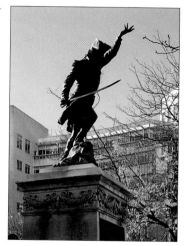

Figure 10-30: The Silhouette effect purposely underexposes backlit subjects.

to be properly exposed, Chapter 7 has some tips for dealing with backlighting.

- **High Key:** A *high key* photo is dominated by white or very light areas, such as a white china cup resting on a white doily in front of a sunny window. This setting is designed to produce a good exposure for this type of scene, which the camera otherwise tends to underexpose in response to all the high brightness values. Flash is disabled.

How does the name relate to the characteristics of the picture? Well, photographers refer to the dominant tones — or brightness values — as the *key tones*. In most photos, the *midtones,* or areas of medium brightness, are the key tones. In a high key image, the majority of tones are at the high end of the brightness scale.

- **Low Key:** The opposite of a high key photo, a low key photo is dominated by shadows. Use this mode to prevent the camera from brightening the scene too much and thereby losing the dark and dramatic nature of the image. Flash is disabled.

After selecting an effect, you can exit Live View to take your picture using the viewfinder if you prefer. Or, to record a movie, remain in Live View mode and just press the red movie-record button to stop and start recording.

Two Roads to a Multi-Image Exposure

Your camera offers two features that enable you to combine multiple photographs into one:

- **Multiple Exposure (Shooting menu):** With this option, you can combine your next two to three shots. After you enable the option and take your shots, the camera merges them into one file. The shots used to create the composite aren't recorded and saved separately. The Multiple Exposure option isn't available in Live View mode.

- **Image Overlay (Retouch menu):** This option enables you to merge two existing Raw images. I used this option to combine a photo of a werewolf friend, shown on the top left in Figure 10-31, with a nighttime garden scene, shown on the top right. The result is the ghostly image shown beneath the two originals. Oooh, scary!

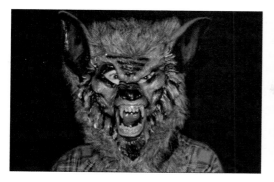 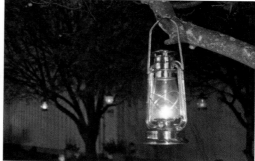

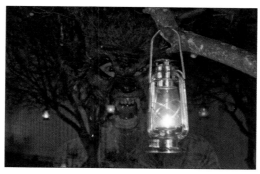

Figure 10-31: Image Overlay merges two Raw (NEF) photos into one.

On the surface, both options sound kind of cool. The problem is that you can't control the opacity or positioning of the individual images in the combined photo. For example, my overlay picture would have been more successful if I could move the werewolf to the left in the combined image so that he and the lantern aren't blended. And I'd also prefer to keep the background of image 2 at full opacity in the overlay image rather than getting a 50/50 mix of that background and the one in image 1, which creates only a fuzzy looking background in this particular example.

However, there is one effect that you can create successfully with either option: a "two views" composite like the one in Figure 10-32. For this image, I used Image Overlay to combine the front and rear views of the antique match striker, shown at the top of the figure, into the composite on the bottom.

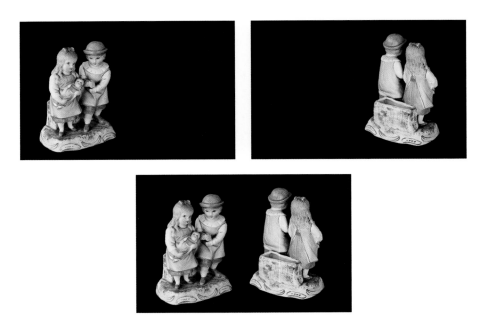

Figure 10-32: If you want each subject to appear solid, use a black background and position the subjects so that they don't overlap.

For this trick to work, the background in both images must be the same solid color (black seems to be best), and you must compose your photos so that the subjects don't overlap in the combined photo, as shown here. Otherwise, you get the ghostly portrait effect like what you see in Figure 10-31.

To be honest, I don't use Image Overlay or Multiple Exposure for the purpose of serious photo compositing. I prefer to do this kind of work in my photo-editing software, where I have more control over the blend. Understand, too, that neither feature is designed to produce an HDR (high dynamic range) image, which lifts different brightness ranges from different images to create the composite. For HDR, you need software that can do tone mapping, not just whole-image blending. (See the Chapter 7 section related to exposure bracketing for more about HDR, including the built-in HDR tool on the Shooting menu.)

In the interest of reserving space in this book for features that I think you will find much more useful, I leave you to explore these two features on your own. The camera manual explains the steps involved in using each of them. Again, though, I think that you'll find photo compositing much easier and much more flexible if you do the job in your photo-editing software.

Ten More Ways to Customize Your Camera

In This Chapter

▶ Creating your own exposure modes and menu

▶ Adding copyright data and hidden text to picture files

▶ Using your own folder and filenames

▶ Changing the behavior of some buttons and dials

*A*s you've no doubt deduced, Nikon is more than eager to let you customize almost every aspect of the camera's operation. This chapter discusses customization options not considered in earlier chapters, including ways to embed a copyright notice in your picture files, create custom folder and file names, and even tweak the function of external controls.

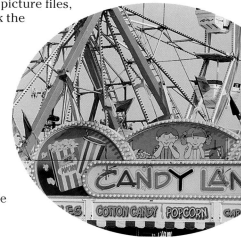

Creating Custom Exposure Modes

After you gain some experience with your camera, you'll find that you usually rely on certain picture-taking options for specific types of photos. For example, you might prefer one set of options when shooting landscapes and another for shooting portraits. If you routinely spend a lot of time adjusting options for different scenes, here's a way to make life easier: You can store two sets of picture options as custom exposure modes, represented on the Mode dial by U1 and U2 (for User 1 and 2), as shown in Figure 11-1.

Setting up your custom exposure modes is easy:

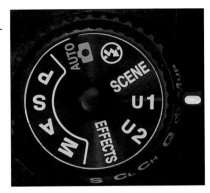

Figure 11-1: You can create two custom exposure modes: U1 and U2.

1. **Set the Mode dial to P, S, A, or M.**

   The mode you choose determines what picture settings you can control, and thus what options you can store as part of your custom exposure mode. For example, in A mode, you control the f-stop, or aperture setting; in S mode, you control the shutter speed.

2. **Select the camera settings you want to store.**

   In A mode, for example, select the initial f-stop that you want the camera to use any time you switch to the custom exposure mode. In S mode, select the initial shutter speed. Also choose settings such as Image Quality, Image Size, Exposure Compensation, Flash Compensation, Flash mode, White Balance, Autofocus mode, and so on.

   A handful of settings can't be stored: Image Area, Storage Folder, File Naming, Manage Picture Control, Multiple Exposure, Remote Control Mode (ML-Le), and Interval Timer Shooting.

3. **Display the Setup menu and choose Save User Settings, as shown on the left in Figure 11-2.**

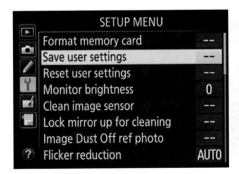
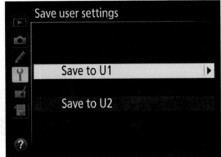

Figure 11-2: Choose the Save User Settings option to store the current camera settings as custom exposure mode U1 or U2.

4. **Press OK to display the right screen in Figure 11-2.**

5. **Highlight the user mode (U1 or U2) that you want to use to store your settings.**

6. **Press the Multi Selector right.**

7. **Select Save Settings and press OK.**

To use the settings you stored, just turn the Mode dial to the custom mode you created (U1 or U2). You can still adjust any settings — you don't have to stick with your default f-stop or shutter speed, for example. The camera just starts you out with the settings that you dialed in when creating the custom mode. You can return to the stored settings at any time by rotating the Mode dial to another setting and then back to your custom mode.

To reset U1 or U2 to the default factory settings for each option, choose the Reset User Settings option on the Setup menu. It lives just beneath the Save User Settings option. (Refer to the left screen in Figure 11-2.)

Creating Your Own Menu

In addition to creating custom exposure modes, you can build your own menu that holds up to 20 of the options you use most frequently. Check it out:

1. **Display the My Menu menu, as shown on the left in Figure 11-3.**

   If the Recent Settings menu appears instead, select Choose Tab, press OK, select My Menu, and press OK again. The My Menu screen appears.

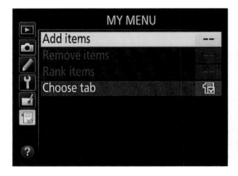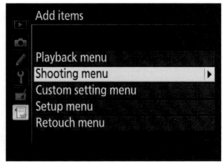

Figure 11-3: You can create a custom menu to hold up to 20 of your favorite settings.

2. **Highlight Add Items and press OK.**

   Now you see the five other menus, as shown on the right in Figure 11-3.

3. **Highlight a menu that contains an option you want to add to your custom menu and then press the Multi Selector right.**

   You see all options on that menu, as shown on the left in Figure 11-4.

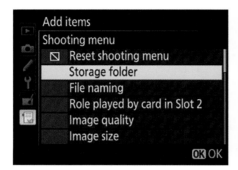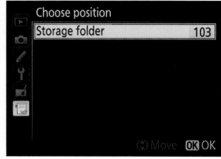

Figure 11-4: Highlight a menu item and press OK to add it to your custom menu.

A few items can't be added to a custom menu. A little box with a slash through it appears next to those items.

4. **To add an item to your custom menu, highlight it and press OK.**

   Now you see the Choose Position screen, shown on the right in Figure 11-4, where you can change the order of your menu items. For now, just press OK to return to the My Menu screen; you can adjust the order of your menu items later.

5. **Repeat Steps 2–4 to add more items to your menu.**

   After creating your custom menu, you can access it by pressing the Menu button and choosing the Recent Settings/My Menu screen. (If you want to switch to the Recent Settings menu, select Choose Tab and then select Recent Settings.)

You can reorder the menu items and remove items as follows:

✔ **Change the order of menu options.** Display your custom menu, highlight Rank Items (as shown in Figure 11-5), and press OK. Highlight a menu item, press OK, and then use the Multi Selector to move it up or down the list. Press OK to lock in its new position. Press the Multi Selector left to return to the My Menu screen.

✓ **Remove menu items.** Again, head for the My Menu screen. Select Remove Items and press OK. You see all the current menu items, with an empty box next to each item. To remove an item, highlight it and press the Multi Selector right. A check mark appears in that item's box. After tagging all the items you want to remove, press OK. A confirmation screen appears; press OK to wrap up.

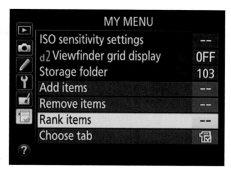

Figure 11-5: Choose Rank Items to change the order of menu items.

Adding Image Comments

Through the Image Comment feature, you can add text comments to your picture files. Suppose, for example, that you're on vacation and visiting a different destination every day. You can annotate all the pictures you take on each day with the name of the location.

Comments don't appear on the image itself; instead, they're stored along with the picture metadata, which is the hidden data that records camera settings in the picture file. You can view that metadata in Nikon ViewNX 2, the photo software that ships free with your camera; see the first part of Chapter 6 to find out how. Additionally, you can view comments in the Shooting Data display mode during playback. Chapter 5 details display modes.

Here's how the Image Comment feature works:

1. **Display the Setup menu and highlight Image Comment, as shown on the left in Figure 11-6.**

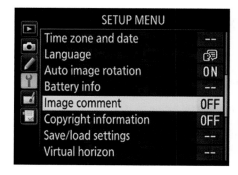 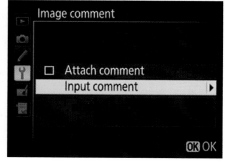

Figure 11-6: You can tag pictures with text comments through this feature.

2. **Press OK to display the right screen in the figure.**

3. **Highlight Input Comment and press the Multi Selector right.**

   You see a keyboard-type screen like the one shown in Figure 11-7.

4. **Use the Multi Selector to highlight the first letter of the text you want to add.**

5. **Press OK to enter the letter into the text box at the bottom of the screen.**

6. **Keep entering letters to complete your comment text.**

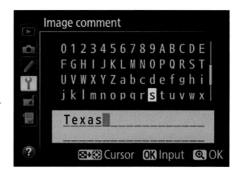

Figure 11-7: Comments can contain as many as 36 characters.

Your comment can be up to 36 characters long. You can use these text-entry tricks:

- *To move the text cursor:* Press and hold the ISO button as you press the Multi Selector in the direction you want to shift the cursor. Release the button to return to the keyboard section of the screen.

- *To delete a letter:* Move the cursor under the offending letter and then press the Delete button.

7. **To save the comment, press the Qual button.**

   You're returned to the Image Comment menu.

8. **Highlight Attach Comment and press the Multi Selector right to put a check mark in the box, as shown in Figure 11-8.**

   The check mark turns the Image Comment feature on.

9. **Press OK.**

   You're returned to the Setup menu. The Image Comment menu item should now be set to On.

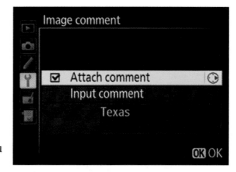

Figure 11-8: Press the Multi Selector right to toggle the Attach Comment box on and off.

The camera applies your comment to all pictures you take after turning on Image Comment. To disable the feature, revisit the Image Comment menu, highlight Attach Comment, and press the Multi Selector right to toggle the check mark off. Press OK to make the change official.

Embedding a Copyright Notice

In addition to embedding image comments into your picture metadata, the hidden extra data recorded with a digital photo file, you can add copyright data that includes your name and a copyright date. As with comments, you can view the copyright data during playback, in Shooting Data display mode, and in many photo programs, including Nikon ViewNX 2. To enter copyright information, take these steps:

1. **Display the Setup menu and highlight Copyright Information, as shown on the left in Figure 11-9.**

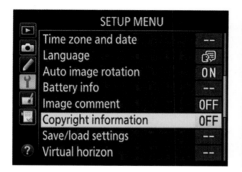
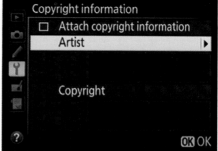

Figure 11-9: Use this feature to embed copyright information into each picture file.

2. **Press OK to display the second screen shown in Figure 11-9.**

3. **Highlight Artist and press the Multi Selector right to display a text-entry screen.**

4. **Enter your name.**

   The text-entry screen works just as when you add image comments:

   - Use the Multi Selector to highlight a letter and then press OK to enter that character. You can enter up to 36 characters.

   - To move the cursor within the text-entry box, press and hold the ISO button as you press the Multi Selector in the direction you want to move the cursor.

   - To delete a character, move the cursor under it and press the Delete button.

5. **Press the Qual button to store your name and exit the text entry screen.**

6. **Highlight Copyright, press the Multi Selector right, and then enter your copyright notice.**

   This time, you can enter a whopping 54 characters.

7. **Press the Qual button to return to the Copyright Information screen.**

   The information you entered should appear, as shown in Figure 11-10.

8. **Highlight Attach Copyright Information and press the Multi Selector right to place a check mark in the adjacent box, as shown in Figure 11-10.**

9. **Press OK.**

   The Copyright Information item on the Setup menu (left screen in Figure 11-9) should be set to On, indicating that the camera will now include your copyright text as part of the file metadata for all subsequent shots.

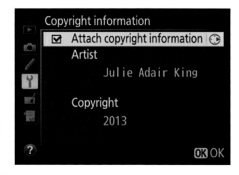

Figure 11-10: Press the Multi Selector right to toggle the Attach setting on and off.

To stop adding the copyright data, just revisit the Copyright Information screen, toggle the Attach Copyright Information box off, and then press OK.

Customizing File and Folder Names

By default, your camera initially stores all your images in one folder, which it names 100D7100. Folders have a storage limit of 999 images; when you exceed that number, the camera creates a new folder, assigning a name that indicates the folder number — 101D7100, 102D7100, and so on.

If you choose, you can create your own folder-numbering scheme. For example, perhaps you sometimes use your camera for business and sometimes for personal use. To keep your images separate, you can set up one folder numbered 200D7100 for work images and use the regular 100D7100 folder for personal photos.

What's more, you can customize the first three letters of your picture file-names. Normally, filenames begin either with the characters DSC_, for photos captured in the sRGB color space, or _DSC, for images that use the Adobe RGB color space. (Chapter 8 explains color spaces.) So, for example, you could set the camera to replace DSC with TIM if you're taking pictures of your brother Tim's family and then change the characters to SUE when you move to cousin Sue's house. The next sections provide details.

Creating a custom storage folder

To create a new storage folder, follow these steps:

1. **Display the Shooting menu and highlight Storage Folder, as shown on the left in Figure 11-11.**

   The number you see for the menu option reflects the first three numbers of the folder name. On the menu, you see only those three numbers; during playback, you see the entire folder name (100D7100, for example) in playback modes that show the folder name.

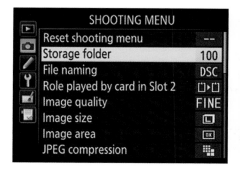 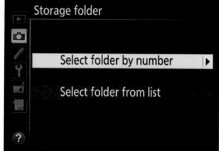

Figure 11-11: You can assign custom folder numbers.

2. **Press OK to display the screen shown on the right in Figure 11-11.**

3. **Choose Select Folder by Number and press the Multi Selector right.**

   You see a screen similar to the one shown on the left in Figure 11-12. Two things to note here:

   - *Folder icon:* A folder icon next to the folder number indicates that the folder already exists. A half-full icon like the one in Figure 11-12 shows you that the folder contains images. A full icon means that the folder is stuffed to its capacity (999 images) or contains a picture with the file number 9999. Either way, that full icon means that you can't put any more pictures in the folder.

   - *Memory card:* If two memory cards are installed in the camera, the one highlighted in the upper-right corner (card 1, in the figure) will be the home of your new folder. This card selection is controlled by the Role Played by Card in Slot 2 option on the Shooting menu. If that option is set to Overflow, the new folder goes on the card in current use. For the other two options, Backup and Raw Slot 1–JPEG Slot 2, the new folder is created on both cards. (Chapter 1 details how to configure the camera for using two memory cards.)

Folder partially full symbol

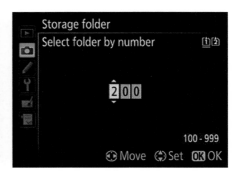

Figure 11-12: Use this screen to create a new folder.

4. Assign the new folder a number.

Use the Multi Selector to highlight one of the three digits and then press up and down to change the number, as shown on the right in Figure 11-12. When you create a new folder, the little folder icon disappears because the folder doesn't yet contain any photos.

5. Press OK.

The camera creates your new folder and automatically selects it as the current storage folder.

If you create custom folders, remember to specify where you want your pictures stored each time you shoot via the Storage Folder option on the Shooting menu. You can use the Select Folder from List option (right screen in Figure 11-11) to see a list of existing folders. See Chapter 5 to find out how to control which folders appear during playback.

Customizing filenames

To customize the first three characters of filenames, follow these steps:

1. Open the Shooting menu, highlight File Naming, as shown on the left in Figure 11-13, and press OK.

You see the screen shown on the right in the figure. The current file naming structure for sRGB and Adobe RGB files appears on the screen. Pictures taken in the sRGB color space start with DSC_; pictures shot in the Adobe RGB color space begin with _DSC.

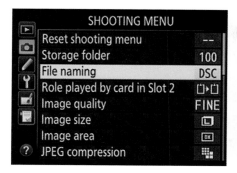
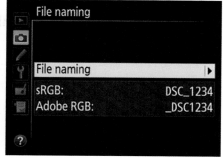

Figure 11-13: This option enables you to change the first three characters of filenames.

2. **Select File Naming and press the Multi Selector right to display the text entry screen shown in Figure 11-14.**

3. **Enter your three custom characters by using these techniques:**

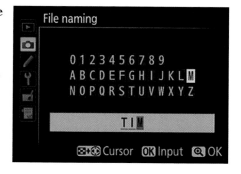

Figure 11-14: Highlight a character and press the Multi Selector center button to enter it.

   • Use the Multi Selector to highlight a character; press the OK button to enter that character in the text-entry box.

   • To move the cursor in the text-entry box, press the ISO button while pressing the Multi Selector right or left.

   • To delete a character, move the cursor under it in the text-entry box and press the Delete button.

4. **Press the Qual button to return to the Shooting menu.**

   The File Naming option should reflect the changes you just made.

Changing the Purpose of the OK Button

You can customize the role that the OK button plays during shooting, playback, and Live View mode through the aptly named OK Button option, found in the Controls section of the Custom Setting menu and shown on the left in Figure 11-15. Highlight the option and press OK to display the screen on the right in the figure.

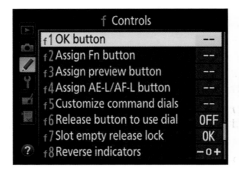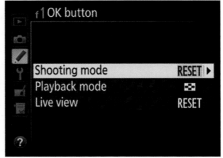

Figure 11-15: You can change the role the OK button plays during shooting, during playback, and in Live View mode.

The settings work like so:

✔ **Shooting mode:** You can choose from three options:

- *RESET (Select Center Focus Point):* At this setting, which is the default, the button automatically selects the center autofocus point. I think that's a pretty handy feature, so it's my choice.

- *Highlight Active Focus Point:* Pressing the OK button highlights the active focus point in the viewfinder. Keep in mind that you can accomplish the same thing during autofocusing by pressing the shutter button halfway.

- *Not Used:* This setting disables the OK button during shooting altogether — although I don't know why you would unless you somehow keep pressing the button by accident.

✔ **Playback mode:** For playback, you get four options:

- *Thumbnail on/off:* This setting is the default; pressing OK toggles the display between thumbnails view and single-image view.

- *View histograms:* Pressing the OK button displays a histogram in both single-image and thumbnails view.

- *Zoom on/off:* Normally, you magnify an image by pressing the Qual button. But if you select this OK Button option, you can press OK to toggle between single-image or thumbnails view to a magnified view of your photo, with the zoomed view centered on the active focus point. After highlighting the option, press the Multi Selector right to select the initial magnification level (low, medium, or high).

- *Choose slot and folder:* Select this option to use the OK button to display the screen that lets you select the memory card and image folder containing the photos you want to view. (You can still use the default method of displaying this screen, which is to press the BKT button and press the Multi Selector up.)

Regardless of your choice, you still press OK to start movie playback. Chapter 4 details movie playback; Chapter 5 covers still photo playback.

✔ **Live View mode:** Finally, for Live View mode, which I detail in Chapter 4, you can choose from these three settings:

  - *RESET (Select Center Focus Point):* This one works as it does during viewfinder shooting: Pressing OK selects the center focus point. It's the default.

  - *Zoom on/off:* Choose this setting to use the OK button to magnify the Live View display, which the magnified view centered on the active focus point. (Normally, you accomplish this by pressing the Qual button.) After selecting the option from the menu, press the Multi Selector right to choose the initial magnification level.

  - *Not Used:* The OK button plays no role during Live View.

Customizing the Command Dials

Through the Customize Command Dials option, found on the Controls section of the Custom Setting menu and shown in Figure 11-16, you can control several aspects of how the command dials behave, as follows:

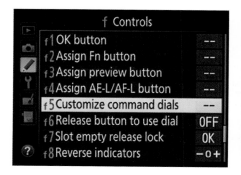
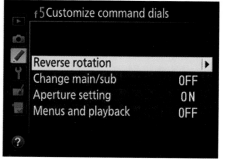

Figure 11-16: You also can modify the functions performed by the command dials.

✔ **Reverse Rotation:** At the default setting, Off, the dials work as indicated throughout this book and the camera manual when you make adjustments to Exposure Compensation, shutter speed, or aperture: Rotating the dial to the right results in a higher value, and rotating to the left lowers the value.

You can reverse this behavior for Exposure Compensation and shutter/aperture control separately. Highlight Reverse Rotation and press the Multi Selector right. To reverse the orientation for one of the settings, highlight it and press the Multi Selector right to place a check mark in the adjacent box. Then press OK.

✔ **Change Main/Sub:** This setting controls which dial you use to adjust aperture and shutter speed. After highlighting the setting, press the Multi Selector right to uncover these options:

- *Off:* This setting is the default. The Main command dial adjusts shutter speed, and the Sub-command dial controls aperture.

- *On (Mode A):* Choose this setting if you want to use the Main command dial to adjust the f-stop when you shoot in the A exposure mode.

- *On:* This setting reverses the dials for the S, A, and M exposure modes. You use the Sub-command dial to adjust shutter speed in the M and S modes and use the Main command dial to adjust the f-stop in the A and M modes.

✔ **Aperture Setting:** For this option, you have two settings:

- *Sub-Command Dial:* This is the default setting; the Sub-command dial controls aperture (assuming that you didn't alter the setting of the Change Main/Sub option just discussed). When you select this option, the Aperture Setting item on the menu appears set to On, as shown on the right in Figure 11-16.

- *Aperture Ring:* This setting relates only to lenses that have an aperture ring; if you select this option, you can adjust the f-stop only by using the aperture ring. The Aperture Setting item on the menu appears set to Off when you select this option.

✔ **Menus and Playback:** For this option, you choose from three settings: Off, On, and On (Image Review Excluded). At the default setting, Off, you use the Multi Selector to scroll through your pictures and change the data-display style during playback. And during shooting, you use the Multi Selector to navigate menus.

At the On setting, you can use the command dials as follows:

- *Playback:* Use the Main command dial to scroll through pictures in single-image view and move the image-highlight box left or right during thumbnails playback. Use the Sub-command dial to adjust the data-display mode during single-image playback and move the highlight box up and down through thumbnails.

- *Menu navigation:* Rotate the Main command dial to scroll up and down through a menu. Rotate the Sub-command dial right to display the submenu for the selected item; rotate left to jump to the previous menu.

If you instead select On (Image Review Excluded), things work the same as they do when you choose the On setting, but the command dials don't work during the image-review period.

You can modify one additional aspect of how the command dials work: Under the normal camera setup, an operation that involves both a camera button and a command dial requires you to hold down the button while spinning the dial to get results. For example, to change the Flash mode, you hold down the Flash button while rotating the Main command dial.

If you find it cumbersome to keep pressing the button while you rotate the dial, you can tell the two controls that you prefer them to dance separately instead of cheek to cheek. The relevant option is located on the Controls submenu of the Custom Setting menu; it's called Release Button to Use Dial. Set the option to Yes, and you let up on the button and then rotate the command dial to adjust a camera setting. So to change Flash mode, for example, you press and release the Flash button and then rotate the Main command dial. Note that the menu item says On instead of Yes when the option is enabled.

There's a gotcha to remember if you accept this variation, however: The setting you're adjusting remains active until you press the button again, you press the shutter button halfway, or the exposure meters turn off. And if you forget and leave the setting "open," you can easily adjust the setting with the command dial when you're meaning to do something else. For this reason, I prefer to use the default setting. Choose No to use this setting; the menu screen then shows Off as the selected option.

Customizing the Fn, Depth-of-Field Preview, and AE-L/AF-L Buttons

You can assign a variety of tasks to the Fn (Function) button, Depth-of-Field Preview buttons, and the AE-L/AF-L button. The next two sections explain your options for still photography and movie recording.

Customizing buttons for still photography

By default, the three buttons are set to perform the following tasks when you're shooting still pictures:

- ✓ **Fn button:** Pressing the button while rotating either command dial toggles the Image Area setting between the DX and 1.3x crop settings.

- ✓ **Depth-of-Field Preview button:** When you look through the viewfinder and press the button, the display changes to give you an idea of how your current f-stop setting will affect depth of field. If flash is enabled, the flash also emits a *modeling flash* (a brief burst of flash light to help you preview how your subject will be lit).

- ✓ **AE-L/AF-L button:** Autofocus and autoexposure are locked when you press the button, and they remain locked as long as you keep your finger on the button.

If you don't use the default features very often, you can assign different functions to the buttons. In fact, you can specify what you want the camera to do when you press the button only and when you press the button and rotate a command dial.

You can get to the modification options in two ways:

- ✓ **Custom Setting menu:** Select Assign Fn Button, as shown in Figure 11-17, to customize the Function button; choose Assign Preview Button to customize the Depth-of-Field Preview button; and choose Assign AE-L/AF-L button to . . . well, you get the drift.

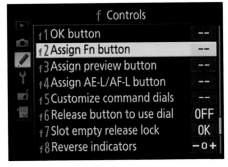

Figure 11-17: You can access the button-modification options via the Custom Setting menu.

- ✓ **Information display control strip:** Symbols representing the current button settings appear in the control strip of the Information screen, as shown on the left of Figure 11-18. To access one of the settings, press the *i* button to activate the control strip, as shown on the right in the figure. Then use the Multi Selector to highlight the button you want to change. I highlighted the Fn button option on the right in Figure 11-18, for example.

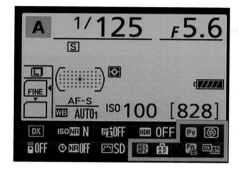 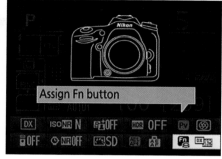

Figure 11-18: You also can view and adjust the button functions through the Information screen.

Either way, press OK to display a screen similar to the one you see in Figure 11-19. Select the operation you want to customize: Choose Press to change the function that's accomplished by pressing the button only; choose Press + Command Dials to set the action that occurs when you press the button and rotate a command dial.

Next, press the Multi Selector right to display a list of all the available functions you can assign. (Your options depend on which button you're modifying.) Make your selection and press OK.

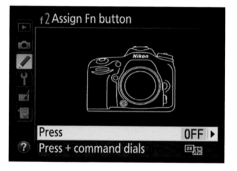

Figure 11-19: You can specify what happens when you press the button with and without using a command dial.

 If you're not sure what a particular option does, press the WB button to display a help screen that spells things out. Your camera user manual also details all the myriad variations you can assign to these buttons.

Customizing buttons for movie recording

By default, the Fn, Depth-of-Field Preview, and AE-L/AF-L buttons serve the following roles when the camera is set to Live View Movie mode, which I cover in Chapter 4:

- **Fn button:** The button is nonfunctional.

- **Depth-of-Field Preview button:** Ditto.

- **AE-L/AF-L button:** Pressing the button locks autofocus and autoexposure, the same as during still photography.

Through the Movie submenu of the Custom Setting menu, you can adjust the role the buttons play during recording, as shown in Figure 11-20. Select the button you want to modify and press OK to display a list of available functions.

 WB

Again, if you're not sure what a setting does, press the WB button to display a help screen, and check your camera manual for complete details.

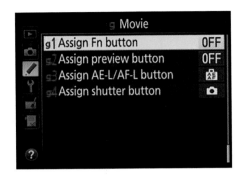

Figure 11-20: Use the options in the Movie section of the Custom Setting menu to define the button roles during movie recording.

Modifying the Role of the Shutter Button

Getting a headache considering all the ways you can customize the D7100 buttons and dials? Me, too. Remember, you *wanted* an advanced camera. LOL, as the kids say. The good news is that only one more button requires discussion — in this chapter, anyway. You can modify the shutter button's behavior in the following two ways:

✒ **Locking exposure with the shutter button:** Normally, pressing the shutter button halfway initiates exposure metering but doesn't lock exposure — the camera continuously adjusts the exposure settings as needed up to the time you take the picture. If you want to lock exposure, you can use the AE-L/AF-L button to do the job, as explained in Chapter 7. When you use single-servo autofocus (AF-S mode), focus is also locked when you press the shutter button halfway. By default, pressing the AE-L/AF-L button also locks exposure and focus.

You also have the option to set the shutter button to lock exposure and focus together. The setting in question is found on the Timers/AE Lock submenu of the Custom Setting menu and is called Shutter-Release Button AE-L, as shown in Figure 11-21. If you set the option to On, your half-press of the shutter button locks both focus and exposure. This option affects movie recording as well as still photography.

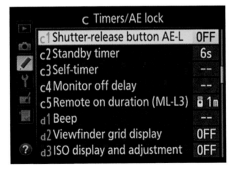

Figure 11-21: This option controls whether the shutter button can be used to lock focus and exposure.

✔ **Using the shutter button for movie recording:** The Assign Shutter Button option, found in the Movie section of the Custom Setting menu and shown in Figure 11-22, determines what role the shutter button plays when you're shooting movies. You have two options: Take Photos and Record Movies. By default, Take Photos is selected, and pressing the shutter button ends movie recording and snaps a still photo. The aspect ratio of your picture is 16:9, encompassing the same image area as a movie frame.

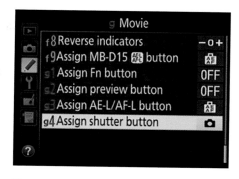

Figure 11-22: And this one determines whether pressing the shutter button in Live View movie mode records a photograph or starts and stops movie recording.

If you choose Record Movies and set the Live View switch to the movie camera position, pressing the shutter button halfway fires up the Live View display. You then release the button and press halfway again to initiate autofocusing. When you're ready to record, press the button all the way down; press all the way a second time to stop recording. To end Live View, press the LV button (in the center of the Live View switch).

At first blush, this option seems pretty meaningless, given that engaging Live View normally requires just a press of the LV button, and starting and stopping recording using the default setting is as simple as pressing the red movie-record button that lies right next to the shutter button. The Record Movies setting may come in handy, though, if you attach a wired remote-release cord to the camera. This setup enables you to put the camera on a tripod and then use the shutter button on the remote to control recording from a distance. You might use this setup to record movies of a hummingbird visiting a feeder, for example, when standing close to the feeder with the camera might scare away the bird.

Unfortunately, this feature doesn't work with the ML-L3 wireless remote control, although it is compatible with the WR-1 and WR-R10 wireless camera remote control units. Also note that when the feature is enabled, you can't display the default shooting information, virtual horizon guide, or grid on the screen. Instead, pressing the Info button simply hides or displays the settings that appear along the bottom of the monitor.

Index

About the Author

Julie Adair King is the author of many books about digital photography and imaging, including the best-selling *Digital Photography For Dummies*. Her most recent titles include a series of *For Dummies* guides to popular digital SLR cameras, including the *Nikon D600, D3200, D5200, and D300s*. Other works include *Digital Photography Before & After Makeovers, Digital Photo Projects For Dummies, Julie King's Everyday Photoshop For Photographers, Julie King's Everyday Photoshop Elements,* and *Shoot Like a Pro!: Digital Photography Techniques*. When not writing, King teaches digital photography at such locations as the Palm Beach Photographic Centre. A native of Ohio and graduate of Purdue University, she resides in West Palm Beach, Florida.

Author's Acknowledgments

I am deeply grateful for the chance to work once again with the wonderful publishing team at Wiley. Kim Darosett, Jennifer Webb, Steve Hayes, Virginia Sanders, and Kristie Rees are just some of the talented editors and designers who helped make this book possible. And finally, I am also indebted to technical editor Dave Hall, without whose insights and expertise this book would not have been the same.

Publisher's Acknowledgments

Executive Editor: Steven Hayes

Senior Project Editor: Kim Darosett

Copy Editor: Virginia Sanders

Technical Editor: David Hall

Editorial Assistant: Annie Sullivan

Sr. Editorial Assistant: Cherie Case

Project Coordinator: Kristie Rees

Cover Image: Main image © iStockphoto.com/EmiliaU; Camera and Back Cover images courtesy of Julie Adair King